Modernity and the Jews in Western Social Thought

Modernity and the Jews in Western Social Thought

CHAD ALAN GOLDBERG

The University of Chicago Press
Chicago and London

The University of Chicago Press, Chicago 60637
The University of Chicago Press, Ltd., London

Published 2017
Printed in the United States of America

26 25 24 23 22 21 20 19 18 17 1 2 3 4 5

ISBN-13: 978-0-226-46041-3 (cloth)
ISBN-13: 978-0-226-46055-0 (paper)
ISBN-13: 978-0-226-46069-7 (e-book)
DOI: 10.7208/chicago/9780226460697.001.0001

Library of Congress Cataloging-in-Publication Data

Names: Goldberg, Chad Alan, author.
Title: Modernity and the Jews in western social thought / Chad Alan Goldberg.
Description: Chicago ; London : The University of Chicago Press, 2017. | Includes bibliographical references and index.
Identifiers: LCCN 2016041901 | ISBN 9780226460413 (cloth : alk. paper) | ISBN 9780226460550 (pbk. : alk. paper) | ISBN 9780226460697 (e-book)
Subjects: LCSH: Jews—France—social conditions. | Jews—Germany—Social conditions. | Jews—United States Social conditions.
Classification: LCC DS140 .G54 2017 | DDC 973/.04924—dc23 LC record available at https://lccn.loc.gov/201604 | 901

♾ This paper meets the requirements of ANSI/NISO Z39.48–1992 (Permanence of Paper).

לדורה

The opponents of nationalism see us as uncompromising nationalists, with a nationalist God and a nationalist Torah; the nationalists see us as cosmopolitans, whose homeland is wherever we happen to be well off. Religious gentiles say that we are devoid of any faith, and the freethinkers among them say that we are orthodox and believe in all kinds of nonsense; the liberals say we are conservative and the conservatives call us liberal. Some bureaucrats and writers see us as the root of anarchy, insurrection, and revolt, and the anarchists say we are capitalists, the bearers of the biblical civilization, which is, in their view, based on slavery and parasitism. . . . Even our merits are turned into shortcomings.

MOSHE LEIB LILIENBLUM, *The Future of Our People*, 1883

De te fabula narratur!

KARL MARX, quoting Horace, in the preface to the first German edition of *Capital*, 1867

Contents

Acknowledgments

It has been many years since I read *Mila 18*, Leon Uris's fictionalized account of the Warsaw Ghetto Uprising, but one passage sticks in my mind. A character in the novel describes his former lover this way: "Most half Jews went to one of two excesses—an abnormal hate of their Jewishness or the embracing of it with an abnormal passion. When Ana discovered her father's Jewishness she became a rabid Zionist." The character adds: "There are times when a woman must be a woman and to hell with Zionism. It's too much to hear it going to bed and waking up." I wouldn't go so far as to call myself rabid, but this passage may help to explain my interest in the sociology of Jews and Judaism. I've long been fascinated by Jewish culture and history, so much so that my spouse, Anna Paretskaya, sometimes hears it going to bed and waking up. I'm fortunate that she shares some of my fascination. This book is informed by and indebted to countless conversations with her. She has heard or read its various parts as they have developed, and her comments, questions, and suggestions have shaped my thinking along the way. I am deeply grateful to have such a brilliant, supportive, and loving partner in my life.

This book started with chapter 2, which began as a paper for an international conference on "Antisemitism and the Emergence of Sociological Theory" at the University of Manchester in 2008. I am exceedingly thankful to Marcel Stoetzler because neither the paper nor this book would have been written without the impetus of the conference that he organized. Since that seminal experience in Manchester, I have presented material from this book at numerous conferences, universities, colleges, and even a few synagogues in Europe, Israel, Canada, and the United States. Although it would be too impractical to name them all individually, I thank everyone who invited me to present my ideas or offered comments and suggestions.

Several research fellowships were indispensable for researching and writing this book. I researched and wrote the first draft of chapter 4 in 2011–12 during a sabbatical generously supported by the University of Wisconsin–Madison and the Martin L. and Sarah F. Leibowitz Membership in the School of Historical Studies at the Princeton Institute for Advanced Study (IAS). My year at the IAS was wonderfully fruitful and productive thanks in part to the intellectual stimulation I received from the permanent faculty and other visiting members. I owe a special debt to Michael Walzer, Steven Lukes, Angel Adams Parham, Phoebe Maltz Bovy, and the members of an informal working group organized by Jeremy Cohen. During my sabbatical year, Jeffrey C. Alexander, Philip Gorski, David Sorkin, Martin Burke, and Tony Michels also provided helpful comments and encouragement. Subsequent research at the University of Chicago's Special Collections Research Center helped me to refine the material in chapter 4.

A Distinguished Visiting Fellowship in the Advanced Research Collaborative at the Graduate Center of the City University of New York in 2013–14 enabled me to research and write the first draft of chapter 3. Director Don Robotham, other visiting fellows, and Graduate Center faculty and students made this task an enriching and enjoyable intellectual experience. David Sorkin was especially generous with his time and advice. Mauricio Pietrocola helped me to conceptualize the transmission of intellectual influences in terms of cultural schemas. Tony Michels and Jeff Weintraub provided useful suggestions from outside the Graduate Center. Gabi Abend provided assistance with housing arrangements in New York City.

A generous fellowship from the European Institutes for Advanced Study in 2015 allowed me to draft the book's introductory and concluding chapters at the Hanse–Wissenschaftskolleg (HWK) in Delmenhorst, Germany. The HWK's rector, staff, and other visiting fellows made it a pleasure to complete this work. I am especially grateful to research manager Susanne Fuchs, who helped me to check English translations of German texts, read and commented on my work, and shared the benefit of her expertise in German social theory. The *Jüdische Gemeinde* of Delmenhorst; its rabbi, Alina Treiger; and its president, Pedro Becerra, gave a warm welcome to my wife and me.

In spring 2013, I shared some of the ideas in this book with the students in my undergraduate theory course at the University of Wisconsin–Madison and with the participants in an adult education class I taught at Beth Israel Center in Madison, Wisconsin. In fall 2014, a graduate seminar I taught at the University of Wisconsin–Madison afforded me the opportunity to discuss my ideas with Jordan Colosi, Yue Du, Jonas Gunzelmann, and Avinoam Yuval Naeh. My ideas were sharpened and modified through these conversations.

Some of the material in this book has already appeared in print. Most of chapter 2 was previously published as "The Jews, the Revolution, and the Old Regime in French Anti-Semitism and Durkheim's Sociology" in the journal *Sociological Theory* in 2011. An abridged version was published with other papers from Marcel Stoetzler's conference in *Antisemitism and the Constitution of Sociology*, published in 2014. Parts of my article "Robert Park's Marginal Man," published in the journal *Laboratorium* in 2012 and subsequently reprinted in *The Anthem Companion to Robert Park*, were incorporated into chapter 4. Some of the material in chapter 3 originally appeared in my article "The Two Marxes" in the *Journal of Classical Sociology* in 2015. I thank the publishers of these articles for permission to reuse this material here, and I am grateful to colleagues, anonymous reviewers, and journal editors for comments I received on it.

Sara Goldrick-Rab took the time to read and helpfully comment on the introductory chapter even as she was working to complete a book of her own.

I extend a special thanks to Doug Mitchell at the University of Chicago Press for his unflagging encouragement, support, and assistance. I am also grateful for the careful reading and thoughtful recommendations of the manuscript's reviewers. Joe Claude, Ryan Li, Carol McGillivray, Trevor Perri, Ashley Pierce, and Kyle Wagner helped to turn my manuscript into the book that is now before you. Thanks also to Rachel Nishan at Twin Oaks Indexing.

This book is dedicated to Dora Goldberg (née Teitelbaum), who more than anyone else sparked my interest in Jewish culture, history, and religion from a young age. Her memory is and will continue to be a blessing.

Chad Alan Goldberg
Madison, Wisconsin
May 2016

1

Introduction

This book compares the portrayal, symbolism, and meaning of the Jews and Judaism in French, German, and American social thought from the late nineteenth century through the early decades of the twentieth century. My primary focus is not on the role of Jews as producers of social thought but rather on Jews as objects of social thought. During this time period, the Jews served as a major point of orientation and reference in debates about what it meant to be modern and what it meant to be French, German, or American. To the social thinkers I discuss in subsequent chapters, *modernity* referred to a set of processes that swept away older historical arrangements to create a new and different social order. These processes were uneven, partial, incomplete, and varied from one place to another in timing and sequence, but they generally included the rise of the nation-state, the spread of democratic and bureaucratic forms of authority, the growth of modern industrial capitalism, secularization, urbanization, and the contact and collision of different peoples and cultures as a result of imperialism, colonialism, and migration. Because many scholars believed that these processes had thrown their societies into crisis, they devoted considerable attention to the possibilities for reconstructing older forms of community or constructing new forms of community under new social conditions. From these concerns sprang their interest in the Jews. The Jews became an intermediary through whom European and American social thinkers discerned in a roundabout fashion the nature, problems, and trajectory of their own societies.

While portrayals of Jews served this purpose in a wide range of social-scientific, humanistic, and literary texts, I concentrate on references to Jews in sociology.[1] This focus is motivated by several considerations. To begin with, sociology has contributed to and comprises an important part of European and American social thought more generally. During the discipline's classical period in the late nineteenth and early twentieth centuries, when its fundamental ideas first took shape, the chief task that sociology set for itself and which was its raison d'être was to interpret and explain the modern world of which sociology itself was a product.[2] Consequently, the symbolic function of the Jews as an intermediary for self-reflection was especially visible in the new discipline at this time. Moreover, the interpretations of modernity that the classical sociologists produced were widely diffused and at times consequential despite resistance to the institutionalization and legitimacy of their discipline. They often considered public influence part of their calling, and they had the means to disseminate their ideas by virtue of their relationships to the state, their participation in the public lecture circuit, or support from private foundations. In France, where the Catholic Church had long been responsible for education, Émile Durkheim's equating of God and society implied that sociologists and public school teachers would assume the roles formerly filled by theologians and priests. From the Sorbonne, he exercised great authority and influence within the university and the French education system overall. Urging his colleagues to advise and educate the masses by means of books, lectures, and popular education, Durkheim declared that "our function is to help our contemporaries to understand themselves."[3] In Germany, university professors served as the spokesmen of the country's educated middle class on cultural questions. From this position, they worked to define "the [German] nation and, through it, the [German] state . . . as creatures and as agents" of the educated elite's cultural ideals. Although sociologists occupied a heterodox position in the German academic field, their mandarin status enabled them to reach a substantial audience. The social thinker Werner Sombart, for instance, became a popular public speaker, comparable to the media stars and celebrities of today.[4] Even in the United States, where intellectuals enjoyed less prestige, sociologists produced studies commissioned by large and influential foundations that directly addressed important public debates about urbanization and immigration. In all three countries, the classical sociologists authorized and promoted visions of the social world—and the place of the Jews within it—that sometimes contributed to producing the reality of that world. This theory effect, as the contemporary sociologist Pierre Bourdieu has called it, was especially likely when the visions that sociologists promoted lent scientific credibility to the aims and ideas of dominant groups.[5] When intellectuals "want to act against the tendencies immanent in society," Bourdieu noted, "they are powerless; but when they act for the worst they are very effective, as they offer an expression and legitimation for society's dark and shameful impulses."[6] To their credit, many of the social thinkers examined in this study resisted the dark and shameful impulses of antisemitism and nativism, but the complicity of others like Sombart in Germany or Edward Ross in the United States had devastating consequences.[7]

Sociology's Jewish Question

Historians and philosophers have investigated the symbolic function of the Jews as an intermediary for self-reflection in a variety of contexts, and this study builds upon their seminal contributions. Ronald Schechter found that French writers and political actors took a pronounced interest in Jews between 1715 and 1815 because the Jews helped them to conceptualize and articulate the Enlightenment idea of human perfectibility: "If the most recalcitrant, *obstinate* people could improve," they reasoned, "then all peoples could improve."[8] Later in the nineteenth century, as Lisa Moses Leff showed, the presence of Jews among French liberals, Saint-Simonian socialists, and anticlerical republicans, as well as the support of these political factions for Jewish rights, enabled them to signify their tolerance, moral standing, and universalism in opposition to the Catholic right.[9] Phoebe Maltz Bovy showed how intermarriage between French Jews and gentiles came to represent an affirmation of the Revolution's ideals, including republican universalism, national fraternity, and the elimination of hereditary social divisions.[10] Likewise, Jonathan Hess found that the German reading public took a strong interest in Jews from the late 1770s to 1806 because "intellectuals concerned with imagining new forms of political community in Germany" based on secular, rational, and universal principles saw in Judaism "the perfect antithesis to the norms of the modern world," namely, "a clannish and coercive form of legalism irreconcilable with the Enlightenment's insistence on individual autonomy, freedom of conscience and the very power of reason itself."[11] According to Yirmiyahu Yovel, the Jews continued to attract the interest of later German thinkers like Hegel and Nietzsche because they "provided Europeans with a mirror . . . in which to see a reflection of their own identity problems. The 'Jewish problem' was . . . a reflection of Europe's own problem with itself, of how, in an age of rapid transformation, Europeans were understanding their own identity, future, and meaning of life."[12] Similarly, Eric Goldstein found that in the United States during the Progressive era and interwar years, the ambivalent racial image of the Jew, at once similar to and different from native-born whites, subverted the color line through which white Americans stabilized their self-image and derived a sense of order, confidence, and superiority. Until native-born whites "could define the Jew and the forces of modernization he represented, they could not clearly define themselves."[13]

Vastly expanding the scope of these findings, David Nirenberg has argued that gentiles have repeatedly invoked Judaism in a wide variety of cultures from antiquity to the present to "make sense of and criticize their world." He concluded that anti-Judaism is "one of the basic tools" with which "the vast edifices of Western thought" were constructed.[14]

Bringing French, German, and American social thought together in a single frame of reference, I extend the insights of this scholarship to classical sociological theory and the history of sociology. To be sure, scholarly attention to the treatment of Jews and Judaism within sociology is not new. There have been important studies of the Jewish backgrounds and contexts of Durkheim, Karl Marx, and Georg Simmel; Max Weber's ideas about Judaism and Jews; the connections that Marx, Simmel, Weber, and Sombart postulated between Jews and modern capitalism; the production of social-scientific knowledge about Jews and its use in political debates over Jewish assimilation; the relationship between sociology and antisemitism; and the historical sociology of Jews and their relations to gentiles.[15] My own study is deeply indebted to these contributions, but they all have limitations that I seek to move beyond. Many of the studies are relatively narrow in scope, focusing on a single author, a single country, or the association of Jews with a single aspect of modern society such as capitalism. Others concentrate on the self-understanding of Jewish intellectuals, or even more narrowly on Jewish social scientists who made Jewish life the main focus of their work, thereby ignoring the important contributions that gentiles made to sociological discourse about the Jews. Those studies that emphasize anti-Judaism or antisemitism neglect positive depictions of Jews, and the sociology of Jewry continues to draw upon ideas from classical sociology without investigating their production or providing a reflexive analysis of its own history. Perhaps in part because of such limitations, these studies have yet to alter or inform prevailing accounts of the origins of sociology as a discipline. In these accounts, sociology appears as a response to the internal transformation of European societies or to colonial encounters with non-European others, but there is little attention in either version to how ideas about the Jews—a people in Europe yet often viewed as foreign to it—helped classical sociologists to construct their understanding of modernity.

Robert Nisbet argued that "the fundamental ideas of European sociology" were "best understood as responses to the problem of order created at the beginning of the nineteenth century by the collapse of the old regime" under the impact of the French Revolution and the Industrial Revolution.[16] Although Nisbet was primarily an interpreter and not a historian of classical sociology, his thesis exemplifies conventional accounts of the discipline's emergence that trace it to social changes within European societies. For this reason, it merits closer consideration. Nisbet's thesis is insightful, but it remains inadequate in several respects. As I show in a subsequent chapter, it disregards the relationship of American sociology to equally profound changes that transformed the United States. Moreover, within the European context, Nisbet neglected the tendency of European social thinkers to link Jews discursively to the two revolutions. The French Revolution initiated the emancipation of the Jews in Europe and was therefore inseparable from Europe's Jewish question; it stimulated debates about the incorporation of Jews into the political community of citizens, much as the Industrial Revolution brought renewed attention to the role of Jews in bourgeois or civil society. Whether Jews were portrayed as agents and beneficiaries of Europe's internal transformations or as a reactionary force obstructing social progress, they loomed large in European discussions of modernization. As I show in later chapters, classical sociologists in France and Germany sometimes challenged this tendency but often contributed to it themselves. Jews were linked in this way to events that Nisbet and others consider the foundation of sociology. This is a major reason for this study's focus on Jews rather than the many other groups that sociologists also discussed.[17]

In more recent years, revisionist scholarship on the history of sociology has faulted conventional accounts for another shortcoming: their inattention to Western colonialism. Seeking to rectify this oversight, revisionist accounts trace the emergence of sociology not to Europe's self-transformation but to European encounters with the non-European world. As R. W. Connell put it in an early version of this critique: "The enormous spectrum of human history that the sociologists took as their domain was organized by a central idea: difference between the civilization of the metropole and an Other whose main feature was its primitiveness."[18] Directing attention to the relation between the metropole and its colonies has produced new insights, yet this perspective risks losing sight of comparable relations of power, knowledge, and cultural domination *within* the metropole. In particular, it neglects the role of Jews in Europe and America as an internal other. To be sure, this role can partly be understood within the conceptual framework that revisionist scholarship provides. As past studies have shown, Jews were often deemed an Oriental presence in Europe.[19] In Germany, for instance, philosophers like Immanuel Kant referred to Jews as "the Palestinians living among us."[20] This sort of characterization enabled antisemites to justify discrimination against Jews by reference to European colonial policies, as when the French writer and political theorist Charles Maurras declared in 1899 that an inferior civil and legal status for Jews in his country would be no different from "the system we apply without worrying, and very reasonably, to our colonial subjects."[21] However, it would be a mistake to treat depictions of Jews in Western social thought as merely another expression of Orientalism because European and American social thinkers also associated Jews with various aspects of the modern West.[22] As I show implicitly in chapters 2, 3, and 4—and argue explicitly in chapter 5—the ambiguous image of the Jew played a distinctive role in the construction of Western social thought that sometimes resembled but at other times differed from representations of colonial subjects. My focus on Jews rather than other groups helps to clarify this role.

This study draws on Bourdieu to move beyond the weaknesses of both conventional and revisionist accounts of the origins of sociology. Bourdieu called for the historicization of inherited categories of thought, concepts, and principles of classification in order to emancipate ourselves from a past that is forgotten and yet continues unconsciously to shape contemporary thought and practice. He described this approach as a "reflexive history that takes itself as its own object," and he used the term *historical anamnesis* to refer to its emancipatory aim. "To avoid being puppets of the past," he wrote, "we must reappropriate the past for ourselves. . . . The work of anamnesis of the historical unconscious is the major instrument for gaining mastery of history, and therefore of the present that is an extension of history." What might this work of historical anamnesis look like? Invoking Durkheim's argument that our basic categories of understanding are neither innate nor a product of individual experience but instead have a social origin, Bourdieu suggested that that one might explain in a similar manner the major dualisms that structure discourse about the social world. For instance, "we could show in this way that the historical opposition between France and Germany has served as a basis (unconscious and repressed) for a certain number of grand alternatives (for example culture versus civilization), and that it is necessary to de-fetishize, or what comes to the same thing, denaturalize."[23] As I show in chapter 3, the antinomy between culture and civilization was also based upon the historical opposition between *Deutschtum* and *Judentum*. The broader point that I wish to make here, and which I elaborate in chapter 5, is that European and American social thinkers contrasted Jews and gentiles in a variety of ways and consciously invoked these differences to elucidate many of the dualisms that characterize modern social thought. What remained unconscious to them was the extent to which their ideas about the Jews, while seeming only to reflect an objective reality, were inherited from the past and helped to organize their perception of reality. It is this hidden influence that the present study aims to recover.[24]

What precisely did the Jews signify to French, German, and American social thinkers in the late nineteenth and early twentieth centuries, and how did they describe Jews in relation to their own societies? We can locate the possible answers to this question along two major axes. The first axis, which Bourdieu has identified, is temporal, while the second axis, theorized by the sociologist Jeffrey C. Alexander, is evaluative. "The prevailing discourse on the social world," Bourdieu suggested, "is produced on the basis of a small number of generating patterns that themselves derive from the opposition between the (outdated) *past* and the *future*—or, in vaguer and seemingly more conceptual terms, between the *traditional* and the *modern*." These oppositions are related so that each can evoke the others: "This is the way for example that the opposition between 'past' and 'future' leads on to the opposition between 'small' and 'large' . . . or again to the opposition between 'local'—i.e. 'provincial' or 'national' (and nationalist)—and 'cosmopolitan,' which, seen from another angle, is identified with the opposition between the 'immobile' and the 'mobile.' From a different angle again, the underlying opposition [between past and future] evokes the opposition between acquired rights, inheritance, 'privileges,' on the one hand, and on the other, 'dynamism' and 'mobility,' 'mutation' and 'change.'" These paired contrasts can be applied, like the oppositions of myth, to diverse objects and experiences in a variety of contexts. "Whatever the particular field to which it is applied," Bourdieu pointed out, "the pattern produces two opposing and hierarchized terms, and at the same stroke the relationship that unites them, in other words the process of *evolution* (or else involution) leading from one to the other."[25] Along these lines, we can distinguish two ways that Jews have been described in European and American social thought: as either a modernized and modernizing vanguard that anticipates the future of the wider social order, or, conversely, as exemplars of an earlier stage of development that Europeans or Americans have left behind.

The characterization of Jews as a vanguard or as latecomers may be given either a positive or a negative interpretation. Among European and American social thinkers, these interpretations drew on what Alexander calls the discourse of civil society. This discourse is produced by a set of binary cultural codes with which one can characterize social actors, relationships, and institutions. A democratic code specifies the virtuous qualities that confer civic worthiness. In contrast, the counterdemocratic code identifies dangerous and polluting qualities that are deemed to threaten the sacred center of civil society. Just as there is no right without left, the sacred ideals, images, and symbols of a society can only be defined in opposition to persons and things that embody their desecration. In social conflicts, actors struggle to "wrap themselves" in a discourse of liberty which they generate with the democratic

TABLE 1.1

	Advanced (A)	*Backward (B)*
Positive (+)	Jews as precursors of a benevolent and desirable modernity	Jews as carriers of traditional virtues that others have regrettably lost or forgotten
Negative (–)	Jews as harbingers of a threatening and frightening future	Jews as a backward and reactionary people

code and to "taint one another" with a discourse of repression derived from the counterdemocratic code, though they usually do not recognize the constructed nature of these qualities: "Social events and actors seem to 'be' these qualities, not to be labeled by them."[26] For Alexander, the history of the Jews in Europe and the United States exemplifies these processes: "Jews have been constructed as anticivil, as the ultimate threat to broad solidarity and the good life" for two thousand years. He traces this "millennia-long demonization" to the "early civil ambition of Christianity and its later political, social, and legal domination." In Europe, he suggests, where demonization of Jews became increasingly "intertwined with the contradictions of civil society," those contradictions became "an inescapable chamber of death" for Jews. "In America," he notes, "Jews did not suffer the same fate, but this was not because their qualities were acceptable. Indeed, until almost halfway through the twentieth century, the status of Jewish Americans was precarious, and in the 1920s and '30s they were increasingly excluded from civil and noncivil life."[27] Only in the aftermath of World War II and the Shoah did Jewish qualities become respectable and sometimes even appealing in the United States.[28] My own findings, presented in subsequent chapters, are broadly consistent with these points: Jews were sometimes portrayed in European and American social thought as malevolent agents of pollution and disorder, more rarely as carriers of positive and valued qualities, and often with ambivalence. Bringing the insights of Bourdieu and Alexander together, we can identify four possible answers to the question of what Jews meant to European and American social thinkers. These answers are arranged in a schematic fashion in table 1.1.[29]

Methods, Sources, and Research Design

This study is a work of interpretive and historical sociology. It is interpretive insofar as I aim to show what Jews meant to the intellectuals who wrote about them. Because the meaning of ideas can only be understood through an investigation of the social and intellectual contexts in which they were embedded, I seek to situate the sociological classics in their historical milieux.[30] To accomplish these tasks, I turn to a range of sources. First and foremost, I rely on primary sources by the classical sociologists themselves, including their major published works, relevant minor texts, and in a few instances, their published correspondence. I also sometimes refer to texts by contemporaries of the classical sociologists that help to clarify the ideas of the latter. While I cite previously published translations from French and German for the sake of consistency and the reader's convenience, I have consulted French sources in the original language when I thought it necessary or when translations were unavailable, and I have checked the accuracy of some quotations from translated German texts with the help of German-speaking colleagues and students. My discussion of the American sociological tradition is further informed by archival research conducted at the Special Collections Research Center at the University of Chicago. The archival materials I consulted include notes, memoranda, letters, diaries, newspaper clippings, and other unpublished materials of Robert Park, William Thomas, and Louis Wirth. I also consulted Wirth's master's thesis and the doctoral theses of Wirth and Everett Stonequist. Wherever I have modified published translations of primary sources or provided my own translations of French texts, I have indicated this in endnotes. Last, I support my arguments and interpretations with evidence from numerous secondary sources, including biographies, relevant works by historians, and previous studies of classical sociological theory. I use the findings and interpretations of past scholarship as a basis upon which to build my own arguments or, in other instances, as foils against which to work out new interpretations or a revisionist perspective. In this way, I seek to further the cumulative development of research on the history of social thought.

Anyone who undertakes a study of classical sociology is compelled to take a position in the debate between historicists and presentists over the proper way to interpret the classics. This study incorporates elements of both approaches while seeking to avoid their respective drawbacks. The aim of the historicist approach is to interpret the classics in their own terms rather than ours, which is to say, in relation to the historical contexts in which they were originally produced. "What historicism abhors," as Alexander puts it, "is the anachronistic introduction of contemporary concerns into the understanding of earlier texts." Historical contextualization is necessary to understand the purposes for which the classics were produced, the questions they were meant to answer, and the opposing ideas against which they were directed, but it offers little insight into the reproduction of enduring habits of thought across multiple social and historical contexts. Moreover, as Alexander pointed out, it is not feasible to investigate the sociological classics in a purely empiricist manner, insulated from the contemporary concerns and presuppositions of the investigator.[31] The presentist approach foregrounds these concerns and presuppositions, interpreting the sociological classics in view of their contributions and usefulness in ongoing controversies today. Yet the presentist's indifference to history is no less problematic than the historicist's ignoring of contemporary concerns.[32] When taken to their logical conclusions, both approaches sunder the past from the present: the historicist aims to relativize contemporary thinking by contrasting it to the past, while the presentist neglects the past as irrelevant to contemporary uses of the classics. This study adopts Bourdieu's conception of reflexive history, described above, in order to transcend the methodological dualism of historicism and presentism. Rather than sunder past and present, I treat the present as an extension of history, albeit a history that is often forgotten and which thus exercises a hidden influence on the present. This continuity between past and present is what allows one to apply the instruments of sociological analysis, which are a product of history, to the history of sociology itself.[33]

Because classical sociology emerged and developed in multiple contexts, it must be interpreted and contextualized in comparative perspective. My main unit of comparison is national sociological traditions, as exemplified in the work of prominent forerunners or representatives of those traditions about whom I say more below. To choose national sociological traditions as the main unit of comparison presumes, as Donald Levine has argued, that French, German, and American scholars "set forth the theoretical underpinnings of the new science of sociology at the turn of the [nineteenth] century . . . in radically different ways" rooted in different religious and philosophical heritages.[34] Of course, this presumption should not be overstated: French, German, and American sociologists were aware of and at times influenced each other's work, and I draw attention to some of those connections in subsequent chapters. Nevertheless, the French, German, and American sociological traditions differed enough to warrant cross-national comparison. My comparisons are universalizing insofar as I seek to show that the Jews served in all three traditions as a touchstone for defining modernity and national identities, but I also aim to show how representations of Jews varied across and within national traditions along the lines indicated in table 1.1. To supplement the cross-national comparisons, the study also includes within-case comparisons. Most notably, each chapter examines how sociological portrayals of Jews resembled or differed from depictions of other groups or categories: Protestants, women, rival nations, and colonial subjects in the French tradition; Puritans and rival nations in the German tradition; and blacks and other European immigrant groups in the American tradition.

These comparisons are individualizing in the sense that they aim to grasp what is peculiar to sociological representations of Jews.[35]

A few words are necessary to explain how I selected the cases for this study. The study aims to investigate the role that representations of Jews have played in sociological thought, but it is not feasible to survey the entire history of sociology in a comprehensive manner. Instead, my strategy has been to concentrate on influential cases that have affected what would be the overall set of findings for the discipline as a whole. In this study, a case may be construed as a national sociological tradition or as a particular author within a given tradition. I concentrate on the French, German, and American sociological traditions because of their centrality to the formation and development of the discipline.[36] By the same token, I have mainly concentrated on authors who were central to their respective national traditions and who often exercised an influence on social thought more generally, though I have sometimes expanded the scope of my study to include precursors, interlocutors, or students of these authors when I thought it was helpful to illuminate the implications of their ideas or to identify broader habits of thought. Émile Durkheim (1858–1917) "may be said to represent a summation of the French tradition."[37] He established "the theoretical primacy of sociology among the social sciences" and "managed thoroughly to identify sociology with his own work, at least in France."[38] He formed a cohesive group of disciples, followers, and collaborators prior to 1914, and the members of his team who survived World War I continued to dominate French sociology until World War II.[39] Furthermore, "his influence and that of his school extended well beyond his own discipline, to affect such neighboring fields as history and anthropology."[40] Perhaps because the educational systems of Germany and the United States were less centralized, classical sociology in those countries lacked a single dominating figure like Durkheim, but leading figures can be identified there as well. Karl Marx (1818–83) was not an academic sociologist, and his thinking ultimately drew on several national traditions, but the German mandarin tradition exercised a formative influence on him through his early formal education, and his ideas exercised an important influence on German sociology despite the conservatism of the German academic establishment.[41] Georg Simmel (1858–1918), Werner Sombart (1863–1941), and Max Weber (1864–1920) were among the founders of the Deutsche Gesellschaft für Soziologie in 1909. Simmel and Weber "appear as the German counterparts to Durkheim" in their role as "agenda-setting sociologists" early in the twentieth century, and Sombart and Weber were coeditors (with Edgar Jaffé) of Germany's leading social-scientific journal, the *Archiv für Sozialwissenschaft und Sozialpolitik*.[42] Although Ferdinand Tönnies was also a seminal figure in

German sociology, he is not included in this study because he initially had little to say about the Jews, and what he later said largely reiterated ideas articulated by Marx, Simmel, or Sombart.[43] My discussion of the American sociological tradition concentrates on the Chicago school of sociology because it was shaped by a distinctively American school of philosophy known as pragmatism, and it played a dominant role in the development of American sociology as a whole from the 1910s into the 1930s. William Thomas (1863–1947) and Robert Park (1864–1944) were two of the most "intellectually dominant figures of American sociology in the early decades" of the twentieth century; they invoked the Jews, among other groups, to elucidate some of the Chicago school's key concepts, and their ideas about the Jews were most fully developed by their students Louis Wirth (1897–1952) and Everett Stonequist (1901–79).[44] Of course, the influence of most of these intellectuals, already significant in their own time, has been magnified for us today by a historical process of canonization. However, because a reflexive approach to history seeks to grasp how history informs contemporary thought and practice, their canonical status is an advantage and not an impediment to the tasks this study undertakes.

While I seek to relate the classical sociologists' ideas about the Jews and Judaism to the larger themes and concerns of their work and to the historical contexts in which they produced their ideas, my exposition of both the ideas and their contexts is bounded in several ways. To reiterate, this is not a study of Jews or their role in the development of modern social thought. Rather, it is a study of how various social thinkers, only some of whom had Jewish backgrounds, portrayed the Jews and Judaism. I do not attempt to deal with all aspects of these authors' works, provide a comprehensive overview of their general contributions to sociology, or elaborate on the overall development, phases, or revisions of each author's thought, except when those shifts are directly relevant for my purposes. Moreover, readers who are primarily interested in the nuances and peculiarities of each individual's thought will be disappointed by the abstraction, simplification, and schematization inherent in nonindividualizing comparisons. This study analytically accentuates certain elements in the ideas of Durkheim, Marx, Weber, and others in order to draw analogies among them. It may be that some complexities of their thought are thereby obscured, but the study's comparative approach compensates for this loss with a corresponding gain: it enables me to throw into relief broader discursive patterns and habits of thought that transcend individuals. To use Durkheim's terms, my interest is less in the idiosyncrasies of particular thinkers than in those *représentations* that he called collective in the double sense that they are socially generated and refer to society.[45] Last, just as I do not provide a comprehensive overview of each thinker's ideas, I do not provide a complete overview of the institutional and organizational setting, field of intellectual production, and macrosocial context in which each thinker produced his ideas.[46] Such an exhaustive account is beyond the scope of this study, and it is unnecessary. The historicist mode of analysis does not aim to reach a "complete and final statement about a classical theorist's ideas and circumstances, but to reclaim, through various contextualizing procedures, *selected aspects* of the theorist's work, many of them covered over, misremembered, or simply forgotten during the subsequent history of sociology and the other social sciences."[47] Many aspects and circumstances have already been investigated by previous scholarship upon which this study builds. My own contribution to the work of historical contextualization is to situate the classical sociologists' ideas about the Jews and Judaism in relation to cultural assumptions inherited from the past and contemporaneous disputes about the perceived and desired place of the Jews in modern society. In this way, I aim to highlight a feature of classical sociology's historical context that has not received sufficient attention, and thereby add to our knowledge of the ideas, practices, and social relations that shaped the discipline and the wider discourse on the social world to which it contributed.

The organization of this study is shaped by one other major consideration: the widespread use in social thought of different root metaphors (or more accurately synecdoches) for modernity. Social thinkers have sometimes singled out a master process that they believe captures or explains the central tendencies of modern society. A part of modern society is thereby made to represent the whole. As Nisbet's thesis about the two revolutions implies, European thinkers relied heavily on the metaphors of democracy, a political category especially favored by conservatives, and industrial capitalism, a socioeconomic category preferred by socialists. Fred Matthews has suggested that liberal thinkers in the United States were disinclined to prioritize the distribution of political and economic power and therefore gravitated instead to the categories of urbanism and mobility: they tended to ascribe to the city or to immigration the problems and tensions that European conservatives blamed on democracy and which socialists attributed to industrial capitalism.[48] While one should be careful not to overdraw this contrast—European social thinkers also wrote about the city, and references to democracy and capitalism appear in American social thought, too—it nevertheless usefully reminds us that social thinkers observed the modern world through different conceptual lenses that shaped what they saw there. Accordingly, I compare representations of Jews not only across different national sociological traditions but also in relation to different root metaphors for the interpretation of modernity. In this way, I show that different metaphors did not render Jews less salient in attempts to grasp the meaning and significance of modernity. While some European thinkers invoked the Jews to elucidate the democratic revolution of 1789 or the emergence and growth of industrial capitalism, others in America saw Jewish immigrants as a quintessentially urban people who exemplified the perils and promise of the modern metropolis.

Overview

The chapters that follow comprise three cases and a conclusion. Each of the three case studies makes particular arguments that are specific to that chapter in addition to supporting the overall claims of the book. Chapter 2 investigates the relationship of the Jews to the French Revolution as it was conceived within the French sociological tradition, particularly in the work of Durkheim. Highlighting the ways that Durkheim's sociology was directed against French antisemitism, I show how he challenged depictions of Jews as agents of revolutionary subversion or counterrevolutionary reaction. Chapter 3 examines the relationship of the Jews to modern industrial capitalism as it was conceived in the German tradition, concentrating on the work of Marx, Simmel, Sombart, and Weber. Their descriptions of that relationship are shown to be patterned in particular ways that reproduced, in secularized form, cultural assumptions derived from Christian theology. Chapter 4 turns to the work of Thomas, Park, Wirth, and Stonequist in the Chicago school of American sociology, where the key metaphor of modernity was neither democracy nor industrial capitalism; instead it was the city. As that chapter demonstrates, they conceived the city and its new modes of social control in part by reference to the Jewish immigrants concentrating there. This chapter reinterprets the concept of assimilation in relation to pragmatist concerns about forming a democratic public under modern social conditions. Each of these chapters can be read on its own, independently of the others, but together they provide a comparative perspective on the role that representations of Jews played in classical sociology. The social thinkers examined in these chapters worked within different national traditions, emphasized different features of modern society, and disagreed about whether the Jews were synonymous with or antithetical to those features, but they all invoked the Jews to grasp the meaning of the new social order emerging around them.

Chapter 5 concludes the book. Seeking to capture the bigger picture that emerges from the case studies and comparisons, it summarizes my findings and elaborates their broader implications for contemporary scholarship on Jews, modernity, and the history of sociology. The chapter also addresses how the recurring patterns and habits of thought documented in previous chapters were reproduced across space and time, why Jews have been such a prominent reference point for European and American social thinkers, why Jews came to signify such varied and inconsistent meanings, and how my findings relate to past studies of Orientalism, Occidentalism, and European perceptions of America. Last, this chapter challenges scholarly claims that new minority groups—most notably, Muslims—have displaced Jews as the main reference point for the construction of European and American identities today. While Muslims have surely emerged as an important touchstone in their own right, I argue that the Jews—and now the Jewish state—continue to serve as an intermediary for self-reflection in the twenty-first century.

2

The French Tradition: 1789 and the Jews

If the basic ideas of European sociology may be understood as a response to the collapse of the old regime under the impact of the French Revolution and the Industrial Revolution, then much the same can be said about nineteenth-century European antisemitism. Antisemitism, historian Stephen Wilson has suggested, was "a rejection of modern society, as antisemites conceived and experienced it," and it offered a "mythical explanation and a scapegoat" to account for and exorcise poorly understood processes of social change.[1] But even when modernity was interpreted in less threatening and more positive terms as an emancipatory and progressive development, the Jews could serve equally well to signify the threat of restoration and reaction. Moreover, this function of the Jews as symbols of modernity or its antithesis was not unique to antisemitism; within classical sociology, too, the Jews could be identified with modernity or a premodern past. All of this suggests that European sociology not only emerged alongside of and within the same milieu as nineteenth-century European antisemitism but also in relation to it. This would mean that the ideas of European sociology and antisemitism were not only responses to the same revolutions, but they were also responses to each other.

This chapter investigates the relationship between sociology and antisemitism in France through a case study of French sociology's central figure: Émile Durkheim. The interplay between Durkheim's sociology and French antisemitism was sometimes explicit, as in Durkheim's analysis of antisemitism during the Dreyfus Affair, but it was more often implicit, requiring careful exegesis to reconstruct.[2] I seek to accomplish this below, focusing on one side of this relationship—Durkheim's response to antisemitism—and one of the two revolutions to which European sociology is said to be a response: the French Revolution.[3]

The chapter proceeds in six steps. I begin by distinguishing and briefly sketching (1) reactionary and (2) radical forms of antisemitism in nineteenth-century France. While this dichotomous conception admittedly simplifies French antisemitism, eliding nuances, ambiguities, and overlapping themes expressed across the political spectrum, it usefully captures those aspects of French antisemitism that are most essential for the purposes of this chapter. Next, I show that (3) Durkheim, though he largely eschewed traditional Jewish religious observance, was attentive to Jewish issues and engaged in efforts to counter antisemitism. I then discuss (4) how Durkheim's sociology responded to reactionary antisemitism and (5) to radical antisemitism. I suggest that his remarks about the Jews directly addressed antisemitic claims about them, their role in French society, and their relationship to modernity. At the same time, Durkheim was engaged in a reinterpretation of the French Revolution and its historical legacies that indirectly challenged other tenets of French antisemitism. In other words, he also challenged antisemitism in a roundabout way by showing that its tenets were derived from and rested upon a fundamentally flawed understanding of the revolution to which it was, in part, a response. Last, while I mainly seek to understand Durkheim's ideas about the Jews and Judaism in relation to French antisemitism, I also briefly consider them (6) in relation to his characterization of Protestants, women, Germany, and Europe's colonial subjects. Because these social categories also served as reference points in Durkheim's thinking about what it meant to be modern and French, this comparison helps to clarify what was peculiar to his representations of Jews. In sum, this chapter proposes a novel interpretation of Durkheim's work: namely, that it contains direct and indirect responses to reactionary and radical forms of antisemitism, which together form a coherent alternative vision of the relationship between modernity and the Jews.

To understand Durkheim's ideas about the Jews and Judaism, one must situate them in their historical context, including the social condition of France's Jewish population. There were fewer than 87,000 Jews in France in 1900–1901, comprising less than one quarter of 1 percent of the country's total population of 38.6 million French people.[4] This Jewish population had diverse origins; it included Sephardic Jews who hailed from southwestern France as well as a larger Ashkenazic population from the northeastern regions of Alsace and Lorraine, and after the 1881 pogroms in Russia, it was augmented by Jewish immigrants from eastern Europe.[5] Disposed toward the republican principles and institutions to which they owed their emancipation, a small number of French Jews dedicated themselves to successful careers in high-ranking public service during the Third Republic.[6] Most French Jews, however, earned their livelihoods in commerce and shopkeeping or in small workshops as artisans. Jewish vagabonds and a few wealthy Jewish bankers and entrepreneurs, respectively, occupied the lower and upper extremes of the Jewish class structure. Highly acculturated and urbanized by the fin de siècle, French Jews settled in especially large numbers in Paris, where their numbers grew from eight thousand at the beginning of the nineteenth century to approximately sixty thousand in 1900.[7] The social and economic advances made by French Jews during the Third Republic coincided with renewed antisemitism in royalist, clerical, and socialist circles, which comprised an important feature of Durkheim's milieu. Among the events that raised Durkheim's awareness of antisemitism and probably shaped the development of his thinking about Jews and Judaism were the 1892 Panama scandal in France and the antisemitic reaction to it; the Dreyfus Affair between 1894 and 1906, in which Durkheim was involved as an active Dreyfusard; Durkheim's work during World War I on behalf of Jewish immigrants from Russia; and developments in Russia itself, including pogroms in 1903 and 1905 and the emancipation of Russian Jewry in 1917. This chapter alludes to some of these events, but it does not aim to provide a complete account of Durkheim's social thought or circumstances in their entirety. The development of his sociological work and the wider context in which he formulated his ideas have been well documented by others and cannot be fully addressed in the scope of this chapter. Instead, this chapter focuses more narrowly on one aspect of Durkheim's cultural and discursive milieu: it seeks to understand his ideas about the Jews and Judaism, at least in part, as a dialectical response to opposing ideas that could be found in the public sphere in nineteenth-century France.[8]

Reactionary Antisemitism: The Jews as Symbols of Revolutionary Modernization

Historians remain divided about how precisely to analyze the nineteenth-century French right and its relation to twentieth-century fascism, but three main currents can be distinguished: the Ultraroyalists, known as Legitimists following the 1830 July Revolution, who were loyal to the Bourbon dynasty, committed to an alliance of throne and altar, and hostile to the French Revolution; the Orleanists, aligned with the house of Orléans and the *grande bourgeoisie* and committed to an elitist parliamentary liberalism; and Bonapartism, which was Caesarist, antiparliamentary, and devoted to national glory. French Catholicism, historically aligned with the right after the 1789 Revolution, was also divided into competing currents. On the one hand, Assumptionist Catholicism was militant and intransigent, demanded repentance for France's alleged infidelity to its Christian tradition, looked for a miraculous return to power of pope and king, and sought to mobilize the masses through pilgrimages and the press. On the other hand, a minority liberal current was averse to public disorder and to apocalyptic and mystical tendencies but largely isolated from the masses. Two other developments further complicated this configuration. In a shift in the 1890s known as the *Ralliement*, some French royalists made their peace with the Third Republic at the urging of Pope Leo XIII. Because not all royalists accepted the papal decision, this move exacerbated the divisions within French Catholicism. Moreover, in the last third of the nineteenth century, a new nationalist-populist right arose, exemplified by the formation of the Action Française in 1899. Although this nationalist-populist current exercised an important influence over the broader rightist spectrum, its relations with older elements of the French right were not always harmonious. In sum, although capable of coming together at times into a potent coalition, the right wing in nineteenth-century France was not monolithic.[9]

Antisemitism found expression across both old and new elements of the French right. In France, as elsewhere in Europe during the nineteenth century, antisemitism was linked to anxiety about and reactions against modernization, in all of its disruptive manifestations: capitalist development, the modern state, urbanization, transformation of the family and women's roles in society, secularization ("dechristianization"), demographic shifts, and so forth.[10] While not every element of the French right opposed all of these changes, each could find aspects of modernity that threatened its particular ideals and interests. Insofar as the Jews came to be seen as a symbol of modernity and one of its governing factors, as both the sign and cause of a "world gone wrong," they became a lightning rod for the anxieties that modernization provoked.[11]

Because the exponents of reactionary antisemitism in France traced many of these same changes to the French Revolution of 1789, they also associated the Jews with the Revolution.[12] Wilson notes that "association of the Jews with sedition, disruption and Revolution had long been a commonplace of antisemitic writing" in France, and historian Esther Benbassa points out that in the late nineteenth century, right-wing opinion continued to consider the Jew "the architect of revolution and anticlericalism, the persecutor of the clergy, and the destroyer of Christian religion and civilization."[13] Charles Maurras, for instance, a leader and theoretician of the Action Française, referred to the French Revolution as "the Jewish Revolution."[14] According to this view, the Jews orchestrated the French Revolution out of self-interest and were its principal beneficiaries. As jurist Edmond Picard put it, the "fearsome Semitic invasion dates only from 1789 and from the reforms realized by the Revolution."[15] Likewise, for the journalist Edouard Drumont, the Jew was "the most powerful agent of turmoil that the world has produced." "Wherever the Jews appear," he insisted, "they spread disorder and ruin in their wake"; "the Semites excel in the politics of dissolution."[16] The Catholic clergy expressed similar views. The abbé Chabauty wrote that "the Revolution in all its reality is the Jewish nation, acting throughout the entire world, under the orders of its leaders, in several army corps and under several banners, inside, outside, and against Catholic and Christian society"; the abbé Lémann, who was himself a Jewish convert, denounced the Declaration of the Rights of Man as "a war machine in the hands of the Jews"; and the popular and influential Catholic newspaper *La Croix*, referring to the centenary of the French Revolution as "the Semitic centenary," informed its readers that the Jews brought about the Revolution not merely to emancipate themselves but to dominate France.[17] Catholic antisemites, in short, held the Jews responsible for all the tribulations that afflicted the Church since 1789. French antisemitism, the writer Bernard Lazare concluded in 1894, was "the creed of the conservative class, of those who accuse the Jews of having worked hand in hand with the Jacobins of 1789."[18]

If the Jews were identified with the Revolution in the discourse of reactionary antisemitism, "the rejected modern world was contrasted with an imagined 'Old France,'" and "'Old France' was set in explicit opposition to the Jews."[19] Antisemites like Drumont contended that the old regime had subordinated the Jews in order to protect itself from them: "If ancient France had been happy and glorious for many centuries, it was because it carefully guarded itself against the Jew."[20] Moreover, reactionary antisemites tended to view Jewish influence as a cause or, alternatively, a consequence of the collapse of the old regime. Drumont tried to show "how, little by little, under the Jewish influence, old France was dissolved."[21] As literary critic Ferdinand Brunetière put it in his review of Drumont's *La France juive*, if modern France "scarcely resembles that of Louis XIV and even less that of St. Louis, the fault, or rather the crime, lies with the Jews."[22] Reversing this reasoning, the monarchist Maurras insisted that it was the revolutionary destruction of the old regime—the "fall of the national dynasty," the "disorganization of the nobility and the clergy," the "persecution of Catholicism," the destruction of intermediary corporate bodies and the "achievement of centralization"—that explained the "rise to power" of the Jews and their allies: Freemasons, Protestants, and foreigners. By transforming France into "a dust of individuals, a desert of atoms," he argued, the Revolution had made it vulnerable to Jewish domination.[23] What was needed, Maurras wrote in the Legitimist *Gazette de France* in 1899, was to treat the Jews as foreigners and restore them to an inferior civil and legal status, "the precaution taken in the Middle Ages," as if one could undo the destruction of the old regime by striking at those whom, in his estimation, its destruction had most benefited.[24]

While this aspiration to restore the old regime and its clearly ordered social hierarchy united reactionary forms of antisemitism, this aspiration expressed itself in different ways, most notably in religious and racial terms.[25] On the one hand, "antisemitism overlapped with the traditional Catholic view" to the extent that the latter was associated with "a backward-looking hierarchical view of the social order." Indeed, "there was a tendency . . . to regard the Church itself as a paradigm of the general social order which antisemites yearned for" and Catholicism as "a necessary bulwark of the social order."[26] On the other hand, the language of racism provided a new and different way of reasserting social order that had the advantages of putative scientific credibility and broad public appeal (even to some socialists), though it existed in uneasy tension with Catholic theology (which stressed, after all, the possibility and duty of converting the Jews). As Wilson explains, racism sought to organize society "as a static hierarchy" and "to justify a kind of 'caste' system": "Late nineteenth-century French society was one in which the hierarchical classification in terms of orders, which had obtained under the Ancien Régime, was obviously inoperative, even in its modified post-revolutionary form." Although postrevolutionary France did not lack a status system, it was "shifting, based . . . to an increasing degree on 'merit' and wealth." If the Jews came to epitomize "uncertainty about social categorizations and ranking" by virtue of their social mobility, then "racial terminology provided an anti-solvent, a new form of absolute and binding classification."[27] In sum, the Christian anti-Judaism expressed in clerical circles sought to reestablish a hierarchical social order modeled on the Church itself, while racial antisemitism revived in a new form the aristocratic principle of hereditary inequality.

Radical Antisemitism: The Jews as Symbols of the Old Regime

Following the 1871 Paris Commune, the French left was divided between syndicalism, which was associated with the Confédération Générale du Travail (formed in 1895) and oriented to industrial organization and economic action (primarily the strike), and socialism, which was oriented to political organization and action.[28] Socialists were themselves divided into a multitude of doctrines and sects, most notably the Guesdists, followers of Jules Guesde, French socialism's most orthodox Marxist; the Blanquists, disciples of Auguste Blanqui, including Albert Regnard, Gustave Tridon, and their leader Edouard Vaillant; the Possibilists, the reformist wing of the socialist movement; the Allemanists, dissident Possibilists led by Jean Allemane; and "independent" socialists, including Auguste Chirac, Alexandre Millerand, and Durkheim's friend Jean Jaurès, "who did not subscribe to any single, well-defined ideology and were not enrolled in any of the nationally or regionally organized Socialist parties."[29] It was not until 1905 that the Guesdists, Blanquists, Possibilists, Allemanists, and independents formed a unified party, the Section Française de l'Internationale Ouvrière (SFIO). Even then, opinion within the prewar SFIO remained divided over socialist participation in bourgeois governments, socialist participation in war, and whether the socialist movement and trade unions should be linked or kept separate. In addition, socialism was sometimes understood to encompass the anarchists, who in 1881 split from the various schools of "orthodox" socialism and in 1892 began a violent campaign of propaganda by the deed; the Radical Socialists, reformist republicans who separated from other socialist parties in the early 1900s; and even some nationalists and former Boulangists.[30] In sum, the French left was just as variegated as the French right in the late nineteenth century.

While the counterrevolutionary type of antisemitism described in the previous section may be its most familiar expression, it would be a mistake to conclude that antisemitism was confined exclusively to reactionaries who rejected the legacies of 1789. In addition, there existed a radical and left-wing variant, the exponents of which—including some of the principal fathers of French socialism—saw themselves as the Revolution's most "faithful and uncompromising heirs."[31] Indeed, "at the beginning of the Third Republic, the most important anti-Semitic writings came from the pens of socialists such as Albert Regnard, Gustave Tridon, and Auguste Chirac."[32] There were socialists across the movement's ideological and organizational divisions who mixed anticapitalism with antisemitism into the 1890s.[33] Ultimately, it was the Dreyfus Affair that separated what was not always clearly distinguishable before then: the "orthodox" socialists, who eventually sided with the Dreyfusards and united in the SFIO, and the nationalist and antisemitic socialists, who sided with the anti-Dreyfusards.[34]

In contrast to the language of reactionary antisemitism, which tended to associate the Jews with the Revolution and with the disruptive modernizing processes it had unleashed, the discourse of radical antisemitism tended to identify the Jews with the old regime or, more precisely, a neo-feudal social order.[35] For example, at a rally in the town of Suresnes in 1898, Georges

Thiébaud and Lucien Millevoye "made declarations of antisemitic revolutionary Socialism, declaring that 'all the principles of 1789 are threatened by the Jewish conspiracy.'"[36] Similarly, when anti-Jewish riots swept through France in 1898, the socialist *Humanité nouvelle* "praised the anti-Jewish demonstrators in France as heirs to the revolutionary tradition of 1789."[37] This view was a continuation of the sort of anti-Jewish views expressed during the Revolution itself by the antisemitic Jacobin Jean-François Rewbell, who prominently opposed the extension of citizenship to the Jews. It harkened back to eighteenth-century perceptions of the Jews, characteristic of the French Enlightenment and subsequently revived in the writings of some nineteenth-century socialists, as archaic, ignorant, superstitious, traditionalistic, particularistic, clannish, and backward—in short, the very antithesis of the modern society that the French Revolution ushered in.[38]

Identification of the Jews with the old regime took different forms, depending on which aspect of the Revolution was stressed. Most commonly, the Jews were denounced as a new royalty or nobility. This view was summed up in the title of Alphonse Toussenel's popular book, *Les Juifs, rois de l'epoque: Histoire de la féodalité financière*, first published in 1845 and reissued in 1847, 1886, and 1888. Toussenel was a self-described disciple of Charles Fourier whose book likely influenced Pierre-Joseph Proudhon.[39] "The French people," Toussenel argued, "supposedly freed by the revolution of '89 from the yoke of the feudal nobility, has only changed masters"; they were now "enfeoffed to the domination of Israel."[40] Using similar language, Proudhon denounced the Jews as "the rulers of the day," "indifferent . . . to the progress and freedom of the people they oppress," and he condemned as "counterrevolutionary . . . all the lenders of money and instruments of labor . . . who recognize the Jews as their leaders."[41] According to this view, the Jews matched and even exceeded the worst traits of the old feudal nobility: they were rapacious, greedy, parasitic, exploitative, and unwilling to engage in productive labor. This perception was common in French socialist circles, articulated among others by Fourier, Proudhon, and Chirac.[42] As Proudhon put it, "the Jew is by temperament an anti-producer, neither a farmer nor a manufacturer nor even a true merchant"—in short, no part of the Third Estate.[43] Toussenel's identification of the Jews with the dominant forces of the old regime was echoed in Proudhon's declaration that "the reign of the Jews" was "the triumph of industrial feudalism" and the title of Chirac's own book, *Les rois de la république: Histoire des juiveries*.[44] Although attacks on the Jews as agents of usury, speculation, exploitation, and profiteering were not confined to the left, denunciation of the Jews as a new royalty or nobility issued frequently from radical quarters as a means of defining the problems of French workers, assigning blame, suggesting remedies, and motivating collective action.[45]

In addition, the discourse of radical antisemitism often associated the Jews with the Catholic Church. "While certain early socialists confused Jews and Jewish bankers with capitalism, others became anti-Semites owing to their anti-religious convictions."[46] This kind of hostility emerged from the French Enlightenment and was especially conspicuous in the work of Voltaire; it reappeared in the anticlericalism of the Revolution, particularly during the Terror and its accompanying persecution of religion; and it resurfaced in the nineteenth century in the language of antisemitic socialists like Proudhon and Tridon.[47] These figures opposed the Jews in part because they understood Christianity to be derived from Judaism.[48] As Proudhon put it, the Jews were the "first authors of that evil superstition called Catholicism in which the furious, intolerant Jewish element always prevailed over the other Greek, Latin, barbarian, etc. elements and served to torture humankind for so long."[49] Likewise, Tridon posited a struggle between Aryan and Semitic civilizations, traced Christianity to the latter, and hailed the French Revolution as heralding a possible return to Aryan wisdom. For Tridon, "Judaism was the deeper source of the evil resulting from the triumph of the Christian world-view in the West."[50] In sum, whether as symbols of feudal nobility or religious obscurantism, the Jews were consistently identified in the discourse of radical antisemitism not with the destructive consequences of revolutionary modernization, but with the most backward and oppressive aspects of the old regime.

Durkheim's Engagement with Jewish Concerns

My argument that Durkheim's work contained direct and indirect responses to French antisemitism gains plausibility if it can be demonstrated that he was attentive to Jewish issues. What do we know about his sense of Jewish identity, especially in relation to that of others in his circle, and how does it square with this chapter's thesis? On the one hand, his attitude toward Judaism has been described as agnostic, uncommitted, and areligious, which apparently made his more observant sister Rosine feel (in her words) "embarrassed about following our old traditions."[51] Some of Durkheim's personal choices may be seen as indicative of this attitude. For instance, his wedding took place in a town hall, and his daughter Marie was also married in a civil ceremony, according to her father's wishes, which so displeased Durkheim's sister that she refused to attend.[52] Durkheim's obituaries in Jewish newspapers noted that he ceased to practice Judaism and lamented that he "did not know the religion of his fathers."[53] More recent commentators have echoed these assessments, suggesting that Durkheim "cut his umbilical ties to the [Jewish] religious community" and transferred his attachment instead to "French republican and secular society," "discarded Judaism," "rejected Judaism as a religion," or distanced himself from religion.[54]

On the other hand, Durkheim's attitude to Judaism was not wholly hostile, he "never repudiated his Jewish birth," and he "never deliberately and irrevocably cut himself off from all his Jewish roots and connections."[55] On the contrary, he maintained strong ties to his "close-knit Jewish provincial family."[56] For instance, he continued to return as an adult to his hometown of Épinal for major Jewish holidays, and he chided his nephew Marcel Mauss for shirking family obligations such as taking his grandmother to synagogue.[57] Durkheim himself took part in family rituals, reportedly looking "happy at the prospect of an upcoming bar mitzvah," and he even attended synagogue, albeit rarely, on family occasions in Épinal.[58] In addition, he chose to marry a Jewish woman, Louise Dreyfus, and such "endogamy reinforced alliances with other Jewish circles."[59]

Durkheim also "kept his affiliation to the Jewish community."[60] He collaborated in his scholarly work with other Jewish intellectuals, maintained close contact with Jewish scholar and Dreyfusard Salomon Reinach during the Dreyfus Affair, and received an invitation from the chief rabbi of Bordeaux to give a lecture on Judaism.[61] During World War I, Durkheim supported the Comité Française d'Information et d'Action auprès des Juifs des Pays Neutres, and he served as president of another committee established in 1916 under the auspices of the Société des Études Juives to document (partly in response to antisemitism) the service of Jews in the war.[62] Like many of his Franco-Jewish contemporaries, Durkheim also took an active interest in the plight of Russian Jews during World War I, both those who had immigrated to France and those who remained in Russia. He served on a commission established in 1915 to study the situation of Russian immigrants in Paris, most of them Jewish, and in that capacity, he challenged the antisemitism directed at them during the war.[63] In 1916, he joined Baron Edmond de Rothschild and the scholar Sylvain Lévi—all three were "prominent members" of the Alliance Israélite Universelle—to discuss the dire circumstances of Russian Jewry with two officials of the Russian government traveling through Paris.[64] When a meeting was held in 1916 "under the leadership of Sylvain Lévi, of Rabbis Dreyfuss and Israël Lévi, and of the philo-Semitic socialist deputy Marius Moutet . . . to organize legal assistance for Russian Jews residing in Paris," "both Durkheim and Lévi expressed the wish that French and immigrant Jews draw closer together," and Durkheim "became the head of the committee established to effect the rapprochement of the two communities."[65] These activities indicate the extent of Durkheim's integration into and solidarity with the organized Jewish community in France.

Durkheim's efforts to diagnose and counter antisemitism suggest that it played an important role in fostering his sense of Jewish identity.[66] Contemporary sociologist Pierre Birnbaum tentatively suggests that antisemitism reawakened "a feeling, however feeble, of particularist identity," "a kind of hidden faithfulness," within Durkheim and Jewish members of his circle, "which sometimes moved them to public action and to unexpected commitments."[67] Likewise, Ivan Strenski contends that "anti-Semitism reinforced or even created," however "incipiently and incompletely," a "sense of Jewish identity" for Durkheim and Mauss that "was, up to that point, weak or moribund."[68] If this interpretation is correct, Durkheim and the Jewish members of his circle were caught up in a larger trend. Antisemitism, especially during the Dreyfus Affair, "compelled a number of Jewish intellectuals . . . to explore the meaning of their differentness in French society," resulting in a new interest in Jewish culture and a new willingness among some of them to reflect publicly about their Jewishness and write on Jewish themes.[69]

In sum, Durkheim's sense of Jewish identity was not traditionalist, but neither was it absent or nonexistent. To be sure, Durkheim continued to see emancipation and assimilation as the solution to the Jewish question as late as 1917, and he welcomed the February Revolution in Russia for making such a solution possible for Russian Jewry.[70] However, biographical evidence suggests that he did not envision assimilation as a complete obliteration of Jewish identity or loss of Jewish particularism. As Pickering has argued, Durkheim's life is best seen as an instance of *accommodation* rather than *incorporation*: in other words, not a complete shedding of Jewish identity and ties to the Jewish community but a process in which the individual "becomes closely associated with the larger society by adopting as much of the gentile culture as is possible without denying Jewish culture."[71] Likewise, though Durkheim's obituary in the *Univers israélite* lamented that he "probably contributed to alienating more than one Jewish intellectual from Judaism," many of the Jewish intellectuals who collaborated with him showed a similar pattern of accommodation in their lives.[72] This pattern was not unusual: even though nineteenth-century French Jewry officially defined itself in religious terms, nonobservant Jews made up a sizable portion of the community by the early twentieth century; these "nonpracticing Jews were still considered coreligionists"; and many of them "continued to identify as Jews" and "often took part in Jewish philanthropic efforts as a nonreligious expression of their Jewishness."[73] Even in the face of virulent antisemitism, Durkheim and several Jewish members of his circle remained wedded to the "policy of integration pursued by French Jewry," a middle way between the kind of Jewish self-determination espoused by Zionism and the "total assimilation" demanded by some elements of French society.[74]

The biographical evidence presented here is consistent with the broader claims of this chapter. If Durkheim's sense of Jewish identity developed in response to the antisemitism of his time, then it is not farfetched to think that his sociological thought developed in reaction to antisemitism as well. This does not mean, of course, that antisemitism was the only element of Durkheim's milieu against which his sociological thought was directed. However, if antisemitism was salient and significant enough to shape his sense of personal identity, it would be strange indeed if it was irrelevant to his sociological thought.

Durkheim's Sociology in Relation to Reactionary Antisemitism

Durkheim was surely familiar with the leaders and ideas of reactionary antisemitism. Drumont's *La France juive* was an enormously popular best seller in Durkheim's time, and it was widely reviewed, including by the Catholic rightist Brunetière, whose views Durkheim criticized.[75] Given the fame that the book brought Drumont, it is inconceivable that Durkheim would have been unacquainted with Drumont's work. Furthermore, Durkheim's correspondence shows that he was familiar with the Action Française and with antisemitic leaders of the nationalist-populist right like Maurras and Maurice Barrès, as one would expect given Durkheim's involvement in the Dreyfusard cause.[76] Durkheim's professional and civic activities also brought him into contact with French Catholicism. He engaged liberal Catholics through his involvement in the Union pour la Vérité—an association whose host, Paul Desjardins, aimed to reconcile Catholics and freethinkers, to whom Durkheim argued in 1905 that the separation of church and state would benefit the former—and through his participation in the Union des Libres Penseurs et de Libres Croyants pour la Culture Morale—an association that brought together believers and secularists, where in 1914 he sought to assure the former that his sociology of religion was not a threat to them.[77] At the same time, Durkheim became closely associated with anticlericalism because of his role in promoting secular education.[78] These activities would have acquainted Durkheim with Catholic ideas, including the antisemitism in clerical circles.

The propagators of reactionary antisemitism were also familiar with Durkheim. Barrès was a careful reader of Durkheim, and sociology occupied an important place in his correspondence with Maurras, though this did not prevent Barrès from castigating Durkheim's sociology in the Chamber of Deputies.[79] The Action Française combined "an attack on the University and its 'official doctrine' in 1912, with an attack on Durkheim and his Jewish influence."[80] Likewise, Maurras denounced Durkheim in 1916 as a Jew and "therefore powerful," an "important professor" and "high dignitary of our University" who spread German ideas and disrespected the French army.[81] In addition, as Durkheim gained authority and influence within the French educational system through his positions on various councils and committees at the Sorbonne and the Ministry of Public Education, attacks on him as "the agent of the anti-clerical governments of the 1900s" became common.[82] Not all such attacks emanated from antisemites, of course, but they would have brought Durkheim and his ideas to the attention of Catholic antisemites, and they certainly fit with and provided a vehicle for antisemitic depictions of the Jew as "the architect of . . . anticlericalism" and "persecutor of the clergy."[83] Admittedly, none of this evidence directly demonstrates that Durkheim's theories were motivated to oppose reactionary antisemites; however, given their familiarity with and opposition to each other, it is likely that reactionary antisemitism was among the elements of Durkheim's milieu against which his thought was directed.

Close examination of Durkheim's sociological work also bears out this thesis. While his sociological views on the Jews were complex, distinguished historical and contemporary elements, and sometimes shifted in emphasis among texts, a continuity is nevertheless discernible in his writings. If the language of reactionary antisemitism set the Jews in opposition to the traditional social order in Europe and identified them with the forces of revolutionary modernization that were rapidly dissolving that order, then Durkheim repeatedly inverted that representation. Again and again, he portrayed the Jews as traditionalistic and backward. Far from constituting the advance guard of a dangerous and disruptive modernity, he suggested, they lagged behind in the process of social development. This view finds its clearest expression in two of his most important works, *The Division of Labor in Society* and *Suicide.*

Durkheim postulated that societies develop over time from simple forms of organization with few or no component parts to highly complex forms of organization with many internal parts.[84] In *The Division of Labor*, he repeatedly suggested that the Jews, by virtue of their segmentary organization based on clans, constituted a relatively simple and primitive social type.[85] "These [segmentary] societies," he pointed out, "are the home *par excellence* of mechanical solidarity"—in other words, the form of solidarity that is the hallmark of the simple societies of the past, based on sameness, uniformity, and conformity, indicated by the prevalence of repressive law, which punishes dissimilarity from the group and precludes the emergence of the "individual personality" and "individual reflection."[86] These characteristics—the distinguishing features of segmentary organization and mechanical solidarity—are in Durkheim's view exemplified by the Jews. "Among the Jews," he noted, "the most abominable crimes are those committed against religion." Because "religion is something essentially social," he inferred that among Jews it is primarily attacks upon society or the group (rather than the individual) that are punished. Jewish law, as codified in the Pentateuch, thus typifies the "wholly repressive" form of law characteristic of "the very lowest societies." In short, "what lies at its heart is the feeling of respect for a force superior to that of the individual."[87]

In *The Division of Labor*, the Jews were said to exemplify another feature of segmentary organization as well: a caste system or "fixed" division of labor that is "passed on by heredity." After pointing to the Indian caste system as "the most perfect model of this organization of labor," Durkheim noted that it is also found among the Jews in the form of the division among *kohanim* (priests), Levites, and Israelites. He suggested that both the low level of functional specialization among the Jews and the role of heredity in the distribution of the priesthood indicate the relatively simple and primitive nature of Jewish society. Moreover, he argued, this organization of labor is not only backward but also a fetter upon the further development of the division of labor. In remarks that clearly foreshadow his criticism later in the book of the forced division of labor that persisted in modern French society, Durkheim added: "For the division of labor to develop, men needed to succeed in throwing off the yoke of heredity and progress to be made by breaking up castes and classes."[88]

Durkheim's references to the Jews (*les Juifs*, *le peuple juif*, or *la nation juive*) in *The Division of Labor* were generally historical in nature, as indicated by the works that he cited and his references to Judea (*Judée*) and the Bible. In contrast, *Suicide* referred clearly to the Jews of modern Europe: its claims about Jews rested on statistical data gathered in the second half of the nineteenth century from Austria and various German states; the Jews of these states were emancipated between 1850 and 1871; and major modernizing changes in Jewish cultural life began to blossom in Germany well before then, most notably the *Haskalah* (Jewish Enlightenment), the *Wissenschaft des Judentums* (Science of Judaism), and Reform Judaism. Moreover, in keeping with its focus on modern European Jewry, *Suicide* switched from the capitalized *Juifs* used in *The Division of Labor*, signifying the Jews as a people, to the lowercase *juifs*, signifying only a religious denomination.[89] Yet despite these shifts, *Suicide* characterized the Jews in similar terms as a community held together by a premodern mechanical solidarity.[90] Their low suicide rate is a product of the "unusual solidarity" and "strict union" of a "small, compact and coherent society" in which "everyone thought and lived alike" and "individual divergences were made almost impossible." "Judaism," he explained, "like all early religions [*religions inférieures*], consists basically of a body of practices minutely governing all the details of life and leaving little room to individual judgment."[91] Although Durkheim acknowledged the role of intolerance and persecution in strengthening Jewish solidarity, he nevertheless regarded it as archaic in form. His account failed to distinguish varieties of Judaism or to acknowledge the struggles within German Jewry between reformers and traditionalists—presumably, he had German Orthodoxy in mind rather than Reform Judaism—but it is not the limitations of his account that I wish to stress so much as its juxtaposition of Judaism with modernity.[92]

Even Durkheim's observations about the high levels of education among European Jews did not lead him to depart significantly from this interpretation of Jewish social life. In *Suicide*, Durkheim argued that education was associated with low social integration, high individuation, and free inquiry, characteristics that are all antithetical to traditional forms of solidarity based on the authority of custom and tradition. This did not mean that free inquiry promoted social dissolution. Rather, Durkheim argued, it was the other way around: "Men generally have the desire for self-instruction only insofar as they are freed from the yoke of tradition. . . . It is certainly not . . . learning . . . that disorganizes religion; but the desire for knowledge wakens because religion becomes disorganized." Moreover, he insisted, it is only in and through free inquiry that social integration can be reestablished. Once the authority of custom and tradition is destroyed, "they cannot be artificially reestablished; only reflection can guide us in life, after this."[93] Thus, in modern societies, mechanical solidarity based on the authority of custom and tradition must be replaced by a new and different sort of solidarity in which greater scope is allowed for individuality and "authority is rationally grounded."[94] In this new form of solidarity, which Durkheim termed *organic*, "reflection" and "criticism" would "exist next to faith, pierce that very faith without destroying it, and occupy an always larger place in it."[95] The Jews would seem to exemplify this possibility because they combined high levels of modern education (Durkheim refers to enrollment in *Gymnasien* and universities) with high levels of social integration, but Durkheim drew a different conclusion. The Jews, he suggested, pursue education and knowledge in order to "protect themselves better against the hate to which they are exposed. . . . The Jew, therefore, seeks to learn, not in order to replace his collective prejudices by reflective thought, but merely to be better armed for the struggle. . . . And since knowledge [*la science*] by itself has no influence upon a tradition in full vigor, he superimposes this intellectual life upon his habitual routine with no effect of the former upon the latter." Thus, education may give the Jew "the intelligence of modern man," but he is still subject to "the severe discipline characteristic of small and ancient groups" and therefore remains "primitive in certain respects."[96]

In summary, while *The Division of Labor* and *Suicide* refer to Jews in different historical periods and places, there is nevertheless a continuity in how the texts characterize them. This continuity becomes more apparent against the background of opposing ideas in Durkheim's milieu: Durkheim's description of the Jews inverts their depiction in the discourse of reactionary antisemitism as symbols and agents of modernity. In Durkheim's writings, mechanical solidarity—the very form of solidarity that reactionary antisemites wished to restore in France—is ironically epitomized by the very group whom they held responsible for its destruction. Likewise, the Jews do not represent money, mobility, and the dissolution of the old regime's rigid status system, as reactionary antisemitism would have it, but rather the permanent, fixed, and hereditary inequalities that characterized the old regime. In both respects, Durkheim's Jews symbolize the past rather than the dominant trends of modern society, for "the progressive decline of castes . . . is a law of history."[97] Thus, for Durkheim, reactionary antisemitism is doubly wrong: not only does it misrepresent the Jews, but it also struggles in vain against the tide of historical development.

Durkheim's challenge to reactionary antisemitism does not rest here, however. Even if the French Revolution was a "Jewish Revolution"—a notion belied by Durkheim's characterization of the Jews—reactionary antisemitism fundamentally misconstrues its nature and consequences. The Revolution, he insisted, was not primarily, or at least not only, a source of social dissolution. Properly understood, it was a moment of "collective effervescence" through which social solidarity might be reestablished.[98] This was Durkheim's response to the Catholic anti-Judaism of clerical circles. He agreed with Catholic reactionaries that "religion alone" could produce the "moral unity" that society needed.[99] However, he suggested, the postrevolutionary secular world was not so irreligious as they might think. The "principles of '89" were themselves "articles of faith," "a religion which has had its martyrs and apostles, which has profoundly moved the masses, and which, after all, has given birth to great things."[100] Indeed, "nowhere has society's ability to make itself a god or to create gods been more in evidence than during the first years of the Revolution." "The Revolution," he pointed out, "instituted a whole cycle of celebrations in order to keep the principles that inspired it eternally young," and even though "that work miscarried," "everything leads us to believe that the work will sooner or later be taken up again."[101] Elsewhere, Durkheim indicated what that work entailed: "it is a matter of completing, extending, and organizing individualism," the system of beliefs "which the Declaration of the Rights of Man attempted, more or less happily, to formulate" and that had "become the basis of our moral catechism." Catholic opposition to this "religion of the individual" was misguided in Durkheim's view, in part because individualism derived from the "Christian morality" of the past, but more importantly because it provided "the only system of beliefs which [could] ensure the moral unity of the country" in the modern age. "To take it away from us when we have nothing else to put in its place," he declared, was to promote precisely what Catholic reactionaries most feared: "moral anarchy."[102]

Durkheim also took aim at reactionary antisemitism in its racial form. He challenged the scientific pretensions of racial antisemitism indirectly in *Suicide* by demonstrating that race did not adequately explain variation in the suicide rate. In addition, he denied that antisemites would find in race a model for the sort of stable and unambiguous social order they desired. Far from eliminating uncertainty about social categorizations and ranking, race exemplified confusion and uncertainty. "Due to crossings in every direction, each of the existing varieties of our species comes from very different origins," and consequently "no one could say with accuracy where they begin and end."[103] The Jews were a case in point; through assimilation, they "lose their ethnic character with extreme rapidity. Only two generations and it's gone."[104] Moreover, Durkheim understood that racial antisemitism sought to revive the sort of hereditary caste system he criticized in *The Division of Labor*, which he argued was not only incompatible with the heritage of the French Revolution (a point that reactionary antisemites would readily acknowledge) but also destined to disappear as the division of labor advanced and society became more complex.[105] Thus, Durkheim's sociology sought to discredit this revival of caste inequality not only on normative grounds but also on the grounds that it was incompatible with the overall development and functional requirements of modern society and therefore futile. For Durkheim, these arguments converged: "The society which morality bids us desire is . . . the society as it is or is really becoming."[106]

Durkheim's Sociology in Relation to Radical Antisemitism

Durkheim was well acquainted with the history, ideas, and leaders of the socialist and syndicalist movements in France. He studied the works of Claude-

Henri de Saint-Simon, Fourier, and Proudhon in preparation for courses he taught or planned to teach; he published articles and reviews about socialism; and he taught a course on the history of socialism.[107] Furthermore, Durkheim was a close friend of Jaurès and reportedly played a key role in persuading him to embrace the Dreyfusard cause; he found some of Guesde's ideas consistent with his own but criticized him in other respects; and in 1905 he debated Hubert Lagardelle, a theoretician of revolutionary syndicalism (and later the minister of labor for the Vichy regime) at a forum sponsored by the Union pour la Vérité.[108] Durkheim also showed familiarity in his correspondence with leading radicals, including Guesde, Jaurès, Vaillant, and the syndicalists Lagardelle and Georges Sorel.[109]

French socialists and syndicalists were also well aware of Durkheim's work. "Many of the Durkheimians . . . lectured to workers in the *École socialiste*" and in the *Universités populaires*, and "they published their sociological work in abridged and popularized form in socialist tracts."[110] Durkheim himself delivered a lecture in 1900 to the Congrès International de l'Éducation Sociale, the audience for which included the socialist minister Millerand, leaders of the Radical Socialist Party, and trade union representatives.[111] The radical reception of Durkheim's ideas was mixed. On the one hand, Jaurès "enthused about Durkheim's work" as early as 1893, and Durkheim's definition of socialism "impressed Guesde and Jaurès, who declared themselves to be in agreement with Durkheim."[112] On the other hand, Sorel published two critical articles about Durkheim's ideas in 1895, including a lengthy study in the socialist journal *Le Devenir social*, and the *Revue socialiste* published Charles Péguy's critical review of Durkheim's *Suicide* in 1897.[113] Given the interest that Durkheim and the radical left took in each other, he would surely have been aware of the antisemitism within radical circles, and one would expect his own thinking about the social question to be directed against it, among other things. However, in the absence of conclusive evidence that Durkheim's ideas were motivated to oppose radical antisemitism, it is only possible to outline an implicit response within his work.

Durkheim's sociology challenged reactionary antisemitism in a straightforward fashion: it disputed the identification of the Jews with revolutionary modernization while denying that the Revolution was a source of social dissolution. Durkheim's relationship to radical antisemitism appears more complicated. Like the radical antisemites, he saw himself as a champion and faithful heir of the Revolution, and his characterization of the Jews as traditionalistic and backward dovetailed with their view of the Jews as symbols of the old regime. However, despite these affinities, and despite his sympathetic stance toward socialism, Durkheim never succumbed to the socialism of fools. The most obvious explanation is Durkheim's Jewish background, which one might expect to have immunized him from the influence of antisemitism. This will not do, however, for there were contemporaries whose Jewish backgrounds hardly prevented them from adopting hostile attitudes toward the Jews. In the pages that follow, I clarify how precisely Durkheim's sociology broke with radical antisemitism, and I suggest that this break had less to do with Durkheim's Jewish background than with their fundamentally different conceptions of the French Revolution and what it would mean to complete it.

While radical antisemitism and Durkheim's sociology both pointed to socialism as a solution to the problems of modern French society, they differed over the meaning of socialism and the means to achieve it. For radical antisemites, the main task of the socialist movement was to dispossess society's privileged class, which they identified with the Jews, and to overturn what they imagined as a neo-feudal social order based on Jewish domination and exploitation. In contrast, Durkheim sought to build socialism without class (or ethnic) warfare. According to his view, "the problem is . . . immeasurably greater than that of the conflicting material interests of the classes; it is not simply a question of diminishing the share of some so as to increase that of others, but rather of remaking the moral constitution of society." This formulation, he added, would divest socialism of its "aggressive and malevolent character."[114] Although these remarks were directed against class warfare rather than antisemitism, they make clear Durkheim's objections to both. By substituting "race" or "ethnic group" for "class" in this passage (categories that radical antisemites themselves routinely confounded), his response to radical antisemitism becomes apparent. While radical antisemites could only imagine a socialist society built on the dispossession and exclusion of the Jews, Durkheim envisioned a more universalistic socialism that would resolve social conflicts in a positive-sum manner. This approach, he stressed, would present "the social question . . . in an entirely different manner. . . . [I]t no longer opposes rich to poor, employers to workers"—or, he might have added, Semites to Aryans—"as if the only possible solution consisted of diminishing the portion of one in order to augment that of the other."[115] "However future society is organized . . . ," he insisted, "there will be a place for all."[116]

While Durkheim was averse to all attempts to resolve the social question through the dispossession of one group by another, he regarded the demand for the dispossession of the Jews as especially misguided because it was a form of scapegoating. (Class warfare, in contrast, was at least based on the reality of conflicting material interests.) In an analysis of modern European antisemitism written at the height of the Dreyfus Affair, Durkheim argued that such scapegoating strengthened solidarity by uniting society around hatred of the Jew. However, he regarded this kind of solidarity as pathological in the context of late nineteenth-century France because it was narrow and exclusionary—a revival of the mechanical form of solidarity that in his view was unsuitable for complex, modern societies.[117] Thus, just as reactionary antisemites ironically promoted social dissolution by their rejection of individualism, the radical antisemites, despite their pretensions to be the most faithful heirs of the Revolution, were in fact profoundly reactionary in their commitment to a premodern form of solidarity deeply at odds with the individual autonomy that the Revolution had promoted.

Durkheim's preference for "remaking the moral constitution of society" over class (or ethnic) warfare flowed directly from his interpretation of the French Revolution. Like the radical antisemites, he saw fundamental continuities between the Revolution and the socialist movement of the nineteenth century, and he considered the Revolution to be unfinished business.[118] But he differed sharply with them over what it would mean to complete the work of the Revolution. While radical antisemitism conceived that work in terms of negation (finishing or reiterating the destruction of the old regime), Durkheim emphasized the need to consolidate, extend, and institutionalize the "principles of '89." In his view, the Revolution "succeeded in striking the final blows at the old system," "abolished all that remained of feudalism," and thereby "extricated" the country "from the past," but it failed to successfully "organize the present," at least "with any stability." With "nothing new" built on "the land thus cleared," the Revolution remained "a *res nullius*" (ownerless property) "suited to all possible ends." "An action so exclusively destructive," he added, "far from attenuating the crisis which had given rise to it, could only make the evil more acute and intolerable."[119] Fortunately, though radical antisemites failed to see the dangers of adopting and repeating this purely negative and destructive approach, other French socialists had perceived the dangers and drawn the appropriate conclusions. Durkheim praised Saint-Simon in particular: "He understood that to reorganize society it was not enough to destroy the old system of forces which unified it. . . . [I]t is necessary to rebuild on new foundations. . . . He reproaches the men of the Revolution for having overthrown the ancient institutions without determining what to put in their place."[120] Durkheim's reproach to the radical antisemites is similar. Like old generals, they imagined that they were still fighting the last war, when what was needed was postwar reconstruction.

Durkheim indicated in a variety of places how the "principles of '89" might be consolidated, extended, and institutionalized.[121] His chief proposal was the reorganization of economic relations through the revival of professional groups. In addition, he sought to "complete, organize and extend individualism," to promote greater equality of opportunity, "to organize economic life and introduce more justice into contractual relations," and "to alleviate the functioning of the social machine, that is still so harsh to individuals, to put within their reach all possible means of developing their faculties without hindrance, to strive to make a reality of the famous precept: 'to each according to his work.'"[122] By realizing a healthy, organic form of social solidarity appropriate to a complex society with a highly developed division of labor, these measures would obviate the need for the pathological forms of solidarity generated by scapegoating, which ultimately divided rather than integrated French society.

A discussion of Durkheim's response to radical antisemitism would not be complete without addressing the anticlerical aspects of the latter, for the Jews symbolized not only a new financial nobility in the language of radical antisemitism but religious obscurantism as well. Interestingly, both Catholic and anticlerical forms of antisemitism viewed Judaism with deep distrust as a corrupting influence (though for very different reasons) which rendered its adherents unfit for civil incorporation into the French community they imagined (in quite different terms).[123] While Catholic antisemitism envisioned a hierarchical social order modeled on the Church from which Jews would be excluded, radical antisemites envisioned a world emancipated from Judaism (and Catholicism). In this respect, too, radical antisemitism was destructive rather than constructive, intent primarily on negating the past. Durkheim's interpretation of the French Revolution as a religious regeneration posed a double challenge to radical antisemitism: it directly contested the conventional view (shared by reactionaries and radicals alike) that the Revolution was fundamentally an attack on religion, and (in contrast to both reactionary and radical antisemitism) it held out the promise of an expanded solidarity in which the Jews could be included. Here, too, Durkheim's response to radical antisemitism was indebted to the ideas of Saint-Simon. Saint-Simonism had attracted considerable interest and support from French Jews in the first half of the nineteenth century, in part because it held out the promise of Jewish integration within the movement's new universalist religion.[124] As Benbassa explains, "the Jew would no longer suffer discrimination owing to his faith and would naturally find his place within this unity. This symbiotic religious vision, untraumatic for Jewish identity, prefigured the secular option that took shape, though not without a messianic aspect of its own, under the Third Republic: Franco-Judaism."[125] Similarly, Durkheim's sociology held out the promise of Jewish integration within the "religion of the individual" propagated by the Revolution, a new, modern, and universalistic civil religion that would transcend the religious divisions of the past.[126]

How precisely would the Jews be integrated into the "religion of the individual" propagated by the Revolution? Was it, as contemporary sociologist Zygmunt Bauman described the meaning of socialism for many European Jewish intellectuals, "a program of *assimilation by other means*," a purely abstract and "universal movement which knew no Jew or gentile," in which "the handicap of Jewishness could be shed" and Jews could turn into "men as such"?[127] Or did Durkheim understand the "principles of '89" and the cult of the individual in dialectical terms as a form of collective consciousness that transcended but also preserved particularistic identities and attachments? His remark that the Jews were losing their ethnic character suggests the former interpretation. However, the latter interpretation is more consistent with his argument that mechanical solidarity based on sameness was giving way to an organic form of solidarity that allowed for pluralism and difference. The biographical evidence from Durkheim's own life supports this latter interpretation as well. The pattern of accommodation exemplified by Durkheim and other Jewish intellectuals in his circle suggests that the "principles of '89" were, in his view, not a purely abstract and universal rationalism that negates particularistic identities and attachments, but the basis for an expanded form of solidarity that both preserves and transcends them. In this respect, Durkheim's understanding of the Revolution conformed to the prevailing view among French Jews of his time that there was no conflict between acculturation and "group survival as Jews" and that "French-Jewish symbiosis was possible and mutually beneficial."[128]

An Excursus on Jews and Other Others

While Durkheim's ideas about Jews and Judaism are best understood in relation to French antisemitism, they may be further clarified by comparing his portrayal of Jews to other groups, social categories, or nations that played a significant role in his thinking. Before concluding this chapter, let us briefly consider four such groups: Protestants, women, Germans, and colonial subjects. With the exception of what Durkheim called religious societies, these categories overlapped empirically with Jews: there were Jewish women as well as men, Jews in Germany as well as France, and Jews in the colonies as well as the metropole. Nevertheless, these categories represent ways of dividing the social world that we can distinguish analytically. In this way, we can compare how Durkheim contrasted men and women, for instance, to how he contrasted Jews and gentiles. These kinds of comparisons will help us to identify what is peculiar to his characterization of Jews.

Protestants held prominent positions in the political and commercial classes of Third Republic France and were also associated, like Jews and freethinkers, with modernity. As we have seen, hostility to republicanism and capitalist development could be directed equally at these groups, who were sometimes lumped together for this purpose. French antisemites "engaged in an essentialist and dualist exercise in classification, and, once an entity had been labeled evil rather than good, it became the equivalent of all the other entities placed under that heading. Thus Jew equaled Freemason equaled Protestant equaled England equaled Germany, and so on."[129] As we shall see in later chapters, this tendency is not peculiar to French social thinkers or to previous centuries. Durkheim, however, challenged the equation of Jews and Protestants. Although he, too, associated Protestantism with individualism, free inquiry, and hence modernity, he described Jews quite differently as bound together by a traditionalistic form of solidarity that allowed little scope for individual dissent.[130] In short, rather than lumping together Jews and Protestants, Durkheim contrasted Judaism and Protestantism to elucidate his conception of modernity.

Durkheim's portrayal of women provides another counterpoint to his description of Jews. Contemporary sociologist Jennifer Lehmann has argued that "in Durkheim's account of society women are largely absent" or invisible, though his work nevertheless contained a "latent" sociological theory of women.[131] When women did appear in Durkheim's account of society, he described them as less socialized than men. According to this account, the adult human being has a double nature: he is a natural being, but he is also a social being who has internalized the influence of a society that he expresses, serves, and needs. This process of socialization initiates us into a "higher existence," Durkheim argued, and therefore the relatively nonsocial existence that "satisfies an animal or a child can satisfy us no more. . . . Our activity needs an object transcending it," namely, society. However, Durkheim maintained that the social component of human existence was less developed in women: "As [woman] lives outside of community existence more than man, she is less penetrated by it; society is less necessary to her because she is less impregnated with sociability."[132] Women's purportedly more natural and less social character made them comparable in his view to "'lower,' 'primitive' societies, with their 'simple' social inclinations, which 'need little for satisfaction.'"[133] Insofar as Durkheim associated both women and Jews with earlier stages of development, they are akin in his thinking. The similarity, however, is mostly superficial, because in contrast to women, whom Durkheim saw as undersocialized, Jews were characterized by high levels of social integration and regulation; they were, in a word, hypersocialized. Furthermore, because Durkheim assumed that society would steadily replace nature "as the basis for the divisions among human groups and as the medium for the transmission of human characteristics," he expected the differences between increasingly socialized men and relatively asocial women to deepen over time.[134] In contrast, he expected socially based ethnoreligious differences to be transcended by a shared republican civil religion. Last, Jews were not missing from Durkheim's account of society, and his ideas about them were accordingly more manifest.

Durkheim's characterization of the German nation provides a third point of comparison with his representation of Jews. After the Franco-Prussian War of 1870–71, Germany became a major European rival against which French identity was constructed. As a Jew with a German name who hailed from the border region of Lorraine, Durkheim was himself denounced as a German agent during World War I when, in fact, he actively supported the French war effort and wrote two publications promoting the Allied cause. One of them investigated responsibility for the war, while the other critically examined German historian Heinrich von Treitschke's lectures on politics.[135] Treitschke (1834–96), an outspoken antisemite and champion of authoritarian power politics, was in Durkheim's view a representative figure whose thinking expressed the mentality of his nation. Durkheim argued that Treitschke, and by extension Germany, accepted no limits on the power or will of the state, to which they subordinated international law, morality, and civil society. Durkheim's prewar writings had already established moral regulation as the socially healthy alternative to anomie, unlimited desire, and the law of the strongest.[136] For this reason, Durkheim described the German mentality as abnormal and harmful. In contrast, he associated France and the Allied cause with morality as a force superior to the state and with democratic and universalistic ideals in particular.[137] Comparing these texts to Durkheim's writings about Jews helps to sharpen our interpretation of the latter. Durkheim never characterized Jews the same way he characterized Germany, which is to say, as a nation that subordinated everything to the aggrandizement of state power. After all, Jews possessed no state of their own in the early twentieth century, and Durkheim roundly rejected the antisemitic view of the republican French state as an instrument of Jewish power. Instead, Durkheim's emphasis on the strong and pervasive moral regulation imposed by Judaism implied an affinity between Jews and France. Yet for Durkheim, there was an important difference between Judaism and the secular morality of the French republic.

He distinguished three elements in morality: a sense of duty, attachment to a collective ideal, and the autonomy that comes from understanding the rational basis that criticism and reflection impart to moral rules. Although the last component was arguably part of the Jewish tradition, Durkheim maintained that it was "the principal differentiating characteristic of a secular morality," for religion put morality within a "realm of mystery, where the ordinary procedures of scientific inquiry are no longer appropriate."[138] By this account, traditional Jews appeared to lag behind the preeminently modern, rational, and secular nation that emancipated them.

Last, Durkheim's descriptions of the Jews in Europe may be compared to his portrayals of colonized subjects outside of the European metropole.[139] According to contemporary sociologist Fuyuki Kurasawa, the relationship between the Durkheimian school of sociology and French colonialism was paradoxical. Even as the Durkheimian school benefited from colonialism, Kurasawa argues, it questioned the opposition between primitive and modern that colonialism presupposed: The Durkheimians demonstrated that "'primitive' societies were already civilized and possessed sophisticated ways of thinking about the world"; they promoted cultural pluralism and relativism, gradually problematizing their earlier commitment to social evolutionism; and they tried to show that primitive and modern forms of thought were different only "in degree, not in kind."[140] At the same time, Durkheim and his followers avoided wholly negative depictions of colonial subjects. Quite the reverse, they used "primitive" practices such as the gift economy and the periodic renewal of collective effervescence among Australian aborigines as a reference point from which to criticize "many of the central cultural assumptions and institutional arrangements undergirding modern European civilization."[141] Parallels with Durkheim's characterization of Jews and Judaism are readily apparent. Although he associated the Jews with earlier stages of development that he believed French society had surpassed, he did not regard Jewish communities and modern France as incommensurable. On the contrary, I have argued, his work allowed for the possibility of a French-Jewish symbiosis.[142] Moreover, Durkheim's characterization of Judaism was ambivalent rather than wholly negative: its repressive law was limited by a democratic spirit, and its constraining mechanical solidarity was also a nurturing source of emotional warmth that discouraged suicide.[143] What is peculiar about Durkheim's representation of the Jews is its argumentative context: his portrayal of the Jews as socially backward was directed against opposing images of the Jews as agents of a threatening modernity. However much the Durkheimians may have questioned the opposition between primitive and modern, neither they nor their opponents ever portrayed colonial subjects as a modernized and modernizing force.

Conclusion

"To understand major contributions to the history of social thought," Robert Nisbet suggested in his study of Durkheim, "one must understand the setting in which these were made," including "the ideas and social currents against which Durkheim's thought was directed. . . . Ideas are dialectical responses, caught up in the logic and circumstance of antithesis. . . . This is not to minimize the importance of data, of fact and experience, which the ideas of social scientists seek to synthesize and clarify. . . . Nevertheless, the genesis of thought is not fact, but idea, that most often provides the challenge, the thesis against which any major idea may be seen as antithesis."[144] In line with this perspective, I have attempted to reveal the interplay of Durkheim's sociology with French antisemitism. Antisemitism was itself divided in its orientation to the modern society that the French Revolution ushered in. While reactionary antisemitism gave it a negative interpretation and associated it with the Jews, radical antisemitism viewed it in positive terms as a potentially liberating advance threatened by the Jews. Durkheim challenged both of these views. In his response to reactionary antisemitism, he contested the identification of the Jews with revolutionary modernization, argued that opposition to the Revolution's "religion of the individual" promoted the very social dissolution that reactionary antisemites feared, and denied that race could provide a viable basis for restoring the fixed social hierarchy of the old regime. In his response to radical antisemitism, Durkheim countered its vision of ethnic warfare to dispossess and exclude the Jews with a more universalistic conception of socialism, derived from his distinctive interpretation of the French Revolution, within which the Jews could find a place.

These findings advance previous scholarship on Durkheim's relationship to the Jews and Judaism. Although Birnbaum and Strenski previously examined antisemitism as part of Durkheim's milieu, neither treated it fully. Birnbaum concentrated on the Dreyfus Affair and right-wing antisemitism, and he provided no sustained analysis of the discourse, themes, and motifs of French antisemitism. Likewise, Strenski's focus on genteel scholarly antisemitism did not permit a thoroughgoing investigation of antisemitic intellectuals outside the academy to whom Durkheim also reacted. This chapter builds upon the pioneering work of Birnbaum and Strenski but also goes beyond it in these respects. In addition, by showing how Jewish and French identity were constructed in relation to each other in nineteenth-century France, this chapter seeks to foster a potentially fruitful dialogue between historicists who emphasize Durkheim's Jewish context and those who emphasize his French context.[145]

In addition to deepening our understanding of Durkheim, this chapter contributes to our understanding of the emergence of classical sociology more generally. On the one hand, Nisbet's thesis of the two revolutions exemplifies conventional accounts that trace the foundation of sociology to internal changes within European society. The French Revolution indeed loomed large in Durkheim's sociology. However, as this chapter shows, Durkheim's ideas were as much a response to French antisemitism and antisemitic interpretations of the Revolution as they were to the Revolution itself. Consequently, even though antisemitism and sociology provided opposing accounts of the Revolution with very different implications, Durkheim's version was also constructed in part by reference to the Jews. On the other hand, revisionist scholarship traces the origins of sociology to Europe's colonial encounters with the non-European world, a theme briefly touched upon in the preceding excursus. According to this view, European sociology defined the modernity of the metropole in contrast to the presumed primitiveness of colonized peoples. In fact, European sociology did not need to look beyond the metropole to find such a counterpoint; the Jews in Europe served a similar role in Durkheim's thinking. What distinguishes the Jews, however, is the contradictory and contested meanings conferred upon them. Durkheim inverted antisemitic images of the Jews as a modernized and modernizing threat, but there was little dispute among French social thinkers about the premodern and primitive character of colonial subjects.

Last, this chapter has implications for nineteenth-century social thought more broadly. What French antisemitism and Durkheim's sociology had in common was that they understood modernity, in part, by reference to the Jews. "Religion," wrote Karl Marx in his discussion of the Jewish question, "is simply the recognition of man in a roundabout fashion; that is, through an intermediary."[146] Durkheim, substituting society for man, made a similar point: religion was "a system of ideas by means of which people represent to themselves the society of which they are members and the opaque but intimate relations they have with it."[147] Representations of the Jews in nineteenth-century social thought played an analogous role. In the context of a social order undergoing revolutionary changes, the Jews served as an intermediary through whom European thinkers could discern—and contest—the image of their own past and future.

3

The German Tradition: Capitalism and the Jews

"Just as the French have their theme, namely 'What was the great Revolution?' so our national destiny has given us our theme for a long time to come, namely 'What is capitalism?'" So remarked Friedrich Naumann, the liberal German reformer and friend of Max Weber, in 1911.[1] Indeed, German intellectuals devoted considerable attention in the two decades before World War I to the social origins and consequences of modern industrial capitalism. Their ideas cannot be understood apart from the economic transformation to which they were responding, which was no less profound in its own way than the political upheaval in France. Between 1871, when Germany was politically unified, and 1914, when it entered World War I, it became a world leader in capitalist industrialization. While not synonymous, capitalism and industrialization were closely related phenomena insofar as industrialization was made possible by capitalist development and occurred in capitalist form. Already in the mid-nineteenth century, an initial wave of capitalist industrialization based on steam power and textiles brought unprecedented productivity and partial emancipation from the personal dependence of guild, village, and family, but it also degraded human labor and eliminated the protection that older social arrangements had provided. By the turn of the century, Germany was in the midst of a second industrial revolution based on chemical engineering, internal combustion, and electrification. New technologies went hand in hand with the growth of factories, greater division of labor, mass production, and the transformation of Germany from a mostly agrarian into an increasingly urban nation. With the advent of the twentieth century, German firms exemplified the features of mature or organized capitalism, including the shift from family to managerial capitalism, bureaucratization and the growth of a white-collar labor force, economic concentration, and the expansion of new, abstract, and impersonal forms of property ownership represented by the limited-liability joint-stock company in which otherwise unrelated individuals traded shares in the stock exchange.[2]

German intellectuals interpreted these changes from a particular social position and a distinctive cultural perspective.[3] The German educated middle class that historian Fritz Ringer called "mandarins" was a tiny but privileged social stratum. Originally a creation of the monarchical German state in its struggle against the nobility and still largely state-employed at the turn of the nineteenth century, the mandarins owed their privileged status primarily to educational qualifications rather than hereditary titles (like the nobility) or money (like the economic bourgeoisie). Classical secondary schooling in one of the country's *Gymnasien* provided access to German universities, which were world renowned by the end of the nineteenth century and controlled access to careers in the civil service, the clergy, the liberal professions, and education.[4] German university professors held a strategically important position within the mandarin stratum because they controlled and upheld "the standards of qualification for membership in the group" and acted as "its spokesmen in cultural questions."[5] In this role, university professors consecrated and inculcated a mandarin tradition centered on the ideal of *Bildung* (cultivation or self-development) through the absorption of *Kultur* (culture). The mandarin tradition counterposed *Bildung* to a merely utilitarian orientation to knowledge, and it defined *Kultur* in opposition to *Zivilisation* (civilization). As a formulation from the late 1920s and early 1930s put it, "civilization is to culture as the external to the internal, the artificially constructed to the naturally developed, the mechanical to the organic, 'means' to 'ends.'" According to Ringer, the mandarins "tended to see uniquely German characteristics in their preference of culture over civilization. . . . [T]he nation and, through it, the state were defined as creatures and as agents of the mandarins' cultural ideals."[6] Conversely, *Zivilisation* was identified variously with France, England, America, and the Jews. As capitalist industrialization and related changes increasingly threatened the mandarins' ideals and social influence, they reaffirmed the opposition between *Kultur* and *Zivilisation* more forcefully. A minority of mandarin intellectuals, including some of the most important figures in German sociology, were prepared by the early twentieth century to accommodate themselves to those aspects of modern life that seemed to them inevitable so as to salvage what they could of the mandarin tradition. However, most of their colleagues remained unwilling to make significant accommodations.[7]

During the nineteenth and early twentieth centuries, "the role of Jews in the formation of modern economies . . . was a burning issue," and references to Jews abounded in German discussions of modern capitalism.[8] Because the context of these discussions included the social and economic conditions of German Jewry, a few words about those conditions are necessary before turning to portrayals of Jews in German social thought. Between 1848 and the establishment of the German Empire in 1871, the Jewish population in German states increased from 400,000 to 512,000, and that number continued to grow—augmented after 1881 by Jewish immigration from eastern Europe—until it peaked at 615,000 in 1910. At no time between 1848 and 1910 did German Jews comprise more than 1.25 percent of the total population. In contrast to France, which emancipated its Jews shortly after the outbreak of the French Revolution, progress toward Jewish emancipation in German lands was slower, piecemeal, and at times rolled back. The constitution of the German Empire guaranteed civil equality without regard to religion in 1871, and Jews were elected thereafter to serve in the *Reichstag*, but Jews continued to experience partial exclusion and discrimination in state service, including the army officer corps, the judiciary, diplomatic service, and academic appointments. German Jews were historically concentrated in commerce and trade, and more than half continued to work in this sector in the late nineteenth and early twentieth centuries, with the remainder mostly engaged in trades and industry (20 to 25 percent of German Jews) or the free professions of medicine, law, and journalism (less than 10 percent). Although half of German Jewry was still poor in 1848, most German Jews had entered the ranks of the bourgeoisie by the last third of the nineteenth century, and some became leading bankers, industrialists, and businessmen. The embourgeoisement of German Jews coincided with their urbanization, a process that began before the mid-nineteenth century and increased rapidly afterward. By the end of the nineteenth century, most German Jews lived in large cities such as Breslau, Leipzig, Cologne, Hamburg, Frankfurt, and especially Berlin, where one-third of German Jews eventually concentrated. In sum, Jews were a tiny minority in Germany with a distinctive social profile: state service remained partially closed to them, and they were heavily engaged in commerce and more urbanized than the general population.[9]

Why did Jews figure so prominently in German discussions of modern capitalism? The distinctive socioeconomic profile of German Jews undoubtedly provided a material basis for the interpretations of Jews and Judaism that appeared in German social thought. Under the influence of Germany's historical school of economics, German intellectuals understood well that this profile was linked to the roles Jews had played in European economic development. As the Jews in Europe were pushed out of land owning by the Church and excluded from medieval guilds, they engaged increasingly by the thirteenth century in commerce and moneylending. The precise relationship of these activities to modern capitalism, and the extent to which they reflected Jewish preferences rather than restricted opportunities, were among the questions debated by German historians and social scientists.[10] As these debates demonstrate, the facts—however important as a basis for interpretation—never speak for themselves because social thinkers must select the facts they think are important and impute relationships among them.[11] Because attention to the Jews was often disproportionate to their involvement in historical events, and because in the social thought of some German intellectuals the Jews were assigned subject positions that went far beyond their actual empirical roles, the facts alone cannot fully account for German social thinkers' interest in or portrayals of Jews and Judaism.

This chapter suggests another reason for the attention to Jews in German discussions of modern capitalism: the Jews served German social thinkers as a touchstone for defining what it meant to be modern and what it meant to be German or European in a context of rapid social change. When portrayed as agents of a modern capitalist *Zivilisation*, Jews appeared as a danger to communal solidarity. Building on previous efforts that trace the persistent symbolic construction of Jews in threatening terms to the history of religious antagonism in Europe, I suggest that cultural schemas derived from Christian theology shaped how German social thinkers described the relationship between Jews and modern capitalism.[12] Cultural schemas are "mental structures . . . which shape the way we attend to, interpret, remember, and respond emotionally to the information we encounter and possess."[13] Although the late nineteenth century witnessed the emergence of new forms of secular and racial antisemitism, close examination of classical German sociology suggests that Christian theological schemas were at least sometimes rearticulated in secular or racial terms rather than abandoned altogether. These schemas, I suggest, were tacitly and widely shared among participants in the German intellectual field.[14]

More precisely, this chapter compares how Karl Marx, Georg Simmel, Werner Sombart, and Max Weber described the relationship between the Jews and modern capitalism. Beginning with Marx, the chapter highlights his use of motifs derived from Christian theology while revealing a significant shift in how he linked European Jewry to the development of modern capitalism. The early Marx, it is shown, echoed the venerable discourse of "judaizing" that began with Paul and periodically reappeared in Christian Europe, most notably in polemics among the early church fathers and again during the Reformation.[15] As constructed in this discourse, the Jews showed the gentiles the image of their own unwelcome future. However, the mature

Marx substituted a new and different narrative in which the Jews, after contributing to the creation of modern capitalism, were subsequently supplanted and surpassed. This later narrative can be understood as a secularized version of Christian supersessionism—the doctrine that the New Testament church is the new Israel that has forever superseded national Israel as the people of God—transposed by Marx to the material realm of economic history.[16] From this perspective, the Jews epitomize a past that the gentiles have already overcome. These two narratives provided the tracks along which subsequent discussions of the Jews and modern capitalism proceeded in the work of Simmel, Sombart, and Weber. While Simmel and Sombart reformulated in different ways the early Marx's narrative of judaization, Weber's perspective was closer to the supersessionist perspective of the mature Marx.

How did cultural schemas derived from Christian theology come to influence these four intellectuals? To begin with, these schemas were transmitted through their Protestant religious backgrounds. To be sure, Marx and Simmel were born into Jewish families, but they were baptized at an early age into the same Protestant traditions shared by Sombart and Weber.[17] Because neither Marx nor Simmel received a Jewish education, their socialization minimized cultural schemas derived from alternative or competing religious traditions, the availability of which might have made the reproduction of Christian schemas less likely.[18] In addition, as members of the German educated middle class, all four thinkers were further inculcated with Protestant traditions via the habit-forming force of formal schooling. A *Gymnasium* education included instruction in religion, and postsecondary schooling at the University of Berlin (where all of them studied) familiarized them with German idealism, a philosophical tradition that was deeply informed by Protestantism and that constituted an important element of the mandarins' scholarly heritage.[19] The relative homogeneity of the German mandarin stratum, the density of social ties among its members, and the academic and intellectual capital that flowed to mandarins who reproduced religiously inspired cultural schemas probably reinforced the effectiveness of this socialization, at least for some of the authors considered here. Last, Christian theological schemas became legitimized by the endorsement of authoritative thinkers and taken for granted as a result of repeated use among other German intellectuals with whom Marx, Simmel, Sombart, and Weber interacted. In light of these considerations, it is not surprising that Marx turned to religious analogies to understand modern capitalism. Because "the criticism of religion is the premise of all criticism," as he put it, "we must have recourse to the mist-enveloped regions of the religious world" to understand economic life.[20] This chapter shows how the Christian theological schemas he adopted for his own purposes shaped, in ways he probably did not fully intend, his account of the origins of modern capitalism, just as they would similarly shape the accounts produced by Simmel, Sombart, and Weber.

Karl Marx: From Judaization to Supersession of the Jews

When Marx wrote his essay "On the Jewish Question" in 1843, it was still a live question in German lands. Revolutionary France had imposed Jewish emancipation in the German territories it conquered, and the Napoleonic military threat induced Prussia to take its own initial steps in that direction in 1812. However, after the Napoleonic threat was defeated in 1815, the Jews in Prussia and other post-Napoleonic German states experienced a combination of political reaction, economic restriction, and cultural exclusion. These setbacks were part of a broader reaction against French conquest which extolled the "organic" society of medieval Christendom over the rationalism of the French Enlightenment. They induced Karl Marx's father to convert to Protestantism, and they also shunted many young educated Jews into journalism, a new profession that remained open to them and that the baptized Karl Marx also entered.[21]

Marx's essay "On the Jewish Question" was a response to another essay on the same topic by his erstwhile mentor, the German philosopher Bruno Bauer, whom he had encountered at the University of Berlin. Both Bauer and Marx were influenced, in turn, by the idealist philosophy of Georg Wilhelm Friedrich Hegel. For Hegel, world history was the process through which human beings became progressively conscious of their freedom. From its nadir in the ancient Orient, Hegel argued, where it was restricted to a single despotic ruler, this consciousness reached its zenith among "the Germanic peoples, through Christianity, who came to the awareness that every human is free by virtue of being human, and that the freedom of spirit comprises our most human nature."[22] This view of history formed the backdrop for Bauer's essay, though unlike Hegel, Bauer rejected Jewish emancipation. The Jews, Bauer argued, were an Oriental people who subjugated themselves to an unchanging body of law seemingly imposed by an external power. On that basis, they separated themselves from others and removed themselves from history. Consequently, they were incapable of realizing their own potential as free agents and rational beings. "The placing of Judaism at the bottom of a sort of hierarchy of religions and states of spiritual being and the notion that the Jewish people were outside history partook of long-established Christian criticism of Judaism."[23] However, in Bauer's view, conversion to Christianity was insufficient to emancipate the Jews. Judaism and Christianity alike were merely phases in humanity's progressive consciousness of its own freedom, both of which had to be transcended if that consciousness was to become complete. Therefore, according to Bauer, the state could not emancipate the Jews as long as it remained a Christian state, and the Jews could not be emancipated as long as they remained Jews.[24]

Marx agreed with Bauer that the modern state was a secular state in which politics was separated from religion. However, Marx argued, this exclusion from the political realm could not be equated with the abolition of religion. On the contrary, he pointed out, religion continued to thrive outside of politics, even and especially in the United States, where the separation of state and church was most fully developed. Moreover, Marx suggested, what is true of religion is true of property as well. When the right to vote and hold office is no longer restricted to property owners, property ownership loses its public significance, or, to put it differently, the state emancipates itself from property. But again, this separation of the modern state from property ownership is in no way equivalent to the abolition of property, which continues to exist and operate in private. The continued flourishing of religion and property was detrimental to Bauer's argument and troubling for Marx because it indicated that alienation had yet to be really overcome even in the most advanced states, where political emancipation had already been achieved. Marx argued that instead of overcoming alienation, political emancipation divided the modern individual into the public role of citizen and the private role of bourgeois. Furthermore, the political community of public citizens, which is supposed to be oriented to the general interest, is illusory; in reality it is subordinated to the bourgeois or civil society of private persons oriented to their own egoistic and particular ends. Failing to provide more than an illusory solution to alienation, political emancipation fell short of what Marx called human emancipation, in which "the real, individual man," the egoistic member of civil society, absorbs into himself the ideal, "abstract citizen."[25] Human emancipation aims at a genuine, nonalienated form of community, which must therefore also be universal, that is, not limited to the political community of public citizens; it must encompass all of social life.

Only in the second part of Marx's essay did he turn his attention squarely to the Jews. Marx, in opposition to Bauer, firmly supported Jewish emancipation as a progressive development.[26] This stance was consistent with the first part of Marx's essay, which made clear that political emancipation entailed only the privatization of Judaism and not its abolition. By the same token, Marx had pointed out, political emancipation was insufficient to liberate human beings from religion or property. Bauer failed to grasp the limits of political emancipation, Marx suggested, because he sought the chains of human beings in their consciousness instead of in their real life. Marx, in contrast, began his criticism not with the Jewish religion, with the "sabbath Jew," but with the practical activity of the "real" or "everyday" Jew. In nineteenth-century Prussia, Jews mainly earned their livelihoods by means of peddling, shopkeeping, inn keeping, commerce, and the livestock trade.[27] Marx summed up this activity in a single pejorative word: huckstering (*Schacher*).

What was the relationship between the religious consciousness of the sabbath Jew and the practical activity of the real, everyday Jew? Huckstering, based on practical need and self-interest, was in Marx's view a material form of self-alienation analogous to the spiritual form found in religion. "Just as man, so long as he is engrossed *in religion*, can only objectify his essence by an alien and fantastic being; so under the sway of egoistic need, he can only affirm himself and produce objects *in practice* by subordinating his products and his own activity to the domination of an alien entity, . . . namely money."[28] Money was in reality, like God in the pious man's imagination, an alienated expression of man himself; it was the "worldly god" of the "everyday Jew" corresponding to the spiritual God of the "sabbath Jew."[29] Bauer had insisted that money made the Jews powerful despite their lack of political rights.[30] Without disputing this antisemitic claim, Marx added that money was not simply a means of Jewish power but became a power in its own right over Jews and Christians alike. Marx thereby extended his vicious characterization of the Jews to civil or bourgeois society in toto and turned the most hateful stereotypes of Jews back upon Christians. With the universal domination of money, he wrote, "the practical Jewish spirit has become the practical spirit of the Christian nations," and "the Christians have become Jews."[31]

Having revealed the nature and source of humanity's alienation, Marx could now clarify the meaning of human emancipation. In his view, religion was a protest against material alienation as well as an expression of it. However, like political emancipation, religion failed to offer a genuine solution to the alienation in man's practical life; it, too, provided only a fantastic and partial form of community, limited in this case not to the citizenry (from whose ranks the sabbath Jew was excluded) but to the faithful. Just as the real, universal form of community to which human emancipation aspires cannot be limited to the political life of public citizens (it must encompass all of social life), neither can it be limited to particular forms of community based on religion (it must encompass all of humanity). Marx did not dispute Bauer's assumption (derived from Christian theology via Hegelian philosophy) that Judaism was a narrower, more parochial, and therefore more backward form of community than Christianity, nor that both religions had to be transcended in favor of more expansive forms of community. But where

Bauer attacked symptoms, Marx struck at the root. Only by "emancipating itself from *huckstering* and *money*, and thus from real and practical Judaism," Marx wrote, would the modern age "emancipate itself. An organization of society which would abolish the preconditions and thus the very possibility of huckstering would make the Jew impossible." In other words, the Jewish religion would be abolished not by demanding apostasy in exchange for political citizenship but rather by eliminating its "profane basis," the material conditions that gave rise to it and that it expressed. Because the spiritual self-alienation found in religious consciousness reflected the material self-alienation found in man's practical activity, the Jew's "religious consciousness would evaporate" once the preconditions and possibility of huckstering were eliminated. For Marx, "the *emancipation* of the Jews is the emancipation of mankind from *Judaism* [*Judentum*]," both in its spiritual sense and more fundamentally in the "real and practical" sense of commerce.[32]

Through the remainder of the 1840s and into the early 1850s, Marx continued to identify hucksterism as the "practical Jewish spirit," which in turn had become the "practical spirit of the Christian nations." *The Holy Family*, coauthored with Friedrich Engels and published in 1845, continued Marx's polemic against Bauer and extended it to other radical followers of Hegel; it revisited the Jewish question only to reiterate the argument that Marx had already made in his earlier essay.[33] Marx's unpublished "Theses on Feuerbach," written in 1845, and *The German Ideology*, written by Marx and Engels in 1845–46, concluded their critical reassessment of the Hegelian philosophical tradition and worked out their own materialist conception of history in opposition to it. The Jews were rarely mentioned in these works, but when they were, it was in connection with hucksterism. Marx's first thesis criticized the German philosopher Ludwig Feuerbach for narrowly conceiving practice "only in its dirty-Jewish [*schmutzig-jüdisch*] manifestation" in contrast to "revolutionary" or "practical-critical activity."[34] Likewise, *The German Ideology* identified the Jews with "small-scale commercial and industrial swindling."[35] In essays and articles written in the 1850s, Marx and Engels continued to identify Jews as a commercial people: middlemen who monopolized the exchange of manufactured goods for agricultural produce in eastern Germany, traders in the Ottoman Empire, merchants in Algeria, and horse dealers in Russia.[36] At the same time, Marx continued to insist that what he called the "practical Jewish spirit" was no longer the spirit of the Jews alone; it was, Marx and Engels wrote in *The Holy Family*, "the fully developed *practice* of the *Christian world itself*." The "present-day world," they declared, was "*Jewish* to the core," and the task of emancipation was therefore "the task of abolishing the *Jewish character of civil society*, abolishing the inhumanity of the present-day practice of life, the most extreme expression of which is the *money system.*"[37] Marx made the point again several years later in a discussion of the British Parliament. British Jews already had civil rights, but after restrictions were lifted on non-Anglican Protestants in 1828 and Catholics in 1829, they remained the only group disqualified from Parliament on religious grounds. Consequently, Jewish banker Lionel de Rothschild, who was elected to the House of Commons in 1847 and repeatedly thereafter, could not be sworn in until the House of Lords agreed in 1858 to omit the words "on the true faith of a Christian" from the necessary oath. "It may be questioned," Marx wrote about Rothschild in 1853, "whether the English people will be very contented with this extension of suffrage to a Jewish usurer." But in another article written shortly thereafter, Marx added: "The exclusion of Jews from the House of Commons, after the spirit of usury has so long presided in the *British Parliament,* is unquestionably an absurd anomaly."[38]

As Marx developed his critique of capitalism from the late 1850s through the 1860s in the *Foundations (Grundrisse) of the Critique of Political Economy,* his economic manuscript of 1861–62, and *Capital,* he continued to identify Jews with commerce and usury; however, these activities were reconceived as historical preconditions of modern capitalism and no longer as its defining features. Marx distinguished two basic presuppositions of the capitalist mode of production: there must be free laborers, on the one hand, who must sell their labor power to survive, and "owners of money, means of production, means of subsistence," on the other hand, "who are eager to increase the sum of values they possess, by buying other people's labour-power."[39] Both figures arose as a result of historical processes. The suspension of slavery or serfdom meant that the producer no longer formed part of the means of production, and the dissolution of small, free landed property or communal land ownership meant that the means of production no longer belonged to him individually or collectively. But how did the laborer, now free in this double sense, find himself up against capital? Where did it come from?

"The monetary wealth which becomes transformed into capital in the proper sense, into industrial capital," Marx wrote, "is . . . the mobile wealth piled up through usury—especially that practised against landed property—and through mercantile profits."[40] The usurer and merchant were uniquely suited for this role because in precapitalist economic formations, wealth appeared as an end in itself only among "commercial peoples," while the principal owners of the surplus product that the merchant sought to appropriate—slave owners, feudal lords, and rulers—were mainly consumers of it.[41] The usurer acquired his wealth through the direct appropriation of others' labor, "but in a form which makes the actual producer into his debtor, instead of making him a seller of his labour to the capitalist"; he thus engaged in "capitalist exploitation without a capitalist mode of production."[42] The merchant's methods were equally unsavory: because new value could only be generated through production and not through exchange or circulation, Marx reasoned that the merchant's profits derived from cheating, fraud, and the advantage gained from inserting himself "parasitically" (Marx's term) as a middleman between the selling and buying producers.[43] Marx described the wealth accumulated by usurers and merchants in this fashion as an initial or antediluvian form of capital, though he stressed that its formation and existence preceded the capitalist mode of production and that it could only become capital in its "modern standard form" or "in the proper sense" under specific historical circumstances, namely, when labor and its conditions were commodified (the other presupposition of modern capitalism) and when the owners of monetary wealth took possession of production itself.[44]

Although Marx was clear that not all merchants and usurers were Jews, it was in this role and only in this role that they appeared in his historical analysis.[45] In an image borrowed from Bauer that reappeared in the *Grundrisse* and again in the first and third volumes of *Capital*, Marx described the Jews as a commercial or trading people living in the pores of medieval or Polish society.[46] With this image, Marx also linked Jews to usury: "it [usury] is a form in which the capital of the Jews was created everywhere in the Middle Ages, where they appear as money-lenders in the pores of purely agricultural peoples. (*Debt slavery* in distinction to *wage slavery*.)"[47] As merchants and usurers in the pores of precapitalist production, Marx suggested, Jews helped to further the development of modern capitalism. The primary contribution of these activities, as we have seen, was to promote the formation and concentration of money capital, but merchants and usurers also advanced the other basic precondition of modern capitalism—free labor—insofar as their activities helped to dissolve the old precapitalist forms of production in which the worker was also a proprietor. Commerce and usury did so in several related ways: by subordinating production to exchange value, ruining feudal landlords and small producers (i.e., the owners of the old conditions of labor), accelerating the separation of worker-proprietors from the conditions and instruments of their labor, and appropriating those conditions and instruments. To be sure, in Marx's view commerce and usury played only a limited role in the transition to modern capitalism: these activities did not create the conditions and instruments of labor; their dissolving effects on precapitalist production depended on the nature of the producing communities between and within which commerce and usury operated and on the current stage of historical development; and therefore by themselves commerce and usury were not sufficient to bring about a new mode of production. Nevertheless, Marx assigned considerable historical significance to these activities and by extension to the Jews who engaged in them. It was "in the pores of the old society," he asserted in 1847, that "a new society has taken shape."[48] *Capital* qualified that assertion twenty years later but did not entirely reject it.

As merchants and usurers, Jews helped to bring the modern capitalist mode of production into existence, but in a familiar Marxian twist, they were eventually subjugated by the very forces they helped to create. "[W]herever merchant's capital still predominates," Marx wrote in the third volume of *Capital*, "we find obsolete conditions. . . . In the pre-capitalist stages of society commerce ruled industry. In modern society the reverse is true."[49] Once manufacture and large-scale industry gained sufficient strength to create a market for itself, commerce became "the servant of industrial production."[50] In the case of usurer's capital, subordination to industry was initially accomplished through "violence (the State) . . . by means of compulsory reduction of interest rates, so that it is no longer able to dictate terms to industrial capital."[51] As an example of this development, Marx noted that in the eighteenth century, the Prussian king Frederick II fixed interest rates at 10 percent, though only for Jewish creditors, not Christians.[52] Later, industrial capital subjugated interest-bearing capital by "the creation of a procedure specific to itself—the *credit system*." The credit system was originally "directed against the old-fashioned usurers (goldsmiths in England, Jews, Lombards, and others)" insofar as it deprived them of their former monopoly. Marx added that "the credit system [was] essentially Protestant" because it implied "faith in the social character of production."[53] In these ways, Jews as representatives of antediluvian merchant's and usurer's capital were superseded by modern industrial capital. As if to underscore this point, Marx noted in the first volume of *Capital* that to the capitalist, all commodities were "in faith and in truth money, inwardly circumcised Jews."[54] The metaphor again identified Jews with money while alluding to a spiritual supersession analogous to the material one that Marx described: the capitalist converted commodities into money (C–M) like Christianity transformed gentiles into a new Israel inwardly marked by their circumcised hearts.[55] Marx thus returned to a key theme of his early essay "On the Jewish Question," namely, that "the Christians have become Jews," but in his later critique of capitalism, Christianity was no longer "reabsorbed into Judaism."[56] Rather, like the sculptures of Ecclesia ascendant over Synagoga displayed at cathedrals in Bamberg, Paris, Reims, Strasbourg, and elsewhere, Christian industry now dominated the Jewish commerce and usury that once promoted it.[57]

Georg Simmel: An Ambivalent Narrative of Judaization

As Marx sought to understand the central tendencies of modern society by grasping the capitalist mode of production, so Simmel attempted to understand it through an examination of money as one of its characteristic aspects or expressions. A money economy and modern capitalism are not synonymous, as Weber noted, but for Simmel and other thinkers of his time, they were closely related. Simmel developed his ideas about the money economy between 1889, when he wrote his paper on "The Psychology of Money," and 1900, when his monumental *Philosophy of Money* was published. Only a small portion of these writings was devoted to the role of Jews in the money economy, and the context of these remarks differed markedly from the circumstances of the early Marx: German Jews were formally emancipated after the unification of the German Empire in 1871, though they continued to experience persistent social discrimination and organized antisemitism. (Indeed, Simmel himself experienced discrimination despite his baptism.) Nevertheless, the discourse of judaization served Simmel, too, as a tool for describing the nature and consequences of the modern money economy.[58]

Like the early Marx but in contrast to the mature Marx, Simmel emphasized exchange over production as the fundamental economic phenomenon. Simmel understood exchange broadly, not only as a form of interaction but also as a process that occurs when an individual sacrifices leisure to gain the benefits of labor or opts to use his energy in one way at the expense of another. In all of these instances, things acquire economic value only through comparison with other things to determine what each can be exchanged for. Money serves to facilitate this comparison and mediate exchange. Indeed, with the eventual ascendance of money's symbolic function over its substantive properties or intrinsic value, "it is nothing but the pure form of exchangeability."[59]

According to Simmel, money can serve as a means of exchange because of its distinctive properties, which it imparts to modern life more widely.[60] First, money is instrumental; it is "a means *par excellence*," the "purest form of the tool," because it is not limited to a specific purpose.[61] On the contrary, money can be put to the widest range of uses, and this instrumentality is enhanced by its divisibility, unlimited convertibility, fungibility, transportability, concealability, and universal validity.[62] Second, even when it is not put to a specific use or exchanged for a specific object, money remains valuable by virtue of what Simmel called its "potentiality" (*Vermögen*), its unlimited possibilities of use which distinguishes money from all other values.[63] Third, because exchangeability is eventually all there is to money, it is abstract and lacks any character of its own. Simmel associated this abstract character, in turn, with the growth of intellectualism.[64] Fourth, money is impersonal in a variety of ways: it encourages the detachment that accompanies an orientation to means rather than ends; it is indifferent to specificity, uniqueness, and personal qualities; and unlike more concrete goods or specialized skills that are difficult to dissociate from their possessor, money neither stamps specific or concrete qualities upon its possessor nor carries his personal stamp with it when it passes into new hands.[65] Fifth, the money economy instills a calculating disposition. When individuals come to depend on market exchanges mediated by money to satisfy their needs, they increasingly understand the value of things in quantitative instead of qualitative terms: "the question of what something is worth is increasingly displaced by the question of how much it is worth."[66] This mode of thinking then spills over into all aspects of social life. In the modern money economy, "the life of many people is filled out with determining, weighing up, calculating and reducing of qualitative values to quantitative ones," and this "contributes to the rational, calculating nature of modern times against the more impulsive, holistic, emotional character of earlier epochs."[67]

Simmel described the modern money economy as alienating in at least two ways. In the first place, it contributed to the multiplication of means and the growing length of their series in modern life.[68] "By contrast to primitive circumstances," Simmel argued, "the intentions of people can no longer be achieved through simple, obvious, direct actions." Instead, an ever-expanding set of means and steps mediates between one's needs and the satisfaction of them. Consequently, the "actual end" that the means are supposed to serve "recedes further and further towards the horizon of consciousness and ultimately sinks beneath it." As we get "stuck in the labyrinth of means" and forget the ultimate goal, we begin to think of money, which is initially a means to acquire other goods, as an "independent good," an "ultimate purpose" in itself. Simmel suggested that this "colonization of ends by means" is one of the most important consequences of the prevailing money economy.[69]

In the second place, the modern money economy contributes to the alienation of subjective from objective spirit. Like Marx, Simmel postulated that human subjects objectified themselves in their "words and works, organizations and traditions," all of which represented "the conservation and accumulation of [their] mental labour."[70] Simmel referred to this accumulated mental labor as objective mind or spirit (*objektive Geist*). In his view, the individual's incorporation, assimilation, or absorption of the accumulated mental labor of the past was indispensable for the enrichment, perfection, and development of the self. However, as in Marx, human subjects find themselves estranged from the objects that should serve to widen and promote their lives.[71] In Simmel's account, this estrangement is a consequence of the steady enlargement of accumulated mental labor, which outpaces the cultivation of the individual subject, as well as the increasingly autonomous and foreign logic of this objectified labor. Anticipating Weber's vision of diverging value spheres producing an incoherent culture, Simmel stressed that the various realms of objective spirit develop their own distinctive norms and standards of value that do not necessarily coincide with the demands of individual self-development.[72] This divergence of subjective and objective spirit, he argued, was a consequence of the division of labor and "an offshoot of the money economy."[73]

What relationship did the Jews have to this alienating money economy? In his study of Simmel's *Philosophy of Money*, contemporary sociologist Gianfranco Poggi notes the following insight of its author: "For every institution there is, at any rate in a highly differentiated society, a set of people who are specifically and exclusively identified with and committed to it; and such people often reflect and embody in a particularly intense manner the institution's distinctive traits—whether because their involvement in the institution has so shaped them, or because they already possessed such traits and on that account have specially involved themselves in it."[74] Simmel, echoing Marx, pointed to the Jews as one such set of people for the institution of money, and he suggested several reasons for this affinity.

Like the early Marx, Simmel maintained that "money is the God of our times."[75] For Marx, as we have seen, the analogy rested on the claim that money was an expression of man's own activity that came to dominate him, an inversion of subject and object that anticipated Simmel's later discussion of subjective and objective culture. But Simmel offered a different analogy. Just as all the varieties and contrasts of the world were once believed to be unified and reconciled in God, so money—as the means by which all the varied objects of life can be obtained—now appears as the intersection, expression, and equivalent of all values, and its possession confers the same feeling of security and calm that the idea of God once inspired in the faithful.[76] Simmel, again following Marx, linked this identification of God and money with Judaism:

> The specific ability and the interest of the Jews in the nature of money has certainly been related to their "monotheistic schooling." The temper of a people who for thousands of years became used to lifting their eyes up to a single supreme being, to finding in him . . . the goal and intersection of all particular

> interests, would be suited to devoting itself to the economic sphere and especially to that value which presents itself as the encompassing unity and the common focal point of all sequences of purposes.[77]

While in this instance Simmel traced a Jewish affinity with the money economy to Judaism, elsewhere he provided an explanation that was based not on the tenets of the Jewish religion but on the social position of Jews in medieval Christian society. In his 1889 essay "On the Psychology of Money" and again in *The Philosophy of Money*, Simmel suggested that it is especially among the members of "socially disadvantaged and suppressed" groups who are excluded from "personal and specific" ends that money becomes the "centre of interest." In other words, when people are excluded from full citizenship, deprived of prestige, or prevented from owning land or working in the occupation of their choice, they focus their attention on money. Simmel suggested three reasons for this phenomenon: it is more difficult to exclude people from money than other goods; when direct access to other goods is barred, the means (money) is the only interest left; and money allows indirect attainment of "positions, influence and enjoyments" for persons who cannot directly achieve "social rank and fulfillment as officials or in positions from which they are barred." Simmel referred to this last reason as the "power of money." He provided many examples of this phenomenon, including Armenians in Turkey, Moors in Spain, Huguenots in France, and Quakers in England, but he asserted that "the Jews are the best example of the correlation between the central role of money interests and social deprivation."[78]

Having in mind the Diaspora, and perhaps in particular the westward migration of *Ostjuden* (eastern European Jews) that began in 1881, Simmel also identified the Jews in Europe as the "classic example" of the social type that he called the stranger (*der Fremde*). The stranger is "the man who comes today and stays tomorrow," the wanderer who settles in a community to which he does not initially belong. As a result, the stranger has a peculiar relation to group members: he is "an element of the group itself" but one "whose membership within the group involves both being outside it and confronting it."[79] In *The Philosophy of Money*, Simmel suggested that the stranger's role "within a social group directs him, from the outset, towards relations with the group that are mediated by money, above all because of the transportability and the extensive usefulness of money outside the boundaries of the group." In addition, the stranger is "predominantly interested in money for the same reason that makes money so valuable to the socially deprived: namely, because it provides chances for him that are open to fully entitled persons or to the indigenous people by specific concrete channels and by personal relationships." Last, the stranger is typically involved in trade because it "can absorb people from outside whose roots do not lie in the group," and trade has a "deep inner relationship" to the money economy: the merchant is the personification of exchange, just as money is its reification. These factors orient the stranger toward money, who in turn comes to embody its indifference and characterlessness.[80] In sum, Simmel suggested that the Jewish religion, the social deprivation of Jews at the hands of Christians during the Middle Ages, and their role as strangers within Christian communities worked together to foster interest in money among the Jews in Europe.

In a final twist to his argument, Simmel argued that the Jewish interest in money has now been universalized. Nearly sixty years after Marx declared that the Christians had become Jews, Simmel described a similar transformation. "Money has not lost the character that originally made it a domain of the stranger," he wrote, but "the contrast that existed between the native and the stranger has been eliminated, because the money form of transactions has now been taken up by the whole economic community." If the stranger is a person who is "predominantly interested in money," and if money estranges us from others, then we are all strangers in today's modern money economy.[81]

Like the early Marx, then, Simmel understood the modern money economy to be in some sense a Jewish economy; the difference between them lay in their evaluation of this point. Marx held a pejorative view of Jewish huckstering as a condition that must be transcended. In contrast, Simmel was more ambivalent about the modern money economy. The money form of transactions, while alienating in some respects, also had positive consequences in Simmel's view. For one thing, the cash nexus ties people together in novel ways, not all of them exploitive.[82] As Simmel sought to show with the examples of the modern joint-stock company, the modern trade union, and the nondenominational charitable organization, money allows disparate individuals to cooperate for a specific and limited goal, even though they might have no other goals in common, and to commit a small portion of themselves (perhaps only a monetary contribution) to many such groups rather than being wholly absorbed within a few groups. Simmel also argued that money makes possible new forms of individuality and freedom.[83] For instance, the new forms of association it permits are looser and less restrictive; the modern money economy replaces personal dependence upon a few particular individuals with general and impersonal interdependence upon many interchangeable individuals, which is experienced as emancipation; and the substitution of monetary payment for personal service means that "the person no longer offers himself, but only something without any personal relationship to the individual."[84] Consequently, Simmel's suggestion that the stance of the Jewish stranger has been universalized cannot be understood as wholly critical of this state of affairs. If Simmel did not quite turn Marx's curse into a blessing, like that of Balaam at Mount Peor, he at least made it appear as a mixed blessing.

Werner Sombart: Judaization as Domination

Far more than Simmel and even more than Marx himself, Sombart combined trenchant criticism of modern capitalism with a vehement insistence on its Jewish pedigree and character. The path that he took to this position was twisting and circuitous. He began his career within the reformist tradition of the so-called *Kathedersozialisten* (socialists of the lectern) under whom he studied at the University of Berlin.[85] Sombart then took a Marxian turn in the 1890s, which earned him the praise of Engels, the moniker "Red Professor," and a reputation as a renegade within the conservative German academic establishment. While other German academics saw class conflict as a dangerous threat to national unity, Sombart hoped that trade unionism and class struggle might reestablish German *Volksgemeinschaft* (national community) on a socialist basis. From 1900 to 1906, as Sombart gained professional prominence, he turned against Marxian socialism. In a series of works, he questioned and then denied the proletariat's capacity to lead Germany from the rationalization and utilitarianism of modern industrial capitalism to higher forms of life, and he lamented the affinity of *Deutschtum* (Germany's national character) with the spirit of capitalism. Finally, around 1910, Sombart overcame his estrangement from a capitalist and industrialized Germany and took a stridently nationalist turn that he never abandoned.

Sombart's figurative return to his fatherland did not mean that he forsook his previous hostility to capitalism. In his magnum opus *Der moderne Kapitalismus*, first published in 1902, he had distinguished capitalism from earlier economic systems in terms of its form, technique, and spirit. According to him, precapitalist forms of organization such as the family, the manor, the village, the town, and the guild were overtaken by new capitalistic enterprises that brought property owners and propertyless workers together through the market; traditional technique, based on personal skill and experience and handed down from master to apprentice, was supplanted by rationalized, scientific, and impersonal technique; and a precapitalist ethos for which economic life was merely a means to satisfy human needs, traditionally fixed according to the social station into which one was born, gave way to a new attitude that made rationalized and competitive acquisition an end in itself.[86] What enabled his reconciliation with Germany was a new distinction between two aspects of the capitalist spirit, first broached in 1909 and reiterated in 1913 in *Der Bourgeois* (translated into English in 1915 as *The Quintessence of Capitalism*). On the one hand, Sombart suggested, the spirit of enterprise meant adventure, conquest, and domination, and its leading principles were acquisition and competition. On the other hand, the bourgeois spirit signified economic rationalism and calculation.[87] Sombart overlaid this distinction upon another: heroic peoples and trading peoples. The former included some of the Germanic tribes, while the latter included the Florentines, the Frisians, and especially the Jews, the last of whom he considered the consummate (*vollendeten*) and pure-bred (*rein gezüchtetes*) type of a trading people.[88] By means of these distinctions, Sombart shifted the blame for capitalist rationality from Germany to Jewry.[89]

Sombart's most sustained discussion of these themes appeared in *Die Juden und das Wirtschaftsleben*. First published in 1911 and translated into English in 1913 as *The Jews and Modern Capitalism*, the book was widely reviewed and provoked mixed reactions from Jewish and gentile readers within and outside of Germany.[90] It argued that the importance of the Jews for the development of modern capitalism was twofold: they shaped and largely constructed its outward form or structure, on the one hand, and they were the source of its inward spirit or prevailing attitudes, on the other hand.[91] Under the heading of capitalism's outward form, Sombart emphasized the Jewish role in promoting international trade and colonial expansion, financing the formation of the modern state as a framework for capitalist development, and inventing or perfecting securities and the stock exchange as major features of modern economic life. With this last point, he reversed Marx's claim in *Capital* about the subordination of commercial and financial to industrial capital: "The Stock Exchange activities of the joint-stock banks are becoming more and more the controlling force in every department of economic life," Sombart averred. "Indeed, all undertakings in the field of industry are now determined by the power of finance." This view was not entirely novel; the Marxist theoretician Rudolf Hilferding arrived at similar conclusions around the same time. But in Sombart's hands, this development took on an additional meaning: "The commercialization of industry," he wrote, "was the gap in the hedge through which the Jews could penetrate into the field of the production and transportation of commodities, as they had done earlier in commerce and finance."[92]

The Jews were also assigned responsibility for the spirit of capitalism. Sombart described in the following way the traditional, Christian economic ethos that he thought still prevailed under early capitalism: production and trade were regarded as means for the satisfaction of human needs; economic life was regulated within religious and ethical bonds; producers and traders were expected to receive fair wages and profits, as determined by tradition and custom; unbounded competition, running after or taking away a neighbor's customers, particularly by means of advertising or underselling, was considered improper; and economic life was slow and stable. "This," he declared, "was the world the Jews stormed."[93] According to Sombart, the Jews regarded profit rather than satisfaction of human needs as the ultimate goal of all economic activity; they did not confine themselves to one kind of activity; they actively sought to attract customers by means of advertising and underselling; and in order to undersell, they substituted inferior goods or introduced cost-cutting innovations. In short, the Jews promoted an ethos of free trade and free competition antithetical to the Christian ethic.[94] Sombart then identified the Jewish ethic with the spirit that he believed prevailed under mature capitalism: "The Jewish outlook was the 'modern' outlook [*'moderne' Geist*]. . . . It was they who introduced the new ideas into a world organized on a totally different basis."[95]

Having postulated an outsized Jewish role in capitalist development in the first part of *The Jews and Modern Capitalism*, Sombart tried to account for it in the remainder of the book. He traced it to three sets of contributing factors: first, objective circumstances that made it possible for Jews to shape the capitalistic system; second, the Jewish religion as an intermediate influence between objective and subjective factors; and third, subjective forces, by which Sombart meant inherent Jewish characteristics or "properties of the soul" (*Veranlagungen der Seele*).[96] Among the objective circumstances, he pointed to the widespread dispersion of the Jews, their social position as strangers and semicitizens (*Halbbürger*), and Jewish wealth, which Sombart asserted was greater on average than that of Christians.[97]

Turning next to religion, Sombart argued that Judaism had deep affinities with economic rationalism and the calculating character of modern capitalism. His interpretation of Judaism, like that of Bauer, Marx, and Simmel, was heavily indebted to the philosophical tradition of German idealism. Consistent with Immanuel Kant's interpretation of Judaism as a form of heteronomy based on slavish obedience to external law, Sombart described it as a system of "external legalism" based on meticulous religious bookkeeping, a "contract between Jehovah and His chosen people" that "must be obeyed without questioning."[98] Furthermore, following Hegel's description of Judaism as a religion that alienated its adherents from nature, Sombart equated the Jewish conception of holiness with the rationalization of life, including the sublimation of natural human needs and instincts. Invoking Sigmund Freud, Sombart especially emphasized Judaism's sublimation of sexual life, which purportedly diverted vast amounts of masculine energy to economic activities. "Before capitalism could develop," he proclaimed, "the natural man had to be changed out of all recognition, and a rationalistically minded mechanism introduced in his stead. There had to be a transvaluation of all economic values." The result was "the *homo capitalisticus*, who is closely related to the *homo Judaeus*, both belonging to the same species, *homines rationalistici artificialis*."[99] Last, Sombart argued that Judaism entailed a dualistic ethic. Unlike economic intercourse with fellow Jews, he argued, Jewish intercourse with strangers was conducted without scruples. His primary example of this double ethic was Deuteronomy 23:21, which forbade Jews from taking interest from "your brother" (אחיך) but permitted the taking of interest from the "foreigner" (נכרי).[100] "The differential treatment of non-Jews in Jewish commercial law," he concluded, "resulted in the complete transformation of the idea of commerce and industry generally in the direction of more freedom [*der Gewerbefreiheit und des Freihandels*]."[101]

For Sombart, however, neither objective circumstance nor religion was the ultimate source of the purported Jewish aptitude for capitalism. Rather than Jewish characteristics being a product of Jewish dispersion or the Jewish religion, the Diaspora and the Jewish religion were for him the result of Jewish characteristics.[102] By virtue of their origin, earliest history, and what he described as their millennia-old ethnic purity, Sombart classed the Jews among what he termed nomadic desert peoples.[103] He then traced what he identified as the four invariant elements of the Jewish character—intellectuality, teleology, energy, and mobility—to these southern desert origins.[104] Even the high level of urbanization among Jews in the early twentieth century could be explained in this way, for "the modern city is nothing else but a great desert."[105] Although Sombart acknowledged the influence of money (an implicit nod to Simmel) and the ghetto on the Jewish spirit, they were in his account secondary and supplemental: the abstract, mobile, and quantitative nature of money was, after all, consonant with Jewish "Saharaism and Nomadism," and the ghetto merely rendered inherent Jewish characteristics more marked and one-sided.[106] In the final analysis, Sombart insisted, "Jewish characteristics are rooted in the blood of the race, and are not in any wise due to educative processes."[107] Spirit (*Geist*) ultimately turned out to be an expression of blood.

Returning to the purported clash of Jewish and Christian economic ethics that he had described earlier in the book, Sombart concluded by recasting the conflict in racial and essentialist terms. Pushing into the north, he wrote, the migrating Jews encountered there forest peoples who were different in virtually every respect: they were settled and rooted in the soil, hence indigenous, and they lived in communion with nature rather than in an instrumental relation to it.[108]

> From the wood which is cleared, from the marsh which is drained, from the soil which the ploughshare turns arose that economic organization of society which was dominant in Europe before Capitalism came—the feudal, manorial system, resting on the ideas that production should be only for consumption, that every man should have his niche to work in, and that every society should have differences in status. . . . From the endless wastes of sand, from the pastoral pursuits, springs the opposite way of life—Capitalism.[109]

The narrative of judaization that the early Marx had spun seven decades earlier thus reappeared in Sombart's account, even though the religious categories were now transmuted—within the very same book—into racial categories. Indeed, Sombart explicitly appealed to the authority of Marx's essay "On the Jewish Question" to bolster his claims.[110] In Sombart's retelling, the Jews appeared as an invasive and polluting presence within northern Europe, the social carriers and purveyors of a modern capitalist *Zivilisation* that destroyed and supplanted the ethical *Kultur* of medieval German Christendom.

To be sure, Sombart was not always consistent about the relative importance of the Jews, nor entirely clear about their relationship to other factors in the development of modern capitalism, and he sometimes described other groups and nations in similar terms. Following a trip to the United States to attend the 1904 Congress of Arts and Science, he declared that "the essence of capitalism" had nowhere "reached as full a development as in North America."[111] Although he declined to attribute this development to the characteristics of an Anglo-Saxon race, Sombart described an American spirit (*amerikanischen Volksgeistes*) which in its privileging of monetary quantity over quality, its self-advancement and unrestricted competition, and its "restless striving" and need for "freedom of movement" (*Ellbogenfreiheit*), resembled what he later described as the Jewish spirit.[112] Furthermore, like the Jews, the Americans were said to have a utilitarian orientation to nature: "The only relationship between the Yankee and his environment is one of practical usefulness," he wrote scornfully; the American could see in Niagara Falls only horse power.[113] Well aware of the similarities in his portrayals of the Jewish and American spirits, Sombart insisted in 1911 that "Jewish elements" gave America its "ultimate economic form," that the United States was "filled to the brim with the Jewish spirit," and that "Americanism is nothing else . . . than the Jewish spirit distilled [*geronnener Judengeist*]."[114]

With Weber's thesis about the Protestant ethic and perhaps America's Puritan origins in mind, Sombart also stressed the affinity between Judaism and

Puritanism. He argued in 1911 that they shared so many elements, especially a commitment to the rationalization of life, that "Puritanism *is* Judaism," or at least it derived from Jewish sources.[115] However, Sombart was not consistent on this point. In 1913, he acknowledged with a nod to Weber that Puritanism "did not altogether suppress the capitalist spirit" and even "unconsciously facilitated its growth," but he denied that it was responsible for the bourgeois spirit, boundless and unscrupulous acquisition, or great undertakings and enterprises. "Protestantism," he flatly declared, "has been all along the line a foe to capitalism."[116]

Last, returning to his distinction between heroic and trading peoples, Sombart castigated England during World War I as the embodiment of the bourgeois spirit. In doing so, he made use of a contrast between the commercial English and the warlike Germans initially drawn by the English sociologist Herbert Spencer and revived during the war by English propagandists. However, in Sombart's own wartime propaganda entitled *Händler und Helden* (*Traders and Heroes*), the distinction underwent a transvaluation: England's mercantile spirit was derided as inferior to Germany's strong sense of duty, patriotism, and martial prowess. This polemic against English commercialism prepared the way for an attack on what Sombart called Germany's inner England, the German Social Democratic Party, which he accused of promoting economic rationalism and utilitarianism in a different guise.[117]

Although America, the Puritans, and England also symbolized for Sombart the menace of modern capitalist *Zivilisation*, his attention to the Jews was greater and more sustained. In addition to *The Jews and Modern Capitalism* in 1911, he published *Die Zukunft der Juden* (*The Future of the Jews*) in 1912, he gave public lectures on the subjects of both books, and he returned to the topic of the Jews in later writings.[118] Moreover, the nationalist stance that Sombart adopted circa 1910 and that intensified during World War I was increasingly inflected with antisemitism. Nowhere was his animus toward Jews more apparent than in *Deutscher Sozialismus*, published in 1934 and translated into English in 1937 as *A New Social Philosophy*. There, Sombart argued that only German socialism, which he now distinguished from its Marxian and Catholic variants, could lead Germany into a new economic age. Again invoking Marx's essay "On the Jewish Question," he envisioned this task as an existential struggle between the German spirit, to which German socialism was said to correspond, and the Jewish spirit, which he described as the controlling spirit of the current economic age. The Jewish spirit would "continue to exist," he warned, "even if the last Jew and Jewish descendant [*Judenstämmling*] were destroyed" because it had been internalized by gentiles and objectified in modern economic institutions. Consequently, he declared, for Germans "to free [themselves] from the Jewish spirit," it was "not enough to eliminate [*auszuschalten*] all Jews"; it was necessary to "so transform the institutional culture that it will no longer serve as a bulwark for the Jewish spirit."[119] Sombart thus used the considerable academic and intellectual capital he had accumulated at the end of his career to legitimize Nazi persecution.

Max Weber: Reviving the Narrative of Supersession

Weber was careful to distinguish capitalism in general from the highly rationalized form it took in the modern West. He defined as capitalistic any economic action that rests on the expectation of profit by the use of opportunities for exchange. Capitalistic enterprises in this general sense could be found "in all civilized countries of the earth," from antiquity to modern times. Capitalistic activity is rational insofar as it is based on capital accounting, which is to say, calculation: "at the beginning of the enterprise an initial balance, before every individual decision a calculation to ascertain its probable profitableness, and at the end a final balance to ascertain how much profit has been made." The more sophisticated the methods and the more accurate and certain the calculations, the more confidently can capitalists predict what decisions are best for them, and the more rationalized capitalism becomes. While Weber acknowledged that some premodern capitalistic enterprises already evinced "considerable rationalization of capitalistic calculation," it was typically hampered by tradition, which discouraged the development of new methods, products, or markets, or by an orientation to political and irrationally speculative opportunities for profit, which he called adventurers' capitalism. In his view, it was first in the West, and only in modern times, that capitalism reached its most rational form, and it was precisely the rationalism of modern, Western capitalism that distinguished it from all earlier forms.[120]

Weber sought in a variety of places to identify the historical preconditions and characteristics of modern rational capitalism. Among the texts in which these discussions can be found are *The Protestant Ethic and the Spirit of Capitalism*, published in 1904–5 and again in expanded form in 1920; *Economy and Society*, which Weber wrote in the 1910s for an economics handbook he was editing and which was posthumously published in 1922; the *General Economic History*, based on students' notes of lectures that Weber delivered in winter 1919–20; and Weber's introduction to the first volume of his *Collected Essays in the Sociology of Religion*, which he worked on shortly before his death and which was first published in 1920. Although the discussions in these texts do not correspond perfectly, there is enough overlap among them to give a sense of the economic, political, and religious preconditions that Weber saw as most important for the rise of rational capitalism in the West.[121]

Among the economic developments that contributed to the rationalization of capitalistic enterprise, Weber underscored the separation of business from the household, rational bookkeeping, and the rational organization of formally free labor. All of these innovations improved calculability. Weber considered the development of a rational monetary system, the organization of large and regular markets, the establishment of permanent rather than merely occasional capitalistic enterprises, and the introduction of rational technology, closely associated with the development of modern science, to be important for the same reason. Other economic developments contributed to rationalization by maximizing economic freedom. Weber emphasized the appropriation of all means of production by private entrepreneurs who were then free to buy, sell, and manage them as they saw fit; the freeing of markets from traditional restrictions such as the monopolization of specific activities or goods by status groups; and the representation of property rights by commercial instruments, such as shares of stock, which were themselves available to buy and sell in a market. These sorts of innovations freed entrepreneurs to maximize profits based on their calculations.

Chief among the political preconditions of modern capitalism was a rational system of law and administration. This system, Weber argued, resulted from the development of a bureaucratic state with equality under the law for rights-bearing citizens. While he did not regard bureaucracy itself as a modern development, he did think the rationality of this form of organization propelled its steady expansion in the modern era. Bureaucracy was instrumentally rational insofar as it made ruling and administering more efficient; the bureaucratic state was formally rational insofar as it applied universal and abstract rules without regard to persons, and without hatred or passion; and bureaucratic authority was legal-rational, meaning that civil servants and jurists were loyal to rules rather than to a specific individual. As a result, personal discretion and arbitrariness were minimized. The concept of citizenship complemented these developments when it was extended from cities, where it first emerged, to the modern state. Citizenship brought individuals from different families or clans together into the same political community, reinforcing the trend toward universal and abstract rules, and it transformed them from subjects of political rule into holders of rights within the political community. A rationalized state with rights-bearing citizens made calculations about profit and loss more certain and predictable by suppressing crimes against persons and property, establishing common markets within national borders, standardizing taxation and money, and regulating contractual exchanges. That both the modern state and the concept of the citizen appeared first in the West, according to Weber, helps to explain why modern rational capitalism first appeared there as well.

These economic and political developments comprised only the external conditions for the rise of modern rational capitalism in the West and did not fully capture its inward basis in the realm of subjective spirit. Therefore, Weber argued, an exclusive focus on them could only yield a one-sided materialistic explanation of modern capitalism. To complete his explanation, he also stressed the crucial contribution of a religiously inspired rational ethic for the conduct of life.[122] According to Weber, this sort of rational ethic was obstructed elsewhere in the world by "spiritual obstacles" that were overcome in the West.[123] One of the biggest obstacles was the belief in magic. As long as the "mysterious incalculable forces" of magic governed the world, modern economic, scientific, and technical rationalism based on calculation was impossible.[124] In addition, fear of "supernatural evils" generated "deep repugnance to undertaking any change in the established conduct of life," making magic a powerful buttress for economic traditionalism.[125] Belief in magic also underlay the ritual barriers that separated clans, tribes, and peoples and thus precluded the concept of citizenship.[126] A second obstacle was closely related to those barriers: the persistence of a dualistic economic ethic that forbade the pursuit of gain within one's own tribe, clan, or religious community but imposed no ethical restrictions in dealings with foreigners. In contrast to Sombart, who viewed modern economic liberalism as a universalization of the external ethic, Weber argued that both sides of the double ethic obstructed the rationalization of capitalism: the in-group ethic because it subordinated economic rationality to custom and tradition, the out-group ethic because it undermined the trust necessary for continuous and regular economic relations.[127] A third major obstacle was the existence of a different kind of ethical dualism: stringent expectations for religious virtuosi combined with relatively lax requirements for the masses. This kind of double standard did not preclude a rational ethic, but it restricted it to the virtuosi and thus limited its everyday impact in the wider world.[128] Only when these spiritual obstacles were cleared away, Weber argued, could a rational ethic for the conduct of life—which is to say, the spiritual and subjective basis for modern rational capitalism—emerge and become widespread.

What role did the Jews play in Weber's account of the rise of modern rational capitalism? What he stressed above all was the contribution that Judaism, especially in its exilic form, made to the disenchantment (*Entzauberung*, literally "demagification") of the world.[129] By rejecting magic as a means of achieving salvation or compelling God, and by insisting that evil was divine punishment rather than the work of demons or malevolent spirits, Judaism fostered a rational ethic of conduct based on learning and observance of religious law. In addition to fostering personal self-control, this perspective implied a world that was governed by rational providence and therefore calculable or at least understandable.[130] Contrary to Bauer's characterization of Judaism as Oriental, the Jewish ethic was in these respects "worlds apart from the paths of salvation offered by Asiatic religions."[131] Judaism thus had "notable significance for modern rational capitalism" and "rendered an important service from the point of view of economic history."[132] Indeed, Weber suggested, from this perspective the religious development of the Jews constituted a "turning point of the whole cultural development of the West," and it was upon this fact that "world-historical interest in Jewry rests."[133]

However, if Weber interpreted Judaism as the religious font of modern Western rationalism, Judaism's promise was in his view only fully realized with the advent of Christianity. As he saw it, the rationalizing potential of Judaism could only be partly fulfilled within the confines of that religion; it was hampered above all by the persistence among the Jews of a double ethic, which signified a narrow focus on the redemption of a single community.[134] To extend its rationalizing influence, he argued, Judaism had to become universal in scope, capable of encompassing within its membership everyone in the world. Following a long-standing Christian tradition that counterposed Christian universalism to Jewish particularism—a tradition that had already reappeared in nineteenth-century German idealist philosophy and Marx's discussion of the Jewish question—Weber regarded universalization as the principal contribution of Christianity to the growth of Western rationalism. For him, Christian universalism was exemplified by Paul's espousal of "fellowship with the uncircumcised," which made possible "a Christian world mission."[135]

If Christianity preserved Judaism's rationalizing influence while transcending its limitations, this process culminated for Weber in the Protestant Reformation. In the first place, unlike the church that "lets grace shine over the righteous and the unrighteous alike," the Protestant sect conditioned acceptance on "strict inquiry into one's ethical conduct" and thereby guaranteed the "business honor and reliability" of its members.[136] Moral certification by the sect did not universalize Judaism's in-group ethic so much as overcome the dualism upon which it rested: while tempering the unrestricted pursuit of gain in dealings with strangers and thereby promoting trust, the Reformation simultaneously overturned the Catholic prohibition against usury and brought "calculation into the traditional brotherhood."

The result was neither traditionalism nor untrammeled ruthlessness but instead, "a regulated economic life with the economic impulse functioning within bounds."[137] This context made economic calculation more predictable without stifling the innovations that rationalization entailed.

In the second place, the Protestant notion of a calling advanced economic rationalization in ways that Judaism could not. The concept of the calling made worldly activity a religiously meaningful and obligatory way of proving one's faith and attaining certainty of grace. Judaism, in contrast, though not averse to worldly economic acquisition, could not regard ethically indifferent economic transactions with strangers as a realm in which religious merit could be demonstrated.[138] Instead, Judaism regarded economic activity as secondary and instrumental to what it considered really worthy: "complete devotion to the study of the Law."[139] Moreover, insofar as the calling required "not single good works, but a life of good works combined into a unified system," it imposed a more rational and methodical patterning upon worldly activity.[140] In contrast, the rationalizing influence of Judaism was limited by its "conception of man's relationship to God as a bookkeeping operation of single good and evil acts," as well as the inconceivability for Jews of "methodically controlling the present world, which was so topsy-turvy because of Israel's sins, and which could not be set right by any human action but only by some free miracle of God that could not be hastened."[141] Last, Protestantism expected everyone to have a calling in life, and it deprived laymen of the quasi-magical and ritualistic means of salvation that persisted in medieval Catholicism.[142] Consequently, while Judaism's hostility to magic exerted a rationalizing influence upon conduct within its own confines, and medieval Catholicism fostered a rational ethic within the monastery, it was the Reformation that carried the rational ethic "out of monastic cells" to the (gentile) masses in "everyday life," where it "began to dominate worldly morality."[143] In sum, the concept of a calling, which Weber insisted was "not applicable to the Jew," conferred religious significance on worldly activity, rationally systematized it, and universalized this ideal of ethical conduct.[144] In all these ways, the calling fostered the rational organization of labor—its specialized, regular, methodical, and conscientious character—which Weber considered a defining feature of modern rational capitalism.

Asceticism was the third component of Protestant Christianity that in Weber's view enabled it to surpass Judaism in the promotion of economic rationalization. In contrast to Sombart, Weber insisted that asceticism was absent in Judaism; its sexual and economic ethics instead remained "naturalistic."[145] He acknowledged that medieval Catholicism contained a well-developed ascetic tradition that prized self-control and rejected spontaneous, impulsive enjoyment, but as part of the systematic organization and planning of conduct it was confined to the higher morality of the monastery.[146] According to Weber, it was the Reformation (particularly Calvinism) that spread Christian asceticism to the masses by incorporating it into the notion of the calling. The layman's daily labor, traditionally a means to satisfy human needs, now served only to increase the glory of God. The ascetic element of the Protestant ethic was, in turn, indispensable for the development of modern capitalism: it encouraged entrepreneurs to productively reinvest rather than consume their profits, thus contributing to the rational organization of capital, just as the religious duty to work hard and methodically in one's calling promoted the rational organization of labor.[147]

The upshot of Weber's argument was that Judaism paved the way for modern rational capitalism but prevented its adherents from completing the path it had prepared. "The Jews," he maintained, therefore "stood on the side of the politically and speculatively oriented adventurous capitalism; their ethos was, in a word, that of pariah-capitalism."[148] In other words, ritually separated from the wider society and occupying an inferior position relative to it, the Jews made their profits from moneylending or political opportunities rather than industrial activities. As Marx, Simmel, and Sombart had noted, Jews were "the agents of the money economy" and as such were involved in banking and the financing of political, military, and colonial ventures; in commerce; and in tax farming. However, Weber argued, there was "nothing specifically modern" or Western about these activities.[149] He acknowledged that external conditions such as the dispersion of the Jews, their minority status, and their precarious social position helped to shunt them into these kinds of activities, but he argued it was mainly the ritual requirements of their own religion—and their belief that faithful observance of those requirements was the *sine qua non* of a future messianic redemption that would elevate the Jews over their persecutors—that made them an outcast commercial people.[150] Without asceticism or the notion of a calling, Judaism provided no spiritual basis for transcending pariah capitalism and developing the rational organization of capital and labor: "here," he wrote, "the Jews have not had a decisive influence."[151] Because they were unable to originate these innovations, "hardly a Jew is found among the creators of the modern economic situation, the large entrepreneurs; this type was Christian and only conceivable in the field of Christianity."[152] More precisely, it was "Puritanism [that] carried the ethos of the rational organization of capital and labour."[153]

Does the origin of modern Western rationalism lie, then, in Judaism or in the overcoming of Judaism? To emphasize either side of Weber's argument at the expense of the other is to miss its supersessionist logic. Although the mature Marx and Weber differed about where the Jewish contribution lay, they agreed that the Jews helped to make modern capitalism possible. Puritanism, as Weber put it, "absorbed" from the Jewish ethic what was adapted to the rational organization of capital and labor, just as the "Puritan nations, especially the Americans, . . . absorbed to the point of the absolute loss of any trace of difference" Jewish immigrants who had "abandoned orthodoxy" and thus (in Weber's view) the religious basis of the Jews' self-imposed pariah status. However, Weber did not conceive of economic rationalization as a process of judaization. Just as modern Christian industry superseded Jewish commerce and usury in Marx's later writings, so Puritan rational capitalism superseded Jewish pariah capitalism in Weber's account. Indeed, Weber insisted, "precisely the non-Jewish element in Puritanism enabled Puritanism to play its special role in the creation of the modern economic temper, and also to carry through the aforementioned absorption of Jewish proselytes, which was not accomplished by nations with other than Puritan orientations."[154] In this way Weber broke with the narrative of Jewish domination: in his view, it was not the reality that Sombart imagined but the fantasy of a resentful pariah people waiting for God to turn the tables on its oppressors. Yet, Weber continued to attribute to Jews the aspiration to dominate, and he seemed unable to envision a future for the Jews other than a stubborn continuation of their pariah status or complete absorption into the Protestant world.[155]

Conclusion

In sum, both the early and the mature Marx defined modern capitalism in relation to the Jews, but Marx's changing views about the nature of that relationship resulted in two different narratives. These alternative Marxian legacies could then be taken in different directions by subsequent thinkers. For the early Marx, the "Jewish spirit has become the spirit of the Christian peoples," and "the Christians have become Jews" because the Jews epitomized civil or bourgeois society.[156] This was a narrative of Jewish domination—not necessarily domination by individual Jews but rather, as Sombart later put it, the domination of a Jewish spirit internalized by gentiles and objectified in modern economic institutions. Simmel's reformulation of this narrative in which the modern money economy universalizes the spirit of the Jewish stranger avoided the pejorative tone of Marx and Sombart because money appeared to him as a source of freedom as well as alienation. Nevertheless, all three accounts may be seen as variations on the theme of judaization.

The Jews did not disappear from Marx's mature work, as is sometimes supposed.[157] But there they appear primarily as usurers and merchants who helped to bring the capitalist mode of production into existence only to be superseded within it later. The mature Marx thus dispensed with the earlier narrative of Jewish domination, but in doing so, he made the Jews an anachronism, a people who, as in Hegel's philosophy of history, remain obstinately on the stage after their world-historical role has been fulfilled. Initially identified with the spirit of the age—a spirit that had to be transcended if humanity was to be emancipated—they later came to represent the past, stubbornly refusing to yield to the progress of history. Notwithstanding the important differences in how Marx and Weber understood modern capitalism, Weber's thesis about the supersession of Jewish pariah capitalism by Puritan rational capitalism may be seen as a variation on this same narrative and in this respect follows the second of the two tracks that Marx laid down.

How might we explain the patterned ways that German social thinkers described the relationship between Jews and modern capitalism? Previous scholarship has emphasized the importance of the local institutional setting, field of intellectual production, and macrosocial context in which ideas are produced.[158] However, thinkers with markedly divergent professional trajectories were shown in this chapter to have produced similar ideas. Notwithstanding his role in founding the Deutsche Gesellschaft für Soziologie, Simmel was a stranger in the academy; he worked for fifteen years as a lowly *Privatdozent* in Berlin before obtaining a full professorship in 1914 at the provincial University of Strasbourg.[159] In contrast, Sombart's trajectory took him from the periphery of German academic life to its center. He began his career at the provincial University of Breslau; in 1906, he accepted a post at Berlin's *Handelshochschule*, an institution not under the Prussian Ministry of Education but instead administered by the Berlin Merchants' Guild; but by 1917, he had joined the prestigious University of Berlin at the highest academic rank, signaling his apotheosis as a German mandarin.[160] Yet in spite of these very different trajectories, Simmel and Sombart both described modern economic life as the universalization of a Jewish spirit. The divergence of Marx and Weber is even starker. In contrast to Marx's aborted academic career, Weber was a respected scholar who lectured at prestigious universities in Heidelberg, Vienna, and Munich. Yet in spite of these differences, both of them described modern capitalism as superseding Jewish contributions that made it possible. For these reasons, I have emphasized macrosocial context over institutional location or position in the German academic field.

Which aspects of their macrosocial context were most important for patterning how German sociologists described the relation between Jews and modern capitalism? One aspect of their milieu emphasized in past scholarship is their orientations to modernity, but like institutional setting and position in the field of intellectual production, this factor can be ruled out on the basis of comparative evidence. While Sombart has been described as either a reactionary modernist or an antimodernist, neither of these terms could plausibly be applied to the early Marx or Simmel, yet all three described economic modernization as judaization.[161] Because thinkers with quite different orientations to modernity produced similar ideas, it is difficult to see how those orientations could have yielded such a result. Accordingly, rather than trace Sombart's ideas about the Jews to his reactionary modernist or antimodern orientation, I have investigated how he used those ideas to construct his understanding of modernity.

Past scholarship has also emphasized antisemitism as an important aspect of the macrosocial context for classical German sociology. Many scholars have deemed antimodernism and antisemitism to be closely related, and antisemitism was widespread among German academics in the late nineteenth century.[162] However, antisemitism also fails to provide an adequate explanation for how classical German sociologists described the relationship between Jews and capitalism. To begin with, not all of the thinkers covered in this chapter can plausibly be described as antisemitic. Although some authors have criticized Weber for taking a radically assimilationist view toward Jews in accordance with his political commitments, and one writer has gone so far as to say that "Weber contributed to anti-Semitism," he was certainly not an antisemite by the standards of his time.[163] Neither, of course, was Simmel. Consequently, discussions of antisemitism have mostly focused on Marx and Sombart, though even here, scholarship is divided.[164] As Lars Fischer has pointed out, the "clear-cut juxtaposition of antisemites and non-antisemites" on which these debates rest hinders our understanding of the past because it elides the "extent to which both self-avowed antisemites and those opposed to political antisemitism" in nineteenth- and early twentieth-century Germany "subscribed to many of the same anti-Jewish stereotypes."[165] Accordingly, the principal aim of this chapter has been neither to convict nor to exonerate Marx and Sombart of antisemitism but to clarify what role their assumptions about the Jews played in the development of their thinking about modern capitalism.

Where did the stereotypes of Jews embedded in classical German sociology come from? Scholars with a materialist bent have emphasized the real historical basis of such stereotypes in the role that Jews played in European economic history and their highly visible concentration in commerce and finance.[166] The problem with this approach is that German intellectuals did not react directly to objective conditions; they reacted to those conditions as apprehended through historically constituted schemas that organized their perception. Other scholars have stressed the impact of ideal factors on classical social thinkers, ranging from internal psychological conflicts to more general cultural, philosophical, and intellectual influences.[167] The problem with this approach is that it tends to reduce ideas to biography, treating them merely as extensions of individual thinkers, or to abstract ideas from social relations. This chapter has taken a synthetic view: it acknowledged that portrayals of Jews in German social thought had a material basis while affirming the idealist insight that the facts never speak for themselves; their selection and interpretation is always shaped by cultural schemas that precede experience. Building upon and extending previous scholarship, I suggested that the relevant schemas in this instance have a religious origin in Christian theology transmitted via the Protestant cultural milieu shared by all four of the thinkers covered in this chapter.[168]

The connections that German social thinkers once made between the Jews and modern capitalism are likely to strike us today as dangerous and politically suspect. Should one reject inquiry into the cultural dispositions of particular groups as racist and instead follow those scholars who, under the influence of neoclassical economics, have abandoned the search for social carriers of capitalist rationality because they conceive such rationality to be natural, timeless, and universal? This would be a grave mistake. The German sociological tradition made a genuine and valuable contribution with its insight that *homo capitalisticus* is not history's point of departure but a historic result. To avoid the pitfalls of that heritage, contemporary scholarship must become more historical, not ahistorical. It must become historical in a double sense: both in regard to the groups that scholars study, for only in this way can one avoid essentializing others as an ongoing mode of exclusion today, and in regard to ourselves, in the sense that social inquiry must become more reflexive, which is to say, more attentive to how the social scientist's own internalized history shapes his or her vision and division of the social world.[169]

4

The American Tradition: The City and the Jews

The Jews served as an intermediary for self-reflection in Europe, where they were associated with the democratic revolution of 1789 or the growth of industrial capitalism, but did they serve a similar function for American thinkers preoccupied with the transformation of their society by urbanization and mass immigration? Seeking to answer that question, this chapter focuses on the Chicago school of sociology.[1] My reasons for this focus are threefold. To begin with, urbanism and mobility were key research topics for the Chicago school, which played a leading role in the development of urban sociology and the ecological study of the movement and displacement of populations over time. Furthermore, although the Chicago school was influenced by European social thought, its starting point was a distinctively American philosophy known as pragmatism, and its interest in the self, the city, and disorganization sprang from an underlying concern about "the nature of America and Americans: what they ought to be, why they are not as they ought, and how they may become more like they ought to be."[2] Last, the Chicago school played an important role in American sociology as a whole. The University of Chicago established one of the country's earliest sociology departments in 1892; that department became the preeminent center of the discipline in America by 1914; and its early establishment, size, and prestige allowed it to dominate American sociology throughout the 1920s and into the 1930s. The Chicago sociology department published American sociology's flagship publication, the *American Journal of Sociology*; its chairman served as the journal's editor; and its members were involved in the creation in 1905 of the American Sociological Society. Twenty of the first forty presidents of the American Sociological Society received their doctoral degrees from Chicago or were on its staff, and in the same period, the University of Chicago awarded more doctoral degrees in sociology and placed more of their recipients in colleges and universities than did any other institution.[3] The Chicago school's ascendancy in American sociology began to wane after the mid-1930s for a variety of reasons, including the departure of key figures, the rise of new theoretical perspectives, methodological challenges, and the development of competing centers of sociological research and graduate training.[4] Accordingly, the scope of this chapter is confined to what is now considered to be the first Chicago school during the peak of its influence from World War I through the 1930s.

The chapter places particular emphasis on the work of four major figures in the Chicago school: Robert Ezra Park; his mentor William Isaac Thomas, who persuaded the University of Chicago to hire Park; and two of Park's students—Louis Wirth, who also knew and was directly influenced by Thomas, and Everett Verner Stonequist. Thomas was one of a handful of the most influential thinkers in American sociology from 1910 to 1940.[5] After Thomas was dismissed from the University of Chicago in 1918, Park became the central figure in Chicago sociology, but it was heavily indebted to both men for its scholarly agenda and intellectual direction; they directed their students toward particular research topics and provided them with the key concepts they used to analyze their empirical findings.[6] Among these students, the German-born Wirth earned his doctoral degree in 1926 and joined the faculty at the University of Chicago in 1931, where he remained until his death in 1952. Stonequist earned his doctorate in 1930 and then joined the faculty at Skidmore College. Examination of the work of these four figures will show that early sociological interest in the Jews stemmed from similar sources in both America and Europe: in the United States, no less than in France and Germany, Jews served as a touchstone for defining modernity and national identity in a time of rapid social change.

The Chicago sociologists directed their attention to Jews at a time when mass immigration was altering their salience, numbers, and social conditions in the United States. Before 1880, the country's Jewish population did not exceed 280,000; its origins lay in the small Sephardic immigration of the seventeenth century and the German-Jewish immigration that predominated from 1820 to 1880. From 1881 to 1924, this population was augmented and soon outnumbered by the arrival of more than two million Jews from eastern Europe. As a result, America's Jewish population rose from an estimated one million in 1900 to 3.25 million in 1915, growing from 1.3 percent to 3.2 percent of the country's total population. By 1925, the number of American Jews had swelled to an estimated 4.5 million, comprising nearly 4 percent of the US population. In contrast to the predominantly bourgeois occupations of

German-Jewish Americans, including law and politics, banking and finance, department store ownership, publishing, medicine, and literary, academic, and scientific activities, the newer Jewish immigrants from eastern Europe made their living in petty trade or joined America's immigrant working class, concentrating especially in the clothing industry. All segments of American Jewry, however, were urbanizing. Already by the 1870s and 1880s, there were sizable Jewish communities in New York, Cincinnati, San Francisco, Philadelphia, Baltimore, and Chicago. Although many of the newer Jewish immigrants who arrived after 1880 came from small towns and villages in eastern Europe, they settled in America's largest cities. In this respect, Jews in America were comparable to their counterparts in France and Germany. "By the time the First World War broke out," as one historian puts it, "world Jewry had become a city people."[7]

From Rural Cultures to Urban Civilization

To determine the meaning and significance of the Jews in the Chicago school of sociology, it is first necessary to understand the broader conceptual framework within which the Chicago sociologists situated them. This framework was to a great extent the work of Robert Park.[8] Like other classical sociologists, Park envisioned the social world as undergoing a transition from the traditional to the modern, or in the terms that he borrowed from German social thought (see chapter 3) and modified for his own purposes, from culture to civilization.[9] As Park conceived them, culture designated a society with a moral order, integrated by means of ritual and tradition, and regulated on the basis of folkways and mores, while civilization signified a new social order that released individuals from the control of local custom while integrating them more loosely through trade and commerce. Upon this basic dualism, Park and other Chicago sociologists overlaid a series of related distinctions: primary/secondary institutions, sacred/secular, consensus/symbiosis, and rural/urban. The couplet of primary and secondary institutions, derived from Charles Cooley, distinguished close relationships such as family ties, in which interaction involved one's entire personality, from more impersonal and narrowly circumscribed relationships, as in the workplace, which did not extend into the rest of one's life.[10] But the linchpin of Chicago school thinking was an assumed historical development from rural life, which was equated with the face-to-face relations and total involvement of the simple primary group, to urbanism, which signified the specialization, fragmentation, rationalism, and impersonality of life in modern civilization.[11] Thus, the city symbolized the modern world: "understand the city and you understand the central tendencies of modern society."[12] When linked together, these antinomies formed a common frame of reference within which Chicago sociologists could place the experiences of a variety of groups, including African Americans, immigrants, and Jews.

If Park and his students equated rural with (traditional) culture and urban with (modern) civilization, then they saw mobility as the chief means of transition from the one to the other. According to this view, the movement of peoples took two main forms: the colonization or displacement of so-called backward peoples and regions by more advanced peoples, as in the case of European imperialism, or the migration of purportedly less advanced peoples to more advanced areas, as when European or Asian peasants from agrarian villages or African Americans from southern plantations migrated to American cities. Regardless of whether the metropole came to them or they came to the metropolis, movement meant a "similar initiation of culture-peoples into the complexities of urban civilization."[13] Migration brought different peoples and cultures into contact and collision; these cultural conflicts interrupted habitual routines and broke what Park, borrowing a phrase from the nineteenth-century British economist Walter Bagehot, called the "cake of custom"; and this loosening of parochial bonds made a less prejudiced and more enlightened perspective possible. "When the traditional organization of society breaks down, as a result of contact and collision with a new invading culture," Park wrote, "the effect is . . . to emancipate the individual man." Because he is no longer bound by "local proprieties and conventions," the "energies that were formerly controlled by custom and tradition are released," and he "learns to look upon the world in which he was born and bred" with less prejudice and more objectivity.[14] "Inevitably he becomes, relatively to his cultural milieu, the individual with the wider horizon, the keener intelligence, the more detached and rational viewpoint."[15] Migration was thus a process of creative destruction: by destroying "the cultures of tribe and folk" it cleared the way for "the rational organization which we call civilization."[16] In sum, the Chicago school understood migration not simply as movement in space but also as a conflict-ridden, emancipating, enlightening, and civilizing movement from tradition to modernity.

The Marginal Man Looks Jewish

The concept of the marginal man presupposed this dualistic vision of the social world. Although German-Jewish sociologist Georg Simmel, Thomas, and the American economist and social scientist Thorstein Veblen anticipated the idea of the marginal man, it was Park who coined the name and provided its most influential exposition in 1928.[17] The marginal man, as Park defined him, was a distinctive personality type produced by the contact and collision of cultures, a "cultural hybrid, a man living and sharing intimately in the cultural life and traditions of two distinct peoples; never quite willing to break, even if he were permitted to do so, with his past and his traditions, and not quite accepted, because of racial prejudice, in the new society in which he now sought to find a place. He was a man on the margin of two cultures and two societies, which never completely interpenetrated and fused."[18] In Park's introduction to Stonequist's monograph on the marginal man, based on Stonequist's 1930 doctoral dissertation and published in 1937, Park stressed not just cultural contact but also cultural conflict in the emergence of this personality type: the marginal man, Park wrote, was "one whom fate has condemned to live in two societies and in two, not merely different but antagonistic cultures." This antagonism existed twice, in social relations and at the level of individual personality, outside and inside of the marginal man. On the one hand, he was a product of the cultural conflicts brought about by conquest, invasion, and migration. In an early description of globalization, Park suggested that "the vast expansion of Europe during the last four hundred years" had "brought about everywhere an interpenetration of peoples and a fusion of cultures," producing in the marginal man "a personality type which if not wholly new is at any rate peculiarly characteristic of the modern world." He was thus "an effect of imperialism" and "an incident of the process by which civilization . . . grows up at the expense of earlier and simpler cultures."[19] On the other hand, the marginal man was himself a microcosm of cultural conflict, which reappeared in his mind as "the conflict of 'the divided self,' the old self and the new."[20] "The external conflict of the groups," as Stonequist put it, "finds an echo in the mind of the individual concerned," and the "duality of cultures produces a duality of personality."[21] Within a quarter century of the publication of Park's 1928 article introducing this concept, it had gained wide circulation in American sociology and was found in nearly all of the discipline's introductory textbooks.[22]

Although Park conceived the marginal man as a general social type, he closely associated the type with the Jews of the modern era. Park had studied with Simmel in Germany, and he explicitly identified the marginal man with Simmel's own notion of the stranger, the "classic example" of which was "the history of European Jews."[23] Following his teacher's lead, Park traced the origins of the marginal man to the same source.[24] Three main points emerged from this discussion. First, in the influential *Introduction to the Science of Sociology*, the leading textbook in American sociology from 1921 until it went out of print in 1943, Park and Ernest Burgess claimed that the Jews in Europe, prior to their emancipation, were largely isolated by gentile exclusion and their own ritualistic self-segregation. They associated social isolation, in turn, with the "provincialism" and "low intelligence" that characterized "the savage, the peasant, and the backward races."[25]

Second, Park and Burgess qualified this view later in their textbook with an excerpt from Werner Sombart's 1913 study *Der Bourgeois*, translated into English as *The Quintessence of Capitalism*, in which Sombart linked the social type of the stranger to migration and the development and spread of the spirit of capitalism. Within this excerpt, Sombart emphasized "Jewish migrations" as one of the three most important "wanderings of large groups" since the sixteenth century. The implication was that from the sixteenth century onward, Jews were already, through their migratory and commercial activity, exposing others to new cultural influences.[26] William Thomas and Florian Znaniecki made a similar point in *The Polish Peasant in Europe and America*, a sprawling masterpiece published in five volumes between 1918 and 1921 that soon came to define early American sociology. Standing "outside of Polish social life" and "Polish society," they wrote, "the Jews were to a large extent representatives of the capitalistic economy." As such, they introduced the peasant to a new, alien, and individualistic ethos of economic rationalism at odds with "the old family economy, in which economic values are still to a large extent qualitative, not yet subordinated to the idea of quantity, and the dominant attitude is the interest in getting a good living, not the tendency to get rich." Indeed, they argued, "much deeper" than the social disorganization produced by the Polish peasant's own migration was "the disorganization . . . produced by strangers" such as "the Jewish shopkeeper," who "settle[d] among the local inhabitants, bringing with them different mores," but "fail[ed] to become assimilated," in the case of Jews, "through racial reasons."[27] This theme reappeared in *Old World Traits Transplanted*, a book largely written by Thomas but published under the names of Park and Herbert Miller in 1921. Polish peasants, they noted, lived in largely self-sufficient communities through much of the nineteenth century, but they "knew by report that there was a great world, and they had some relations with it, through Jews and manor owners."[28] Wirth, citing Sombart, likewise emphasized the migratory and commercial activity of Jews, including their role as cultural intermediaries between the Orient and the Occident.[29] In all these works, Jews were depicted as key agents breaking down the social isolation of others, introducing them to new cultural influences, and thereby promoting their social disorganization. How Jews were able to play this role without exposing themselves to new cultural influences was not explained. Park simply asserted that "the history of the Jews proves that it is possible to maintain . . . a form of tribal culture, with an extraordinary degree of mobility and a lively interest in, and aptitude for, trade."[30]

Jews may have promoted the contact and collision of cultures as early as the sixteenth century, Park suggested, but they themselves did not fully experience and internalize it until their emancipation began at the end of the eighteenth century. This was the third point to emerge from his discussion of the Jewish role in the modern, worldwide mixing of races and cultures. According to Park, it was the emancipation of the Jews in Europe that broke up *Jewish* isolation and provincialism, dissolved the cake of *Jewish* custom, and thrust the Jews into closer contact with gentiles.[31] In this respect, emancipation affected the Jews in the same way as their own activity had affected others; it was functionally equivalent to migration and had similar consequences, stamping modern Jews—in contrast to their socially isolated and provincial forebears—with the enlightened, rationalistic, and cosmopolitan outlook that was the hallmark of the man living in two worlds. The emancipation of the Jews was thus critical to Park's conception of the marginal man and his identification of him with the Jew. "When . . . the walls of the medieval ghetto were torn down and the Jew was permitted to participate in the cultural life of the peoples among whom he lived," Park wrote, the "new type of personality" appeared. "The emancipated Jew was, and is, historically and typically the marginal man, the first cosmopolite and citizen of the world."[32]

Although Park and his students extended the concept of the marginal man to others, it continued to have a strongly Jewish connotation. Park had characterized Jews in similar terms in 1926, and in the 1930s he returned to the example of the Jews in his writings about race relations in the American South, Hawaii, and throughout the world.[33] Furthermore, Park's student Louis Wirth, who was himself Jewish, provided a comparable description of Jews in his classic study *The Ghetto*, which was published in 1928, the same year as the article in which Park introduced the concept of the marginal man. For Wirth, a confluence of internal and external processes broke down the social isolation symbolized by ghetto walls, but those processes were partly offset by countervailing forces that tended to reproduce ghettoization even in the New World, including antisemitism and discrimination, new immigration, and the reconcentration of Jews in new neighborhoods as an unintended consequence of their flight from immigrant ghettoes. Thus, he concluded, "the rise and decline of the ghetto seems to be a cyclical movement." The persistence of the ghetto within a gentile world, and the Jew's recurring emergence from and retreat to it, produced the cultural friction internalized by the marginal man. Wirth was skeptical that such friction could be eliminated. The Jew, he wrote, "lived on the periphery of two worlds, and not fully in either. . . . His self is divided between the world that he has deserted and the world that will have none of him."[34] Nearly a decade later, Stonequist pointed to the Jew as the "typical" and "classic illustration" of the marginal man, as did Park's erstwhile coauthor Herbert Miller in his review of Stonequist's study.[35] Even Park's student Everett Hughes, who after World War II unmoored the concept of marginality from Park's starting point of racial and cultural mixing, reaffirmed that "the Jew emerging from the Ghetto" was the "prototype" of the marginal man.[36]

The Jewishness of the marginal man was apparent not only to Chicago sociologists but also to American Jewish intellectuals. Already in the first two decades of the twentieth century, a number of American writers, including Jewish immigrants like Abraham Cahan, Mary Antin, and Horace Kallen, had provided vivid portraits of the ethnically, nationally, or racially divided personality; at the same time, Jewish psychologists in America drew attention to such personalities and shaped the interpretation of them. Hence, as both objects of psychological study and as contributors to the development and popularization of psychology in the United States, "Jews figured into public speculation about the idea that the human psyche and the American nation were divisible rather than solid, pluralistic rather than unified."[37] Jewish participation in such discussions fed into a broader social-scientific turn beginning in the 1920s in how American Jews publicly talked about Jewishness and explained themselves to gentiles.[38] In this context, it is not surprising that American-Jewish intellectuals would themselves take up the marginal man concept. Some took issue with the concept for portraying Jews in an undesirable manner as maladjusted, psychologically damaged, insecure, unstable, and prone to deviance.[39] Others embraced the concept as a positive characterization that implied tolerance, insight, and freedom.[40] Their disputes notwithstanding, all seemed to agree that the marginal man looked Jewish. "While various individuals and groups are characterized as marginal," noted sociologist and rabbi David Golovensky nearly a quarter century after the publication of Park's seminal article, "the Jewish group in the diaspora" remained "the classic example and 'ideal type' marginal personality."[41]

An Excursus on Jews, African Americans, and the Marginal Man

No discussion of the marginal man would be complete without a comparison of Jews and African Americans, not only because of the Chicago school's extensive study of the latter, but also because of the intellectual origins of the marginal man concept itself. Although the Chicago sociologists repeatedly pointed to the Jew as the classic example of the marginal man, the concept was also inspired by Park's interest in Americans of mixed black and white ancestry and by W. E. B. Du Bois's notion of double-consciousness.[42] The American Negro, Du Bois suggested in his 1903 book *The Souls of Black Folk*, was only permitted to see and evaluate himself through the eyes of an "American world" that regarded him with "amused contempt and pity"; the result was a feeling of "two souls, two thoughts, two unreconciled strivings; two warring ideals in one dark body, whose dogged strength alone keeps it from being torn asunder."[43] Notwithstanding his close ties to Du Bois's rival Booker T. Washington, Park invoked Du Bois and his notion of double-consciousness a full five years before introducing his own concept of the marginal man.[44] Park's students were also familiar with the notion of double-consciousness.[45] Thus, it was likely under Du Bois's influence that Park and Stonequist identified the mixed-race individual as a marginal man—not by virtue of heredity, they insisted, but because of the social situation in which he typically found himself.[46] Moreover, Park and his students extended the concept over time from mixed-race individuals to African Americans, perhaps because the line between the two populations was difficult to draw. In 1934, Park pointed to the "Negro peasants of the southern plantations" as one of several "marginal peoples" who were "in transit between simpler and primitive and more sophisticated and complex cultures, such as characterize our modern industrial and urban civilization"; Wirth and Herbert Goldhamer, stressing the diminishing differences between mixed-race individuals and blacks as the economic and educational opportunities of the latter improved, insisted in 1944 that "in a sense *every* Negro, whether light or dark, is a marginal man in American society"; and Stonequist noted in 1964 that "with the spread of education and the progress of the Negro," it was not just mixed-race individuals but all blacks who "enter[ed] into the marginal position."[47]

Why, then, did Park and his students repeatedly refer to the Jew rather than the mixed-race individual or the African American as the prototype of the marginal man? Why did Park place so much emphasis on Jews when he introduced the marginal man concept in 1928, making ten references to them in a thirteen-page article but only a single reference each to "the Mulatto in the United States" and "the Negro"? Several likely answers suggest themselves. First, Park believed that the mixing of races, nationalities, and cultures in America was recapitulating similar processes that had already taken place in Europe.[48] As promoters and products of mobility, commerce, and cultural contact in Europe, Jews were already marginal men before they arrived in American cities. Consequently, as I show below, Jews could symbolize the city and civilization (which is to say, modernity) for the Chicago school in a way that African Americans could not.[49] To be sure, African Americans were also in transit, as Park put it, from the rural South to northern cities, but as late as 1940—two decades after the nation's population as a whole had become predominantly urban—a majority of blacks still lived in rural areas.[50] Park and his students therefore regarded African Americans as latecomers to urban civilization, similar in this respect to the rural peasants from eastern and southern Europe who began to concentrate in American cities at the end of the nineteenth century.[51]

A second consideration also helps to explain the exemplary status that Park and his students assigned to Jews. For Park, as we have seen, the Jew was a meeting point of two cultures; as such he personified the cultural contact and collision that Park thought was so characteristic of the modern world. African Americans, in contrast, could not serve this symbolic function for Park because he was skeptical that they had an indigenous culture of their own; in his view, slavery had largely obliterated any African traditions that blacks might have brought to the United States.[52] To be sure, in 1913 Park welcomed the black man's efforts to "fashion his own ideals and in his own image rather than in that of the white man," but such efforts were in his view a response to segregation, which attenuated cross-racial relations while bringing blacks into "closer and more intimate contact" with one another.[53] For Park, to put it differently, the transformation of African Americans from a caste (under slavery) into a racial minority group (in the era of Jim Crow) did not so much bring an existing black culture into conflict with others as stimulate African Americans' autonomous cultural development in the first place.[54] In short, Jews could exemplify the marginal man more fully than African Americans because Jewish-gentile relations were, according to Park and his students, a matter of culture conflict and not merely the conflict that arose from race prejudice.

A third consideration may also help to explain why Park and his students designated Jews rather than African Americans as the classic example and prototype of the marginal man. The marginal man, as I show below, was an ambiguous social type, a Janus-faced figure who suggested the potential not only for disorganization but also for the integration of previously antagonistic groups within a new and more expansive social order. An emphasis on "the Mulatto in the United States" would have raised the explosive issue of miscegenation as one form that such integration might take. Although this implication could not be entirely avoided, Park and his students downplayed it in two ways: by placing their emphasis instead upon Jews and by subsuming racial differences under the heading of cultural differences.[55] Entrenched racial segregation made African Americans an equally problematic symbol of (potential) integration. To be sure, Jewish Americans also experienced discrimination in the 1920s and 1930s, and Thomas and Park wavered about the prospect of their assimilation. Assimilation is an equivocal term that warrants further parsing below, but suffice it to say here that the integration of Jews in some form within a new social order, while uncertain, was at least conceivable to Thomas and Park.[56] A similar integration of African Americans (and Asian Americans)—even without miscegenation—appeared to Park far more difficult because the inescapable "racial uniform" or "racial mark" of these groups transformed individual competition into racial competition, which in turn led to racial conflict.[57] Consequently, Park did not expect the assimilation of blacks: in a sense, he wrote, "the Negro, even though culturally he be a purely native product, is not assimilated," though he added that after three centuries in which blacks had lived, worked, and interbred with whites in the United States, it was difficult to say in just what sense.[58] At least initially, Park thought that a biracial organization of society was more likely than assimilation of blacks: "the Negro in America," he suggested, was becoming in Booker T. Washington's words "'a nation within a nation.'"[59] For these reasons, Americans of racially mixed or African ancestry probably seemed less suited than Jews to signal the positive and creative side of the marginal man as a potential agent in the construction of a new and expanded social order.

While Park and his students distinguished Jews as the classic example and prototype of the marginal man, they nevertheless linked Jews and blacks together by subsuming both groups under the marginal man concept. Both Jews and blacks were diasporic peoples, Park pointed out, and it was by virtue of their dispersion that both groups became national or racial minorities—an alternative configuration of race relations, Park seemed to suggest in 1937, to both caste inequality and complete assimilation.[60] In much the same way that Thomas, Park, and Miller described immigrants' institutions and nationalist movements (among which they explicitly included Zionism) as positive steps to combat social disorganization, garner equal respect, and participate in American life, Park viewed race consciousness and racial movements as serving a similar function for blacks.[61] Black solidarity and race consciousness may have been a product of segregation and the race prejudice of whites, but in his view, they also provided a basis for African Americans to improve their status, modify the power relationships in American society, and ultimately perhaps even make individual rather than racial competition possible.[62] Indeed, by 1935, Park saw in the migration of blacks to cities, their enfranchisement there, and the rise of a new black political leadership a "career . . . in America" that was unequaled by "any other element in our population, except the Jew."[63] However, writing in 1937, two years after the introduction of the Nuremberg Laws in Nazi Germany, about the racial etiquette that served to fix the African American in his place, Park was less sanguine: "the position of the Jew in Europe," he noted in an implicit rebuke of his own country, "may be said to constitute a race problem in the same sense as the position of the Negro constitutes a race problem in the United States."[64] Wirth, too, stressed the comparable predicaments of Jews and blacks in the 1940s while at the same time expressing hope for a kind of solidarity which, though he did not live to see it, would later be realized in the American civil rights movement: "For both peoples the goal of a happier adjustment to the world in which they must live is seen to be further distant than either had expected. They have the consolation that they can travel at least part of that road in companionship."[65]

Jews, the City, and America

Returning now to the main line of argument, I would like to emphasize that the Chicago school of sociology closely associated the Jews, the city, and civilization. "The Jews," Thomas, Park, and Miller wrote in 1921, "tend even more than other immigrants groups to settle in cities."[66] "The Jew," Park reiterated a year later, was "by tradition a city dweller" with a "predilection for trade," an activity he associated closely with urbanization.[67] In 1928, Wirth described the Jews in similar terms as "a dominantly city people," though he was careful to add the qualification that "the Jews of Eastern Europe occupied until recently the status of a village people."[68] Following the publication of his 1938 essay "Urbanism as a Way of Life," Wirth reaffirmed this view, noting that "the Jews, having grown up with the city, find urban life their natural milieu."[69] One reason for this association of Jews with the city was empirical: There was in fact a high level of urbanization among European and American Jews by the late nineteenth and early twentieth centuries, and no city exemplified this trend more than New York: its Jewish population—mainly immigrants and their children—grew from no more than sixty thousand in 1880 to one and a half million in 1915, when it comprised 40 percent of America's Jews and 25 percent of the city's population, making New York the largest urban Jewish community that had ever existed. Park proclaimed it the "racial capital" of the Jews in 1925; the Jew, he added, "is more at home in New York than he is in Jerusalem."[70]

A deeper theoretical logic also underlay the association of Jews with urbanism. According to the Chicago school, the Jew (as the quintessential marginal man) and the city were both sites in which cultures came into contact and collision, and it was out of this collision that civilization emerged. The

Jew and the city were thus perceived as sharing many of the same qualities. In his seminal 1915 article "The City," Park suggested that "the intellectual characteristics of the Jew and his generally recognized interest in abstract and radical ideas"—including, he added, "that most interesting of abstractions, money"—were connected to the geographical mobility of the Jews and "the fact that the Jews are, before all else, a city folk."[71] Park reaffirmed this point when the article was reprinted in 1925, and he repeated it in slightly different form in 1928: "Most if not all the characteristics of the Jew, certainly his preeminence as a trader and his keen intellectual interest, his sophistication, his idealism and lack of historic sense, are the characteristics of the city man, the man who ranges widely, . . . the cosmopolite."[72] This affinity, in Park's view, is what drew Jews to the city. The marginal man, of whom the Jews were the "historical and classical example," migrated to the metropolis, "the final refuge of the detribalized, denationalized, and emancipated," and the locus of a "new and cosmopolitan civilization," because he found there the opportunity to play the role of an "intermediary and interpreter between the two races and the two cultures" that were "represented . . . in his own person."[73] But Jewish immigrants were not initiated into civilization by their arrival in American cities; because of their previous historical experiences, it was already embodied within them. As Park put it, other immigrants "bring to this country the cultures of peasant peoples," but "the Jew brings with him a civilization."[74] No group therefore was better suited to urban life. As "the city is . . . the natural habitat of civilized man," Park claimed, so "the marginal man is always relatively the more civilized human being. He occupies the position which has been, historically, that of the Jew in the Diaspora. The Jew, particularly the Jew who has emerged from the provincialism of the ghetto, has everywhere and always been the most civilized of human creatures."[75]

Park and his students not only associated the Jews with the city, but they also associated the city with America. If the Jew in whom two cultures clashed was a microcosm of the great urban melting pot of races and cultures—both Park and Wirth described the city this way—then America was becoming the city writ large.[76] Two important trends underlay this view. First, the United States underwent a rapid transformation after the Civil War from an overwhelmingly agrarian into an increasingly urban society. From 1860 to 1910, America's rural population merely doubled, but its urban population grew sevenfold, and it was in the larger cities that population growth tended to be most pronounced; the population of Chicago, for instance, more than doubled in just one decade from 1880 to 1890.[77] By 1920, the national census revealed for the first time that more Americans lived in urban areas (defined as cities and towns with at least 2,500 residents) than rural areas. The dramatic growth of the country's urban population was, in turn, fueled by a second and related trend: massive migration, both overseas and internal. From the early 1880s until the outbreak of World War I, twenty million immigrants arrived in the United States, and by the mid-1890s, most of them came from southern and eastern Europe rather than the northern and western European sources to which Americans were accustomed. Many of these new immigrants were rural peasants who concentrated in the ghettoes and slums of America's burgeoning industrial cities. Even after World War I and the national quotas legislation of 1921 and 1924 curtailed the massive influx of European immigrants, the Great Migration of African Americans from the rural South, pulled by the labor shortages of urban industries, continued to fuel urban growth. Park alluded to both of these trends—urbanization and migration—when he quipped that America was comprised of two classes of people, "those who reached the city and those who have not yet arrived."[78] Because the Jews were already a city people, one might say that they showed Americans who were not yet urbanized the image of their own future. The "Jewish spirit has become the spirit of the Christian peoples," Karl Marx wrote in 1843, and "the Christians have become Jews."[79] Park implicitly agreed, not because Jews epitomized civil or bourgeois society, as Marx had argued, but because they epitomized urban civilization.

Not all Americans were comfortable with this destination. The very trends that in Park's view were a hallmark of modernity—the contact and collision of different peoples and cultures, showcased above all in the metropolis—stoked anxieties in the United States about the new, more exotic, city-dwelling immigrants, of which Jews comprised a substantial portion, and fears that their loyalties might be divided during World War I.[80] These attitudes expressed in part a long-standing urban-rural conflict in American life, and in part the status anxieties among native-born Protestant Americans that sociologist Joseph Gusfield revealed in his classic study of the temperance movement, but they were also and more fundamentally anxieties about the threat that racial and cultural mixing was perceived to pose to national identity.[81] Perhaps no one signaled this more stridently than the anthropologist Madison Grant, who complained in 1916 in his best-selling book *The Passing of the Great Race* that "immigrants adopt the language of the native American; they wear his clothes; they steal his name; and they are beginning to take his women, but they seldom adopt his religion or understand his ideals."[82]

Of course, the metaphor of the melting pot, suggested as early as the eighteenth century and given forceful expression in 1908 by the English-Jewish playwright Israel Zangwill, presupposed racial and cultural mixing as a source of American identity, not a threat to it, at least when such mixing was confined to Europeans; it envisioned America as a new nation forged from the best that the Old World had to offer.[83] But as immigration rose and its sources changed in the early twentieth century, growing numbers of Americans began to doubt the efficacy and desirability of the melting pot. Three alternatives can be distinguished. First, some social thinkers renovated the nation's tradition of ascriptive Americanism or racial nationalism with new ideas drawn from eugenics and anthropology; they began to insist that the nation's identity was Anglo-Saxon or Nordic, it was fixed, and its purity had to be preserved by the exclusion of immigrants who were too dissimilar. This view was especially hostile to Jewish immigrants from eastern Europe.[84] Although a number of American social scientists wholly or partly endorsed this perspective, it was at odds with the Chicago school's stress on social and historical experience rather than heredity to explain social behavior.[85] Second, alongside attempts to exclude new immigrants, an Americanization movement undertook deliberate measures to suppress the foreign heritage of previous arrivals and transform them into "100 percent Americans." Although the Americanization movement was largely led by Frances Kellor, a sociologist and social worker trained at the University of Chicago, Thomas and Park were critical of its methods, which they considered counterproductive and disorganizing. The Americanization movement reached a crescendo during World War I before collapsing in late 1920 to 1921.[86] Third, a small minority of dissenting intellectuals including the essayist Randolph Bourne and the philosophers John Dewey, Alain Locke, and Horace Kallen, promoted the doctrine of cultural pluralism, a view with roots in American pragmatism. Although their views were not identical in every respect, the pluralists agreed that American identity should rest on an ideal of harmonious diversity rather than racial or cultural homogeneity. Despite the Chicago sociologists' own roots in American pragmatism and the pluralistic tendencies that appeared in Park's thinking, their relationship to the cultural pluralists was complicated by the Chicago sociologists' references to assimilation and the equivocal nature of the term itself.[87]

To understand why the proponents of racial nationalism and Americanization feared the mixing of peoples and cultures that Park took to be a defining feature of the modern world, it is necessary to understand what such mixing meant to them. Grant articulated a widespread view when he described immigration as a kind of conquest in which Jewish and other immigrants displaced and usurped old-stock Americans. Sociologist Edward Ross had expressed similar fears in 1914 when he accused American Jews of trying to control US immigration policy for the benefit of "their brethren from the Pale [of Settlement]" while gentile Americans struggled to compete with the underhanded "Jewish invader." The language of conquest was subsequently echoed by historian Lothrop Stoddard, lawyer Charles Gould, and even the Chicago school's own descriptions of ecological succession within the city, and it dovetailed with allegations of Jewish economic power that circulated during the 1920s in the antisemitic propaganda of Henry Ford and the Ku Klux Klan.[88]

Furthermore, racial and cultural mixing was often seen as a solvent threatening national unity.[89] Jewish immigrants in particular were described in such terms. Economist John Commons and eugenicist Charles Davenport contrasted the putative individualism of eastern European Jews to the community ideals of the American pioneer, while Ross saw in the behavior of Jewish immigrants a welter of egoistic and acquisitive impulses expressed outside of and often in opposition to existing institutions. For instance, the experience of tsarist repression purportedly instilled in the Jewish immigrant a hatred of government and a disregard for the law that were ill-suited for the American democracy in which he found himself.[90]

Above all, racial and cultural mixing was feared as a source of moral, social, and biological pollution. The metropolitan city that Park described as a melting pot of races and cultures was for Grant the "*cloaca gentium*" (sewer of the nations) producing "racial hybrids" and "ethnic horrors that will be beyond the powers of future anthropologists to unravel."[91] Likewise, the racial hybrid was for Stoddard "a walking chaos."[92] Grant and other writers regarded eastern European Jews as a racially mixed type already and therefore less pure than smaller and earlier waves of Jewish immigrants of Sephardic or German origin.[93] Eastern European Jews, it was feared, would contaminate America with "Mongoloid" or "Asiatic" blood, degenerate its "higher" and more advanced racial stock, and contribute to the mongrelization of the nation.[94] The interpenetration of peoples to which Grant and others drew attention in the early twentieth century was real, though not always sexual, and it had real consequences for public affairs, but those consequences depended on how it was interpreted. After World War I, the processes that were pulling America into world affairs and pulling the rest of the world into America produced a fierce reaction that took various forms: the coercive and conformist Americanization campaign; the onset of Prohibition (an issue that divided native-born Protestants from Catholic immigrants) in 1919; bloody race riots in Chicago and elsewhere in 1919; deportations of hundreds of foreign radicals during the Red Scare of 1919 to 1920; postwar isolationism, symbolized by the US refusal to ratify the Covenant of the League of Nations in 1919 and 1920; congressional refusal to reapportion seats in the rural-dominated House of Representatives on the basis of the 1920 census; overt and assertive expressions of antisemitism and nativism, including the revival of the Ku Klux Klan as a mass movement in the 1920s; increasingly shrill and ultimately successful demands for the drastic restriction of immigration in 1921 and 1924; and the sound defeat of the urban, Catholic, and "wet" Al Smith in the 1928 presidential election.[95]

Unlike their contemporaries who defined America in opposition to Jewish immigrants pouring through New York harbor, the Chicago school underscored the affinities between them. After all, the Jewish marginal man, like America as a whole, was a meeting point of cultures, a site of cultural contact and collision, and both Jews and America were similarly characterized, according to the Chicago school, by urbanism, mobility, and civilization. To be sure, none of the Chicago sociologists pushed this logic as far as the cultural pluralist Randolph Bourne, who regarded the Jew, by virtue of his "dual life," as the model for a new "trans-national" America.[96] Nevertheless, the logic of the Chicago school's claims pointed to this kind of identification. If Park's theory of marginality was extended to cover the transition from rural to urban, as Park sometimes suggested, it would "appear to consign a considerable portion of the American people to the marginal status" in the early decades of the twentieth century; "in America, most of us would be marginal men."[97] "In one sense," H. A. Wyndham noted in his review of Stonequist's *The Marginal Man*, "we are all marginal men in the shifting world of today."[98] Wirth made the same point in December 1947 in his presidential address to the annual meeting of the American Sociological Society: in "contemporary society," he noted, where there was greater mobility and more "contact between diverse racial and cultural groups" than in the past, "all of us are men on the move and on the make, and all of us by transcending the cultural bounds of our narrower society become to some extent marginal men."[99] Sociologist Arnold Green, who had written about the marginal man in the pages of the professional journal *Social Forces* in 1947, proclaimed a year later in *Commentary*, a magazine founded by the American Jewish Committee in 1945, that alienation was typical in America and not confined to Jews.[100] Reaching a similar conclusion after World War II, Everett Hughes treated the marginal man as merely a special case of the more general problem of role conflicts and status dilemmas.[101] David Golovensky reiterated this line of thought in the early 1950s, proclaiming that "the 'average' American, not merely the Jews and other minorities, must be considered marginal. An analysis will show that a substantial proportion, if not an actual majority, of Americans are either wholly or partially marginal."[102]

The historical context in which the marginal man concept was produced helps to explain why it could be so readily identified with America. Some of the sociologists who encouraged this identification (Wirth, Green, Golovensky) were Jewish, and in so doing, they likely sought to counter claims of a Christian America with a pluralistic vision of national identity in which Jews could be accepted as insiders.[103] But why were gentile commentators also inclined to see America in the marginal man? Comparable notions of a divided or fragmented self (of which Du Bois's double-consciousness was merely one example) had proliferated in American culture well before Park introduced the marginal man concept in 1928. Historians have traced these notions to a variety of sources: the isolation of American intellectuals who in the early twentieth century began to reject middle-class mores without thereby joining the social outcasts whose viewpoint they tried to adopt; urbanization, consumer culture, and the contradictory demands that bourgeois morality placed upon public and private selves; an intense conflict between tradition and innovation in American culture during the first two decades of the twentieth century; anxieties among the educated middle class about overcivilization, understood in gendered and racialized terms; Anglo-Americans' need to reconcile their ethnic supremacy with the liberal and democratic ideals they considered part of their ethnic heritage; and the confluent rise in the United States of modern psychology and mass immigration, which encouraged Americans to reconsider traditional assumptions about the unity of self and nation and to see them instead as similarly fragile and divisible.[104] While these accounts differ, they are not all mutually exclusive. They suggest that educated Americans would likely have seen Park's marginal man as a variation on a familiar theme, a theme moreover that spoke to their own concerns and anxieties. Last, it is significant that identification of the marginal man with America, while beginning in the 1930s, became more frequent after World War II. This frequency likely reflects changing American attitudes toward Jews as a result of the Shoah and its interpretation as well as broader support for cultural pluralism in the postwar era.[105]

Precariously Balanced

While Bourne's transnational America was a hopeful vision, the Chicago sociologists sometimes seemed to see in Jews and America a more foreboding image of modernity. As previously noted, some Jewish scholars were highly critical of the marginal man concept because of the pathological tendencies with which marginality was associated. Wirth, for instance, citing his own study of Jewish immigrant families in Chicago, linked culture conflict to delinquency.[106] Likewise, Park's onetime coauthor Herbert Miller described the inner conflicts of the marginal man as a "psychopathic problem" that could only be cured by "the slow passage of time."[107] Park's view of civilization became similarly pessimistic. The movement and migration of peoples, the expansion of trade and commerce, and the growth in modern times of metropolitan cities had indeed destroyed traditional local cultures and emancipated the modern individual from their grip, but Park struggled to find the wider horizons and keener intelligence that he had once associated with these processes; instead, he suggested, "modern civilization . . . lacked integration and drifted uncontrollably."[108] He lost his former confidence that increasingly complex networks of social and economic interdependence could provide sufficient unity, and in his view, America, like the Western world more generally, "remained precariously balanced between the forces of cohesion and dissolution."[109] He feared it would become a metropolitan civilization lacking a common culture among its increasingly diverse population, "an aggregate of people who use the same artifacts and have no solidarity at all."[110] As marginality seemed to result in personal disorganization for the Jew, urban civilization appeared to bring social disorganization to America.

Yet it would be a mistake to conclude that the Chicago school viewed personal and social disorganization as the inevitable result of cultural contact and collision. Although many of their contemporaries regarded culture conflict as undesirable, the Chicago sociologists saw conflict in pragmatist fashion as a potential impetus to creative action.[111] This was evident in both the life cycle of the marginal man and the race relations cycle said to be set in motion by the contact of different ethnic and racial groups.[112] Veblen, who was not part of the Chicago school of sociology but spent fourteen years at the University of Chicago from 1892 until 1906, suggested as early as 1919 that the intellectual preeminence of Jews in the modern world stemmed from the conflict of cultures that they experienced as a result of their dispersion and migration. In his view, culture conflict imbued Jews with a healthy skepticism toward Jewish and gentile conventions alike, which in turn was a primary requisite for creative contributions to intellectual life.[113] Park also envisioned the possibility that the marginal man might become a creative agent, particularly through his leadership of nationalist or racial mass movements.[114] Likewise, Wirth was careful to acknowledge that "not every case of culture conflict inevitably leads to delinquency. . . . Delinquency represents merely one way in which the conflict may be expressed if not resolved." Echoing Park, he added that a person experiencing such conflict, "far from becoming a criminal, may develop into a prophet, a reformer or a political leader."[115] Stonequist offered a similar prognosis. According to him, the marginal man typically experienced a three-stage life cycle: an initial phase in which he was unaware of cultural conflict; a crisis phase in which he consciously experienced the conflict; and a final phase that comprised the "adjustments, or lack of adjustments, which he makes or attempts to make to his situation."[116] As Stonequist made clear, the crisis phase could lead to a variety of outcomes in the third phase. At the most negative extreme, the marginal man's "mental conflict" could become a "disorganizing force" preventing his "psychological integration." Alternatively, the marginal man could strive to overcome his inner conflict by reconstructing the external ethnic relations which had produced it. "Those [marginal] individuals who have the potentialities to reconstruct their personalities and 'return' as creative agents not only adjust themselves but also contribute to the solution of the conflict of races and cultures. . . . Thus the practical efforts of the marginal person to solve his own problem lead him consciously or unconsciously to change the situation itself."[117]

Like the culture conflict experienced by the marginal man, the transitional period experienced by the migrant was also a crisis in the pragmatist sense: as an interruption of the normally smooth flow of habitual activity, it required a creative adjustment if it was to be resolved successfully. Thomas, Park, and Miller characterized it this way in 1921: "The new situation has the nature of a crisis, and in a crisis the individual tends either to reorganize his life positively, adopt new habits and standards to meet the new situation, or to repudiate the old habits and their restraint without reorganizing his life—which is demoralization."[118] The process of reorganization, as Thomas and Znaniecki had pointed out, did not "consist in a mere reinforcement of the decaying organization, but in a production of new schemes of behavior and new institutions better adapted to the changed demands of the group."[119] Borrowing a term from American pragmatism, they called this process social reconstruction. Reconstruction entailed rational and voluntary cooperation in lieu of coercion; active and intelligent solidarity rather than unthinking conformity; and instead of the suppression of individualistic attitudes, their redirection toward common and socially useful purposes. Therefore, Chicago school sociologists did not regard urban civilization as a permanent state of social disorganization, at least not necessarily. Disorganization was a transitional phenomenon that—if the crisis was successfully resolved—was "followed in the course of time by the reintegration of the individuals so released into a new social order."[120] As Dewey put it in 1922, the "elements of disintegration" could be turned into a "constructive synthesis."[121] Park and Burgess's famous race relations cycle—from competition and conflict to accommodation and eventually assimilation—was one way, though not the only one, in which Chicago sociologists described this process of creative adjustment.[122]

The Jews, whom Thomas and Znaniecki saw as disorganizers of others in the Old World, came to exemplify the potential for creative reorganization in the New World. Although Thomas never completed and published his intended study of the Jews in Europe and America, *Old World Traits Transplanted* provides some indication of the analysis he was developing in collaboration with Park and Miller.[123] Commissioned for the Carnegie Corporation's Americanization Studies project, the study identified the Italians, the Poles, and the Jews as the three largest groups of new immigrants in America; they were roughly equal in numbers, each comprising from 3 million to 3.3 million members at the time of the book's publication in 1921.[124] However, the authors suggested that the three groups epitomized different stages in the transition of immigrants to America's urban civilization. The Italians were identified with the stage of primary-group organization at the beginning of the transition: they retained its advantages "longer than many other nationalities," their "family and community life" was "affectionate and intimate," and its bonds were generally "strong enough to prevent that demoralization of the second generation which characterizes the Poles and, to some extent, the Jews."[125] The Poles were seen to exemplify more than the other two immigrant groups the transitional crisis phase of social disorganization: the Polish communities in America failed to "provide various types of organizations which would assist their members in adjusting themselves to the complex American life"; they neglected their demoralized members, instead abandoning them to American "charity organizations, legal aid societies, and juvenile courts"; but otherwise the Polish immigrant showed "little tendency to participate in American life and institutions."[126] Last, the authors suggested, the Jews exemplified the third phase of reconstruction: "the Jews, far more than any other immigrant group, are resorting to reflective social activity and supplementing the old social forms, spontaneously reproduced, with new, conscious organizations."[127]

Thomas, Park, and Miller pointed to the Jewish Kehillah of New York—an experimental attempt from 1909 to 1922 to provide the city's massive Jewish population with a unified and democratic community structure—as the prime example of this reflective social activity.[128] The Kehillah was formed in reaction to a public allegation made in 1908 (and subsequently retracted) by police commissioner Theodore Bingham that half of the city's criminals were Jews—an indicator of perceived social disorganization that troubled Jewish notables. For the first time, the Kehillah provided a permanent institutional basis for cooperation between the city's affluent, assimilated, uptown German Jews and its poor, eastern European, Yiddish-speaking downtown Jews. More concretely, it sought to organize philanthropic and religious affairs, improve Jewish education, mediate Jewish labor disputes, and reduce Jewish crime. Leaders of the Kehillah pursued these endeavors, especially in the field of education, under the influence of the same Deweyan pragmatism that informed Thomas, Park, and Miller's account of their enterprise.[129] Furthermore, the Jews were distinguished in this account not only by their progress in social reorganization, but also by the fact that it was largely their own accomplishment, in contrast, for example, to the Polish peasant, whose reorganization in Poland was mainly led from above and by outsiders, namely, the Polish "upper strata."[130] Probably with the Kehillah in mind, Park noted in 1925 that the "old structure of Jewish life" was "crumbling" in America, "but out of the ruins of the older cultural life a new, richer, freer, cultural life has sprung up."[131]

Alongside the New York Kehillah, Thomas and Park saw the city's Yiddish press as another promising sign of creative reorganization. Thomas was especially interested in the *Forverts*, the largest of New York's four major Yiddish dailies in terms of circulation, and its *Bintl Brief* ("pack of letters") section in which the editors provided information, advice, and help in response to readers' letters, which described typical problems that immigrants or their children experienced adjusting to the New World. As Thomas saw it, the *Bintl Brief* provided individuals with definitions of situations and mobilized public opinion to enforce them; in this way, the Yiddish press operated as a new instrument of social control.[132] Park also viewed public opinion, expressed through the press, as a new source of social control, particularly in urban settings where secondary relations supplanted primary relations.[133] By social control, Thomas and Park did not mean domination or coerced conformity but rather, the capacity of a group to regulate itself according to its desired principles and values. Social control in this sense was not a product of "ordering-and-forbidding," to use Thomas's expression, but instead required the conscious reflection and active participation of individuals in the community; it depended, as the pragmatist philosopher and social psychologist George Herbert Mead put it, on the ability of individuals to "assume attitudes of others who are involved with them in common endeavors."[134] In this instance, "the editor as an enforcer of desirable standards of family and community interaction operate[d] with the aid and consent of public opinion and participation."[135]

The Yiddish press was an instrument not only for the self-regulation of the community but also for its expansion. Park saw the public as the crucible that brought "individuals out of old ties and into new ones"; generated new traditions, customs, and institutions; and formed new groupings out of the members of already-established groups.[136] In his 1922 book *The Immigrant Press and Its Control*, he suggested that the Yiddish press, particularly in New York City, exemplified these processes: "No other press has . . . created so large a reading public . . . or reacted so powerfully upon the opinion, thought, and aspiration of the public for which it exists."[137] Park believed this to be true in two senses. On the one hand, the immigrant press fostered a "sense of racial and national solidarity" among its readers at the expense of narrower and more provincial forms of identification. "This explains why the Jewish people, although they use three distinct foreign languages—German, Yiddish, and Ladino—have attained in the United States a degree of solidarity and community organization more efficient than they have attained anywhere else since the Dispersion."[138] On the other hand, the American public was "beginning to take notice of the foreign-language papers" and to discuss and quote the opinions expressed therein. "If immigrant editors and readers know that their paper is read outside its own language-group; that America is interested in what it says and takes account of its opinions—that very fact establishes a measure of control."[139] By this, Park did not mean Anglo-American control over immigrants. Rather, he envisioned immigrants and native-born Americans becoming members of the same wider public through which they could communicate and collaborate for the purpose of regulating their common affairs.

By creatively reorganizing their own social life, the Jews pointed the way for others. *Old World Traits Transplanted* noted with approval the wish expressed by an Italian newspaper editor in 1907 that "the Italians would organize as do the Jews."[140] However, Thomas, Park, and Miller did not merely see Jews as a model minority for other immigrants. More importantly, they saw Jewish reorganization as a model for the social reconstruction of America itself. They acknowledged that Jews, like other immigrant groups, had experienced disorder, demoralization, and strife as a result of the swift deterioration in America of Old World traditions. But, they concluded,

> in our examination of the Jewish type of organization we gain an impression that the experiments of this community upon its own problems contain an interest not limited to the Jewish community, but extending to American society as a whole. Our interest in the organization of other immigrant communities is limited to the possible discovery of devices which may assist these groups until they are able to enjoy the benefits of American institutions. In the case of the Jewish group, we find spontaneous, intelligent, and highly organized experiments in democratic control which may assume the character of permanent contributions to the organization of the American state.[141]

According to Thomas, Park, and Miller, the Italian newspaper editor who admired how the Jews organized themselves (and by extension nativists like Ross who feared Jewish organization) erred in thinking that Jews did so "at the expense of Americans."[142] Jewish reorganization was not an assertion of separatism or ethnic chauvinism. On the contrary, immigrant institutions represented "an effort to participate in American life."[143] In this respect, too, Jewish experiences in Europe and America were a study in contrasts. On the one hand, as Thomas and Znaniecki had recognized, Jews were largely excluded from the wider national community being organized in newly independent Poland.[144] On the other hand, to the extent that the reorganization of immigrants promoted their participation in American life, it could be equated with assimilation. But what did assimilation mean in this context?

A careful reading of *Old World Traits* suggests that its authors did not primarily conceive assimilation as a means of preserving an existing Anglo-Saxon culture or promoting conformity to it, but rather as a means for organizing a democratic public, a pressing need that Dewey would later explore more fully in his 1927 book *The Public and Its Problems.* Indeed, this task is what linked the New York Kehillah and the Yiddish press: the former through its annual conventions was intended to create Jewish public opinion, while the latter was supposed to express it. Thomas, Park, and Miller began with the assumption that some social transactions had consequences for individuals not directly engaged in them; the public, comprised of all those who were so affected, organized itself to understand and deal with those consequences that were important enough to need social control. They (and later Dewey) argued that the vast expansion of interdependence in modern societies multiplied and magnified such consequences, making the organization of a new and expanded public urgently necessary. The "locomotive, the post, the telegraph, the press . . . dissolved distances," they wrote, so that the conditions of individuals' daily living were "vitally affected by events occurring without their knowledge, thousands of miles away," thus depriving them of control over the system of relationships in which they found themselves.[145] Immigration was one aspect of the larger problem of organizing a democratic public under these new conditions. No public was possible without the capacity for mutual understanding, and mutual understanding in turn required "a body of common memories." "This is particularly true in a democracy," they wrote, "where it is intended that the public institution should be responsive to public opinion. There can be no public opinion unless the persons who compose the public are able to live and think in the same world." To this end, immigrants had to learn "the language of the country" and "the history of the people among whom they have chosen to dwell," just as native-born Americans had to familiarize themselves with "the history and social life of the countries from which the immigrants come."[146] Because the purpose of this assimilation was to make the immigrant a member of the public, and a democratic public requires active participation in collective problem solving through the medium of communication, assimilation could hardly be a passive experience. On the contrary, Thomas, Park, and Miller expected the immigrant to *contribute* to as well as share "a fund of knowledge, experience, sentiments, and ideals common to the whole community."[147] A year later, Park reaffirmed this expectation when he insisted that "it is participation rather than submission or conformity that makes Americans of foreign-born peoples."[148]

Perhaps nothing better illustrated the process of contributing as well as sharing than the Jewish experiment in communal reorganization. "From our standpoint," Thomas, Park, and Miller wrote, "the Jewish community is serving the Jew by enabling him to identify his interests with America."[149] At the same time, by hailing the New York Kehillah as a promising experiment in democratic reconstruction that America might replicate on a grand scale, they implicitly identified America's interests with the Jews.[150] If New York City's vast, diverse, and frequently divided Jewish population could succeed in forging a more expansive and encompassing form of community for itself along democratic and pluralistic lines, then America could hope to do so as well. Thus, as Jews were assimilating to America, America was urged to become, in a sense, more like the Jews. Returning to this theme in 1925, Park called on Americans to transform the world rather than seek uncreatively to escape from it; he suggested that immigrant communities might serve as a model for this endeavor; and he praised Jews as "the most able and the most progressive" immigrants in the United States.[151] In the 1940s, Park again linked Jews, democracy, and America with a renewed sense of urgency. With Nazi persecution surely in mind, Park suggested that "the problem of the Jew" was "identical with the problem of Democracy"; and the problem of democracy was, in turn, "an American problem because, if there is any place on the planet where people of different races and religions are destined to live and work together in peace and understanding, it is here."[152] More than ever, America needed the sort of creative reorganization that Thomas, Park, and Miller thought they had glimpsed among the Jews of New York.

Conclusion

This chapter has examined how two major figures and their students in the Chicago school of sociology portrayed the Jews, and how this portrayal related to broader debates in their historical context about urbanization, immigration, and national identity. Following an overview of the main dualisms that structured the Chicago school's understanding of social life, the modern

Jew was shown to be the model for and classic example of Park's marginal man between two worlds, Old and New, traditional and modern. The affinities that linked the Jews, the city, and America in the work of Thomas, Park, Wirth, and Stonequist were also described. For these social thinkers, the modern Jew was a microcosm of the modern metropolis, that vast melting pot of races and cultures that urbanization and migration had produced in America. Like the mobile and increasingly urban nation in which he had arrived, the Jewish immigrant was himself a site in which different cultures came into contact and collision. He thus mirrored the ambiguous forces, simultaneously sinister and promising, that were transforming America itself, and he reflected the indeterminate and open-ended nature of the modern civilization taking shape there. Like his adopted homeland, he, too, was precariously balanced between the forces of disintegration and integration. As portrayed in the Chicago school of sociology, the Jews were the specter of dissolution haunting America and at the same time "pioneers and creative agents in that new social order which seems to evolve as narrower group loyalties gradually give way to larger human values."[153]

How do these findings advance previous scholarship on the Chicago school of sociology? Andrew Abbott has usefully divided the historiography of the Chicago school into three main periods: an early period in the 1960s and 1970s that established the Chicago school as an object of historical inquiry; a second period beginning in the late 1970s that brought greater clarity and comprehensiveness to the study of the Chicago school; and a third period, beginning in the late 1980s, in which revisionist scholarship produced more complex accounts of the Chicago school.[154] This chapter builds on the work of all three periods, but it is especially indebted to the last of them, not least for challenging the long-standing but fundamentally mistaken view that the Chicago school was antitheoretical. Like earlier revisionist studies, it aims at "reinserting the Chicago school into the flows of larger histories."[155] While others have generated new insights into the Chicago school by reembedding it within America's social survey and social reform tradition, the tradition of American liberalism, and the tradition of turn-of-the-century newspaper reporting, this chapter situates the Chicago school in relation to a different but no less important aspect of its historical milieu: the Jewish question.[156] This dimension of its historical context has been largely neglected by previous studies, perhaps because the place of the Jews in modern society was assumed to be a uniquely European question that did not arise in America. In fact, antisemitism and nativism were potent forces that raised this question openly and stridently within the Chicago school's milieu, and Jews experienced significant exclusion from civil and noncivil life in America until

World War II.[157] When the Chicago school is reinserted into this context, the interest that its members took in the Jews becomes understandable.

What the Chicago sociologists saw in the Jews becomes more clearly visible when a comparative perspective is adopted. In contrast to the emphasis placed by many European social thinkers on the categories of democracy and capitalism, the sociologists of the Chicago school relied heavily on the metaphors of urbanism and mobility to interpret modernity. Notwithstanding these different root metaphors, Jews played a similar symbolic role on both sides of the Atlantic as a touchstone for defining modernity and national identity. This similarity reflected in part the influence of European and especially German social thought on the Chicago school, but it would be a mistake to conclude that the Chicago school was merely an importer of European ideas. European social thought was creatively reoriented and transformed through its combination with American pragmatism and its transposition to the American context.[158] The Chicago sociologists drew upon Sombart's work, for instance, but in the process they gave his depiction of the Jews as nomads and disorganizers a potentially positive interpretation at odds with his animus, for in their view, it was only out of such activity that a new, freer, more rational, and wider community could arise. What appeared in Sombart's work as an alienating and destructive force was recast by the Chicago school as emancipating and potentially constructive.

While offering a historical interpretation of the Chicago school, this chapter also highlights its ongoing relevance today. As immigration and cultural diversity have again become important topics of social inquiry in both Europe and America, the concept of assimilation has received renewed scholarly attention.[159] What this chapter contributes to that discussion is a novel attempt to reinterpret assimilation in relation to pragmatist concerns about forming a democratic public under modern social conditions. As contemporary sociologist Craig Calhoun has argued, the public is a different mode of social belonging than interpersonal relationships or large-scale categories of personal identity.[160] Historians and social scientists must distinguish the public from these other modes of belonging in order to avoid misunderstandings about what assimilation meant for the Chicago sociologists and what it could mean for us today. Furthermore, the creation of a democratic public was itself one aspect of what Thomas called social reorganization or reconstruction. From this perspective, the debate about whether the Chicago school envisioned the persistence or disappearance of ethnic minorities is misformulated.[161] As the examples of New York's Kehillah and Yiddish press suggest, Thomas and Park identified a third alternative: rather than perpetuating the ethnic community as it existed in the past or dissolving it altogether, one could in collaboration with others reconstruct it in a new form. At the same time, through the incorporation of such communities into a wider public, it was possible to transform culture conflict, not yet mediated by what Dewey called "socialized intelligence," into cooperative problem solving. This hopeful vision, no doubt reassuring to Americans in the early decades of the last century, may yet be of value today.

5

Conclusions

This study has examined in depth several of the most prominent and influential social thinkers in France, Germany, and the United States from the late nineteenth to early twentieth centuries. Each chapter has addressed a different though related set of questions: What is the relationship between Durkheim's sociology and French antisemitism, and how did that relationship shape his account of the meaning and significance of the French Revolution? What explains the patterns in how Marx, Simmel, Sombart, and Weber described the relationship between Jews and modern capitalism? What did Jews signify to Thomas, Park, Wirth, and Stonequist, and how did their view of Jewish immigrants inform their thinking about the prospects for social reconstruction and the formation of a democratic public in modern America? Each chapter can be read on its own, as a freestanding study independent of the others. However, when the chapters are read together and the ideas of these authors are compared, it is striking that regardless of which aspect of modernity they emphasized—democratization, capitalist development, or urbanization—they turned repeatedly to the Jews as a touchstone for interpreting the new social order. They found in the Jews a reflection of French, German, or American society, as they conceived it to have existed in the past or as they imagined it might exist in the future. The Jews served as an intermediary through whom these intellectuals discerned in a roundabout fashion the nature, problems, and trajectory of their own wider societies.

If this commonality among French, German, and American social thinkers is striking, the contrasts are no less so. Let us return to the four possible perspectives presented in the introduction on the relationship between the Jews and modernity. On the one hand, this relationship may be formulated so that Jews appear as forerunners of a positive and desirable modernity (A+

TABLE 5.1

	Advanced (A)	*Backward (B)*
Positive (+)	Thomas and Park: Jews as exemplars of cosmopolitan civilization and creative social reorganization	
Negative (–)	Simmel: Jews as agents and symbols of modern money economy	Durkheim: Jews as traditionalistic exemplars of mechanical solidarity
	Early Marx: Jews as agents and symbols of modern money economy	Weber: Jews as pariah capitalists
	Sombart: Jews as creators of modern capitalism	Mature Marx: Jews as merchants and usurers in the pores of precapitalist production

in table 5.1), or in an equally positive manner, so that they appear to preserve archaic or traditional virtues that other groups or societies have regrettably lost or forgotten (B+). On the other hand, it is equally possible to construct a negative image of Jews as a threatening avant-garde in which the unwelcome future of a judaized Europe or America can be seen (A–), or as a culturally and socially backward people stuck at an earlier stage of development that Europeans or Americans left behind with the achievement of their own hard-won and cherished modernity (B–).[1] While Simmel and Durkheim disagreed about whether Jews epitomized a modern or traditionalistic orientation, both thinkers straddled the line between positive and negative interpretations: Simmel because of his ambivalent view of the modern money economy, Durkheim because his characterization of Judaism was similarly ambivalent.[2] Still, both authors were critical to some degree of what the Jews signified to them. The early Marx and Sombart, for whom the Jews were the agents and symbols of an alienating commercial or capitalist spirit, unmistakably belong to type A–. The mature Marx and Weber just as clearly belong to type B– because the Jews represent for them premodern forms of economic activity that, though not entirely vanishing in modern society, are hardly models to be admired or revived. Only the American authors Thomas and Park offer a positive interpretation of both Jews and modernity (A+): whatever their doubts and fears about the social consequences of immigration and urbanization, they admired New York's Jewish Kehillah as a vanguard model for the reconstruction of social life along more expansive, democratic, and pluralistic lines.[3] The only type to which none of our social thinkers belongs is B+, most likely because they rejected the romantic antimodernism that it entailed. Although critical of the modern money economy, Marx had no sympathy for the "medieval rubbish" swept away by the "gigantic broom of the French Revolution."[4] He thought the route to emancipation lay forward and not backward. Sombart is a possible exception to this general rejection of antimodernism, but for him, the Jewish spirit dissolved rather than preserved what Marx called the "feudal, patriarchal, idyllic relations" of the past.[5]

These findings raise a series of related questions that the remainder of this chapter will seek to address. First, what does this study contribute to ongoing discussions among contemporary sociologists, historians, and philosophers about the relationship between Jews and modernity? Second, what does this study add to our understanding of classical sociology, its historical origins, and its relationship to the social contexts in which it was produced? What new light does it shed in particular on the diffusion of enduring habits of thought across space and their reproduction over time? Third, what accounts for the apparently widespread and recurrent interest of classical sociologists in Jews? More precisely, why did Jews serve in France, Germany, and the United States as a major reference point for constructing the meaning of European or American modernity? Furthermore, what accounts for the welter of contradictory meanings that Jews came to signify? As we have seen, social thinkers tilted every which way in their portrayal and characterization of the Jews. Personifying premodern traditionalism for some authors, Jews epitomized modernity for others. They appeared to many intellectuals as a grave threat but inspired hope in others. What is the underlying logic—the secret (*Geheimnis*), as Marx might say—that could explain this semblance of incoherent meaning? Fourth, how does the depiction and interpretation of Jews in classical sociology compare and contrast to the treatment of other groups, nations, or social categories? How do Jews differ from other others in the sociological tradition, and how do these findings intersect with studies of Orientalism, Occidentalism, and anti-Americanism? Fifth and last, do Jews continue to serve as touchstone for debates about the meaning of late modernity in Europe and America today, or have other minority groups—most notably, Muslims—now assumed this symbolic role in contemporary discussions?

Contemporary Perspectives on Jews and Modernity

This study has underscored the multiple and apparently inconsistent meanings—traditional and modern, negative and positive—that Jews came to signify in classical sociology. Since the close of what historian Eric Hobsbawm called the short twentieth century, several important studies have similarly emphasized the ambiguous image of the Jew and the way that Jews have straddled, confounded, or evaded the prevailing divisions of the social world.[6]

Much of this scholarship is implicitly or explicitly indebted to German social thought, particularly Simmel's characterization of European Jews as the classical example of the stranger and Marx's contention that Jews lived in the "interstices" and "pores" of society.[7] For instance, sociologist Zygmunt Bauman contends that "the Jews have been the prototypical strangers in Europe split in nation-states set on annihilation of everything 'intermediate,' underdetermined, neither friendly nor inimical."[8] The history of European Jews thus exemplifies the problems, costs, and ultimate failure of the modernist project of imposing social and symbolic order; they embodied the ambivalence generated as a by-product of that project, while their cultural and intellectual responses anticipated the postmodernity that Bauman favors. Likewise, sociologist Werner Cahnman has emphasized the persistent position of Jews as intermediaries and the ambivalence it elicits from others: "Wherever we may look in the wide panorama of Jewish history . . . the Jew as the role of the mediator who transmits spiritual and material goods is assumed. . . . The intermediacy between East and West, ruler and ruled, nobleman and commoner, producer and consumer, artist and the public (to mention just a few of the roles of which the entire complex role is composed) has been a cause of irritation and antagonism in many places but it also shows the appreciation with which Jews have been met at all times."[9] Historian Yuri Slezkine has described Jews in similar terms as Mercurians, by which he means perennial "border crossers," "go-betweens," and service nomads who undertook tasks that Apollonian "natives were unable or unwilling to perform." Modernization, he argues, meant that everyone, "first in Europe and then elsewhere, had to become more like the Jews: urban, mobile, literate, mentally nimble, occupationally flexible, and surrounded by aliens."[10] According to Slezkine, Jews excelled at the entrepreneurial and professional pursuits that "made up the foundations of modern states"—here he echoes Sombart's assertion that "arm in arm the Jew and the ruler stride through the age which historians call modern"—but the nationalist garb that modern states adopted to ease the transition to modernity excluded Jews.[11] These accounts have several features in common: an insistence that Jews, by virtue of the positions they occupied, have not fit easily into a Procrustean social order, especially when that order was reimagined along national lines, and often a suggestion that the Jewish predicament has broader significance, illuminating the difficulties and contradictions of the modern condition itself.

A related set of contemporary studies is indebted more to Park's notion of the marginal man, with its emphasis on inner conflict, than to Simmel or Marx.[12] These studies characterize Jews as internalizing rather than mediating the divisions of the social world. For instance, historian Paul Mendes-Flohr explored how the modern Jewish intellectual has negotiated the tensions between his or her "primordial identity as a Jew" and more universalistic commitments.[13] Sociologist Pierre Birnbaum examined the same tension, reformulated in terms of the relationships that modern Jewish social thinkers have had with the Enlightenment. "A long history is probably coming to an end," he wrote: "that of the encounter between the Jews and the Enlightenment, conceived strictly on the universalist mode and anchored in a demanding vision of regenerative assimilation. Another history . . . is appearing with difficulty, one however which is also inspired by the Enlightenment . . . without, however, justifying the eradication of cultures or, especially, the end of Jewishness."[14] Split identity is also a key theme of philosopher Yirmiyahu Yovel's work on the so-called Marranos, the Jews in Spain and Portugal who converted to Christianity at the end of the fifteenth century to escape death or expulsion but who continued to practice Judaism in secret. For Yovel, the Marrano was a figure caught between two religions, a person with a nonintegral identity who transcended any single culture.[15] These studies trace the division of the Jewish self to a variety of historical turning points, from the Inquisition and the Enlightenment to the social movements of the nineteenth and twentieth centuries, all of which pulled Jews out of the concentric social circles of the medieval ghetto and into the intersecting circles that characterize modern life. Although Mendes-Flohr and Birnbaum evinced little interest in whether the inner tensions of the modern Jew have broader significance, Yovel has argued that the Marrano experience anticipated or prefigured major aspects of Western modernity.

How does this study of past representations of Jews in classical sociology relate to contemporary perspectives on Jews and modernity? First, it shows that contemporary perspectives have a historical lineage in classical and especially German social thought. Given the momentous upheavals of the twentieth century, including the genocidal destruction of European Jewry, the extraordinary reestablishment after two millennia of a national home for the Jewish people in Palestine, the dispersion of Jews from the former Soviet Union, and the consequent shift in the Jewish world's center of gravity from Europe to America and Israel, the continuities between classical and contemporary thinking about Jews and modernity are surprising. These continuities raise the question of how habits of thought endure beyond the social conditions that produced them. I address this question in the next section of this concluding chapter, "Classical Sociology within and across National Contexts."

Second, this study has mainly confined itself to cultural representations rather than the social reality and lived experience of Jews; it has not made claims about Jews but instead about how classical sociologists imagined, interpreted, and depicted Jews. If representations of Jews are ambiguous—if social thinkers have represented Jews in equivocal and inconsistent ways—does the intermediary social position of Jews as strangers, Mercurians, and marginal men explain this ambiguity? Much of the contemporary scholarship on Jews and modernity suggests an affirmative answer.[16] However, it is worth reversing the question and asking instead whether cultural representation helps to constitute the social position. In an essay rethinking Simmel's concept of the stranger, sociologist Jeffrey C. Alexander challenges the assumption that a "social structural status" creates the stranger and "determines the orientation adopted by members of the host society" toward him. While "material circumstances are very much involved" in the social production of strangeness, "it is not structural position per se," but rather its cultural interpretation that "leads the occupants of this status to assume a strangeness in the core group's eyes." Strangeness, in other words, is "also and always produced in culturally mediated ways." Indeed, once individuals come to be seen as strangers, "their social position is often altered to be more congruent with their cultural status." Therefore, Alexander argues, "to understand strangeness we must focus on the cultural interpretation of social structures." This interpretive work, he adds, makes use of enduring "symbolic structures that draw from a centuries old discourse."[17] The approach I have taken in this study is similar to Alexander's. As I have already suggested in chapter 3, it is not only structural forces and material relations but also cultural interpretation that creates the stranger, the Mercurian, and the marginal man. I elaborate on this approach below in the section entitled "Why the Jews Are Good to Think." There, I suggest that modern intellectuals have linked Jews and modernity on the basis of categories and symbolic structures that predate the "Jewish Century," modern nationalism, the Enlightenment, or even the Inquisition.

Third, this study revisits a question raised in contemporary discussions of Jews and modernity: Does the Jewish experience of modernity have broader, perhaps even universal, significance? Many of the studies noted above suggest that the Jewish experience or situation is indeed paradigmatic in one way or another; it seems we are all becoming Mercurians with nonintegral identities. In this respect, too, contemporary scholarship follows the lead of classical social thinkers like Marx (in his early years), Simmel, Sombart, and Park, to whom the Jews signified more general processes of modernization. But of course the Jews have not been the only signpost for social thinkers struggling to grasp the modern condition. As we have seen in previous chapters, classical sociologists also used other groups, nations, or social categories to take their sociological bearings: Protestants (or Puritans), women, colonial subjects, other European immigrant groups, African Americans, rival countries or continents, and so on. Are these groups interchangeable with Jews, each a variant of the other, all serving in similar ways to distinguish the traditional from the modern? Or did classical sociologists engage in a more complex process of triangulation, determining their social coordinates in relation to multiple and different reference points? Only a comparative approach can answer this question. I return to this issue below in the section entitled "Jews and Other Others." There, I argue that despite some overlap in the meanings and symbolism conferred upon Jews and other groups, Jews were represented in distinctive ways within the sociological tradition, and these differences were rooted in the peculiarities of the historical relationship between Jews and Christians.

Classical Sociology within and across National Contexts

One aim of this study has been to situate classical sociology more fully in the historical and social contexts in which it was produced. More precisely, it has aimed to illuminate an aspect of these contexts that has not been adequately explored, namely, conversations and arguments about the Jews and Judaism, and thereby to expand our knowledge of the ideas, practices, and social relations that shaped the sociological enterprise. This perspective reminds us that what classical sociologists wrote about Jews was not simply a set of hypotheses about the social world; it was also a set of moves or position takings within the social world that reflected practical goals. Their claims about Jews were interventions in the public sphere, where a range of competing claims about and representations of Jews, some of them produced by antisemitic and nativist movements, also circulated. In addition, this perspective yields new insights into the historical origins of sociology. While the conventional account, exemplified by Nisbet's thesis of the two revolutions, describes sociology as a response to the internal transformation of European societies, revisionists suggest that it emerged instead from colonial encounters with non-European others.[18] As I noted in chapter 1, both the conventional and the revisionist accounts have blind spots. The conventional account neglects how popular discourse linked Jews to the French and Industrial Revolutions. The revisionist account neglects the role of the Jewish other in the origins of sociology or else treats representations of Jews as simply another instance of Orientalism. I elaborate below on the limitations of both accounts and how this study advances beyond them. This study has also revealed how ideas about Jews and Judaism informed the French, German, and American sociological traditions in more specific ways. Chapter 2 showed that some of Durkheim's most important sociological ideas were partly developed in response to public expressions of antisemitism in Third Republic France. He used Jews as a reference point for defining the kind of solidarity appropriate to the modern and democratic order inaugurated by the French Revolution. Chapter 3 showed that classical sociologists in Germany used Jews as a reference point for defining modern capitalism and distinguishing it from traditional economic arrangements. Their thinking was shaped not only by the socioeconomic position of Jews but also by cultural schemas about Jews inherited from the past. Chapter 4 showed how American social thinkers used Jews as a reference point for identifying the perils and possibilities that arose from urbanization and immigration. By examining the sociological classics as practical interventions, rethinking the origins of sociology, and showing how ideas about Jews and Judaism informed national sociological traditions, this study deepens our understanding of classical sociology.

While employing historicist means to understand the sociological classics, this study has sought at the same time to transcend the limitations of an overly rigid historicist approach. Historicism seeks to understand past social thinkers in their own terms rather than ours. The point of such historical contextualization is not to address contemporary questions and concerns but to foster awareness of "forms of intellectual life *different* from our own."[19] This perspective generates useful insights, but there is a danger in exaggerating the extent to which the past is a foreign country. The past continues to inform the present, even and perhaps especially when it is forgotten and its effects are therefore unconscious. This is true of social science no less than other social phenomena that the social sciences seek to understand. As Bourdieu put it, the forgotten history of social science constitutes the hidden or unconscious social conditions of its production in the present. Following Bourdieu, I have therefore emphasized the need for a *reflexive* history, especially the historicization of inherited categories of thought, the aim of which is historical anamnesis.[20] From this perspective, the point of historical inquiry is not to discover forms of life different from our own, as in historicism, but to recover what has been forgotten in order to emancipate ourselves from it.

Reflexive history differs from strict historicism in another way as well: it draws from the history of social science the means as well as the material for critical historical analysis. This is evident, for example, in Bourdieu's frequent invocation of Durkheim in discussions of reflexive history, not only as a historical figure whose ideas need to be explained but also as a source of insight whose contributions remain useful for a contemporary sociology of social science. The implication is that Durkheim and other classical sociologists, though undeniably products of their times, produced ideas that were not limited in their application and relevance to the specific historical context in which they wrote. On the contrary, insofar as they discerned fundamental and enduring features of social life, their ideas remain highly relevant for understanding the present. This study rests on the same assumption. Accordingly, in the next section of this chapter, I apply insights drawn from Durkheim and other past social thinkers to the history of European and American social thought, treating their ideas as tools for as well as objects of sociological analysis.

Last, reflexive history expands the explanatory scope of historicism. Historicism rests on the assumption that ideas are explained by the specific social and historical context in which they are produced. This emphasis on context is indispensable for understanding how and why ideas about modernity and the Jews have varied. However, it provides little insight into the reproduction of enduring habits of thought across multiple social and historical contexts. Previous scholarship has pointed out such long-term continuities in European thinking about Jews. Muller, for instance, has traced the enduring association in the Christian West of Jews with usury, "one of the most long-lived paradigms for the condemnation of market activity."[21] Similarly, Nirenberg described anti-Judaism as a set of long-standing and widely diffused "habits of thought, put to work in changing historical circumstances."[22] My own study, though more limited in scope and cognizant of important differences, has also revealed continuities in the depiction of Jews across contexts. The early Marx, writing in Germany in the 1840s, and Thomas and Park, writing in the United States in the 1920s, portrayed Jews as an advance guard of modernity. Conversely, Durkheim in Third Republic France, the mature Marx in Victorian England, and Weber in Wilhelmine Germany all represented Jews as exemplifying a premodern stage of social or economic development. These continuities present a puzzle for the historicist approach: if some habits of thought recur across different social and historical contexts, then the specificities of each context do not suffice to explain them. The key to understanding such continuities lies in the recognition that "habits (in the sense of habitus) can readily survive the social conditions that produced them."[23]

How are categories and habits of thought produced in one set of social conditions reproduced under new social conditions? A full examination of this question is beyond the scope of this study, but a three-part answer seems plausible. First, even though national traditions of social thought remained distinctive in recognizable ways, ideas about Jews produced in one context circulated through transnational networks similar to those that underlay the international diffusion of social politics in the same time period. These networks included study abroad (Durkheim and Park, for instance, studied in Germany), international conferences (Weber and Sombart traveled to the United States to attend the St. Louis Congress of Arts and Science), academic journals, institutionally sponsored commissions and investigations, and the entanglement of German and American sociology with social Protestantism.[24] To be sure, classical sociologists modified or amended ideas they borrowed from other contexts, and they based their claims about Jews in part on empirical observation of their own settings, but the intellectual carriers of national traditions were not isolated from each other, and shared preconceptions about the Jews shaped their selection and interpretation of facts. Just as intellectuals at the national level may take opposing positions while tacitly adhering to the same presuppositions, so too in a global intellectual field it is possible for adherents of opposing national traditions to take for granted some of the same assumptions and conceptual categories.

Second, Nirenberg's term *habits of thought* provides another clue for understanding the reproduction of ideas across social and historical contexts. Habits persist to the extent that they remain useful, which is to say, until they are blocked by new conditions that require creative and reflective adjustment.[25] Habits of thought that are adapted to the original social conditions in which they were produced are also adapted to comparable conditions.[26] If French, German, and American intellectuals adopted similar habits of thought, it is not only because a common set of ideas was broadly diffused and therefore readily at hand. They reached for similar tools because, in spite of the many ways their milieus varied, they experienced analogous problems. As noted in chapter 1, the chief task that sociology set for itself was to interpret and explain the modern world that arose from the upheavals of the long nineteenth century from 1789 to 1914.[27] This task was comparable across national contexts because the same processes revolutionizing the world were also knitting it more closely together. The French Revolution had "overrun the whole world with its apostles, militants, and martyrs," seeking "nothing short of a regeneration of the whole human race."[28] Capitalist development, Marx observed, created a world market, battering down all Chinese walls. "*De te fabula narratur!*" he proclaimed to readers outside of England who were indifferent to conditions there.[29] Similarly, "if America was once in any exclusive sense the melting pot of races," Park acknowledged, "it is no longer. The melting pot is the world."[30] Although the emergence of mass democracy, industrial capitalism, and urbanization varied in timing, sequence, and form across France, Germany, and the United States, social thinkers were similarly compelled in each country to ponder the implications of these changes for national identity and well-being. In each case, the Jews provided a familiar and expedient fulcrum for reflection on the problems that modernity posed and the possible solutions.

The reproduction of habits of thought across varied social and historical contexts may be the result of a third process as well. The value of habits can lie not only in their usefulness for a task at hand but also in the legitimacy they confer. Organizations within the same institutional environment tend to adopt similar practices and procedures, regardless of their efficiency in order to gain validity, resources, and improved survival prospects.[31] This insight can be applied as well to the producers of classical sociology insofar as they aspired to legitimize, professionalize, and institutionalize the new discipline; they were aware of and oriented to each other's work across national boundaries; and they sought to emulate what they perceived to be relatively successful models elsewhere. Classical sociologists did not necessarily regard specific ideas about Jews per se as a source of scientific and professional legitimacy. Rather, it is more likely that partly preconscious assumptions, schemas, and scripts about Jews and Judaism were embedded within the concepts, categories of thought, and principles of classification they did see as legitimizing. I have already suggested in chapter 3 that this kind of process was at work within the German intellectual field, where cultural schemas derived from Christian theology became legitimized by the endorsement of authoritative thinkers. Given the international prestige of German *Wissenschaft* in the late nineteenth and early twentieth centuries, the academic pilgrimages that non-German scholars like Durkheim and Park made to German universities, and the translation or review of German sociology in the *Année sociologique* and the *American Journal of Sociology*, it is plausible that similar pressures for isomorphism may have operated more widely. Thus, in addition to providing a touchstone for defining what it meant to be modern, ideas about Jews may also have functioned across national contexts as myth and ceremony.[32] However, while the actual operation of organizations is often decoupled from the formal structure that legitimizes them, it is not clear that sociological research was similarly decoupled from the categories, concepts, and habits of thought that legitimized it. On the contrary, as I have repeatedly stressed, these legitimizing concepts also organized sociologists' perception, selection, and interpretation of empirical evidence.

Why the Jews Are Good to Think

Sociology's use of the sacred as a perspective for understanding presumably nonreligious phenomena distinguished it from other social sciences in the nineteenth century.[33] Most notably, Durkheim came to see religion as a model of how secular symbolic processes work.[34] Following suit, I would like to make explicit a suggestion already implied in previous chapters: namely, that the symbolic function of Jews and Judaism in social thought can be understood by way of an analogy to totemism. As Durkheim pointed out, animals or plants served in totemic systems as emblems that created and clarified a society's awareness of itself.[35] Just as nineteenth-century social thinkers asked why specific animals or plants were chosen over others to serve as totemic emblems, so we may ask why Jews were chosen to serve a comparable symbolic function within social thought. In the same way that early accounts of totemism tried to answer the former question by reference to the properties of the chosen animals or plants (e.g., their usefulness to the group), it is also possible to explain what Jews came to symbolize in social thought by virtue of their actual characteristics (e.g., the benefits they accrued from the French Revolution, their highly visible concentration in commerce and finance, or their high rates of urbanization). This kind of explanation may be termed substantialist in the sense that it privileges substances over relations. No such explanation will be attempted here. Instead, following the anthropologist Claude Lévi-Strauss, I suggest that a relational approach is more fruitful.[36]

Lévi-Strauss argued that the choice of animals in a totemic system was neither arbitrary nor based on a "natural stimulus" (fear, admiration, or envy). Rather, it was how animals contrasted to each other that made them meaningful to indigenous groups. These relationships among animals formed a kind of code for signifying kinship relations, but the code rested on resemblances between different relationships, not one-to-one correspondences between the things in those relationships. As Lévi-Strauss put it, it is not that an animal and a kinship group resemble each other; rather, there are "animals which differ from each other," and there are human beings "who also differ from each other," and "the resemblance presupposed by so-called totemic representations is *between these two systems of difference.*" Thus, there is no reason to expect a direct relation between a bear totem and a bear clan; the clansmen need not be ursine or dependent upon bears. But when the bear totem is contrasted to the eagle totem of another clan, the relationship between animals might resemble the kinship relation: bear is to eagle as bear clan is to eagle clan. "Natural species are chosen" to be totemic emblems, Lévi-Strauss famously concluded, "not because they are 'good to eat' but because they are 'good to think.'"[37]

James Pasto has argued that "Judaism . . . was good to think" for German Bible scholars and political writers who "used the Jewish past as a metaphor upon which to build their universal history and identity."[38] Also invoking Lévi-Strauss, historian Ronald Schechter claimed that "the Jews were 'good to think'" for French writers and political actors, which is to say, they were "means of thinking about the prevalent ideas of the age."[39] However, neither Pasto nor Schechter fully developed this analogy to totemism. Here, I seek to extend their insights by elaborating on the relational logic that made Jews good to think. When Jews and Christians distinguished themselves from each other in the first centuries of the Common Era, they produced two opposed but related categories. Likewise, when European thinkers began to distinguish their own era as qualitatively different from the past, they produced two opposing terms, the premodern and the modern, while also positing the relationship that united them, namely, a developmental process from one to the other. As a people whose existence spans both premodernity and modernity, Jews do not necessarily resemble either of these terms. The sociologist looks in vain for such resemblances because for every resemblance discovered, one can find a counterexample from historical and social research. Instead, following the approach set out by Lévi-Strauss, I suggest that the *relationship* between Jews and Christians formed a code for signifying the *relationship* between premodernity and modernity. This suggestion will become clearer by examining each of these relationships in turn.

To understand the historical relationship between Jews and Christians, one must consider its theological point of departure, the sacred status conferred upon Jews within that relationship, and the ambivalence that characterized the relationship. Because the differentiation of religion from other aspects of social life is a relatively recent development, it would be anachronistic to describe the relationship between Jews and Christians in exclusively theological terms, but its social, economic, political, and other aspects were inseparable from theology. In Europe, Christian theology molded the initial socioeconomic and political aspects of the relationship in its image, even if those other aspects later came to assume a causal significance of their own.[40] Christianity consecrated the Jews (that is, set them apart) in a double sense: the Jews were initially set apart in the Old Testament as the original people of God, a nation of priests, and subsequently in the New Testament as a people who rejected the incarnation of God in Christ.[41] The Jews thus embodied what Durkheim called the ambiguity of the sacred, a category that comprises both the pure and the impure.[42] This ambiguity, which provides the basis for both identification and repulsion, can be traced in turn to distinctive features of the relationship between Jews and Christians. As sociologist Shmuel Eisenstadt pointed out, the Jews were "not just a national or religious minority in some 'alien' environment. They became such a minority in civilizations whose historical roots and basic premises were," on the one hand, "closely interwoven with Jewish history and faith, which . . . developed historically out of the Jewish fold." On the other hand, "continuous Jewish existence always constituted an ideological challenge" to Christians (and Muslims), for "the Jews' adherence to their faith and mode of life" implicitly called into question the legitimacy of the hosts' own creed and civilization. Consequently, "both Christianity and Islam . . . displayed an ambivalence toward the Jews that they did not feel toward other minorities." This ambivalence was rooted in "common historical origins, continuous mutual reference, and latent competition."[43]

Let us now turn to the relationship between the premodern and the modern. By the sixteenth century, Europeans had begun to distinguish modernity as a particular historical period from antiquity and the Middle Ages.[44] As noted in chapter 1, the opposition between the premodern and the modern, along with related dichotomies derived from it, then formed the basis upon which European and American intellectuals produced the discourse on the social world (including classical sociology) that prevailed in the nineteenth and early twentieth centuries. Because the application of this dualism usually entailed at least implicit evaluation as well as description, and this evaluation could always be inverted, the terms *premodern* and *modern* were widely deployed in struggles over the meaning and legitimate definition of a society's sacred ideals, images, and symbols, including the principles of 1789 in France, *Bildung* and *Kultur* in Germany, and the melting pot in America. Particularly during ritual moments when such struggles intensified, intellectuals invoked the opposition between tradition and progress to maintain or recast the meaning of these sacred ideals, alter the relation of social actors to them, and advance their own material or ideal interests in relation to those of other groups.[45] Previous chapters provide several examples of such moments, including the Dreyfus Affair in France; World War I for intellectuals in France, Germany, and the United States; and the nativist, isolationist, and antiradical hysteria that engulfed the United States after the war. Even as they struggled with one another over the valuation of modernity, intellectuals were themselves often of two minds about it.[46] Durkheim, as we have seen, aligned himself with the French Revolution, yet he worried about the anomic tendencies that followed in its wake. The most important figures in German sociology belonged to what Fritz Ringer called the "modernist" wing of their country's mandarin stratum, yet they shared many of the same concerns as their "orthodox" counterparts.[47] Even Robert Park and his students, perhaps the most optimistic of the social thinkers examined in this study, expressed deep anxiety over the urban disorganization they observed. It is this ambivalence that led Robert Nisbet to describe classical sociology as modernist in its objectives and values but conservative in its "essential concepts" and "implicit perspectives."[48]

I have suggested that the relationship between Jews and Christians was not only something in the world but a way of seeing the world; in particular, it formed a code for signifying the relationship between premodernity and modernity. It was precisely the resemblances between these systems of difference that made Jews good to think for intellectuals as they struggled over the meaning of premodernity and modernity. "The Church is the daughter of the Synagogue," as the French writer Bernard Lazare wrote in 1894, yet the continued existence of the Jews placed them in latent competition with Christians.[49] Likewise, modernity developed out of premodern roots and premises, some of which survived into the modern era, yet modernity was conceived as a negation of the premodern. Furthermore, because Judaism was both the source of Christianity and its latent competitor, and because competition could be imagined to yield inverse results—judaization or supersession—the relationship between Jews and Christians could signify the relationship between premodernity and modernity in more than one way: Christians may become Jews as the premodern becomes modern, for instance, or Christians may supersede the Jews as the modern supersedes the premodern. The ambiguities and tensions in the relationship between Jews and Christians made it an equivocal code that allowed the Jews to be associated with both premodernity and modernity. Last, the relation between Jews and Christians is linked to the relation between the premodern and the modern by way of a third fundamental relation between the sacred and the profane. As should now be apparent, the ambiguity of the sacred is manifested in parallel fashion in Christian ambivalence toward the Jew and in the ambivalence of many fin-de-siècle intellectuals toward modernity. The parallel between Christian ambivalence toward Jews and intellectuals' ambivalence about the modern world does not mean that the former caused the latter, still less that ambivalence toward modernity produced ambivalence toward Jews, though these attitudes may have reinforced each other in the minds of some thinkers. It is more accurate to say that the historical ambivalence toward Jews is one of the factors that rendered them good to think for intellectuals who had similarly ambivalent attitudes toward modernity.

As a code for signifying the relationship between premodernity and modernity, the relationship between Jews and Christians was not the monopoly of Christian thinkers; it was also available to the Jewish thinkers discussed in this study. To begin with, continuous mutual reference within the relationship between Jews and Christians ensured that it was a part of Jewish tradition no less than Christian tradition. The formal properties of the relationship remained the same for Jews and Christians, though of course they did not interpret the relationship the same way. Christianity's ambiguous consecration of the Jews was incompatible with Jewish self-understanding. However, the Jewish prophetic tradition produced its own ambiguity, combining an interpretation of Jewish exile and dispersion as divine punishment, on the one hand, with the expectation of messianic redemption, on the other hand. The house of Israel is dry bones without hope (the past), but the divine breath will make them live again (the future).[50] Furthermore, social thinkers with Jewish backgrounds were able to take the role of the Christian other, often learning Christian perspectives directly through formal schooling. As shown in chapter 3, the baptized Marx and Simmel learned liberal Protestantism in their respective *Gymnasia.* But even recipients of a Jewish education, such as Durkheim and Wirth, were not insulated from Christian traditions: Durkheim fell under the influence of a Catholic schoolmistress and considered conversion when he was an adolescent, and the young Wirth attended an evangelical school while also studying with a rabbi.[51] Last, Christian theological perspectives on Jews did not vanish with secularization. In Europe and North America, they formed part of what sociologist John Torpey calls latent religiosity, "the geological substrate left behind by centuries of religious influence," and (as shown in chapter 3) theological schemas took secularized forms embedded in broader philosophical or political traditions.[52] In these ways, Christian perspectives could indirectly influence Jewish thinkers. None of this means that Jewish intellectuals adopted Christian perspectives uncritically or that their ideas were always identical to those of gentiles. Jewish thinkers could and did challenge the hegemony of what historian Susanah Heschel calls the "Christian theological gaze."[53] But even when they did so, they and their opponents fought over and through the same pair of consecrated opposites: Judaism and Christianity. This pair of opposites remained the shared basis for signifying the relationship between the premodern and the modern, even as it allowed that relationship to be signified in multiple and opposing ways.

Jews and Other Others

Although references to Jews appeared prominently within and across different national traditions of social thought, they were not the only point of reference for sociologists seeking to define what it meant to be modern. As this study and previous scholarship have acknowledged, "other groups, other 'others,' served similar conceptual purposes."[54] The previous chapters have discussed some of these other groups, comparing in depth how classical sociologists described them and Jews. They include women and colonial subjects (chapter 2), Protestants or Puritans (chapters 2 and 3), rival nations or continents (chapters 2, 3, and 4), and other European immigrant groups and blacks (chapter 4). As noted in chapter 2, most of these categories overlap with Jews: there were Jewish women as well as men, Jews in the colonies as well as the metropole, Jews in Europe as well as America, and so on. Nevertheless, these categories can be distinguished analytically as alternative ways of dividing the social world. In this way, it is possible to compare how classical sociologists contrasted Europeans and their colonial subjects, for instance, to how they contrasted gentiles and Jews. Here, I elaborate on these comparisons in the framework of scholarship on Orientalism, Occidentalism, and anti-Americanism. I begin with a review of this scholarship and its implications for the history of sociology and Jewish history. I then proceed to clarify how my own study both builds upon and challenges the insights of past scholarship. Finally, I offer some conclusions about how the representation of Jews in classical sociology resembled and differed from the representation of other others.

Edward Said's now-classic and highly influential study of Orientalism provides a useful point of departure for this discussion. Said conceived of Orientalism as an essentializing and dehumanizing body of theory and practice that divided the social world into two opposing terms, East and West, linked in an asymmetrical and hierarchical relationship of power and knowledge. Orientalism represents the East as primitive and backward, in contrast to an advanced West; as "static, frozen, fixed eternally," incapable of development, and therefore in need of "Western attention, reconstruction, even redemption"; and as unitary and monolithic, thus obscuring differences within the East "in the interest of one [overriding] difference" between East and West.[55]

Building on Said's critique of Orientalism, some contemporary sociologists have developed a "postcolonial critique of sociology" or a "self-critique of sociology . . . as a product of empire."[56] As noted in chapter 1, an early version of this critique appeared in the work of R. W. Connell, who argued that sociology did not originate in the internal transformation of European societies but rather in colonial encounters with the non-European world: "The enormous spectrum of human history that the sociologists took as their domain was organized by a central idea," Connell claimed: "difference between the civilization of the metropole and an Other whose main feature was its primitiveness."[57] More recent work has elaborated these claims, insisting that classical sociology was Orientalist, Eurocentric, and elided the colonial relationships and imperial dynamics that were integral to and constitutive of the modern world.[58] According to this view, "Marx, Weber, and Durkheim—far from simply providing neutral observations on society—effectually portrayed non-Western societies in their theories as homogeneous essences . . . as static and backwards, hence reserving dynamism, social creativity, energy, and enlightenment for European societies alone."[59] These Orientalist assumptions, it is argued, blinded classical sociologists to how East and West were mutually constitutive. Rather than showing how modernity was formed in and through the metropole's relations to its colonies, the classical sociologists sought to explain "Europe's industrial and democratic revolutions" as the product of a "special dynamism" internal to the West but "lacking in other societies."[60] In this way, classical sociologists were able to treat European or American history and experience as a "universal template" for understanding and reconstructing non-Western societies.[61] Last, the critique adds, sociology is rooted in and remains tied to an "Enlightenment scientism" that has been "complicit with western imperialism."[62]

In addition to influencing the self-understanding of sociology, Said's analysis of Orientalism has also had an important impact on contemporary understandings of Jewish history. Although his critique focused primarily on the West's cultural domination of Arabs and Muslims, he emphasized the close resemblance between European antisemitism and the "Islamic branch" of Orientalism.[63] After all, he pointed out, "'Semites' were not only the Jews but the Muslims as well."[64] He argued that Orientalism explained the behavior of Jews and Muslims alike on the basis of a "pre-existing 'Semitic' essence" and "in terms of their primitive origins."[65] Said fell silent about antisemitism after the defeat of Nazism, but he argued that Orientalism continued to legitimize "atavistic designations" in contemporary "discussions of Islam, the Arabs, or the Near Orient."[66] In his view, Zionist leaders and Israeli policy makers adopted toward Arabs the same Orientalist attitudes once directed at Jews, leaving Arabs as the principal remaining victims of Orientalism.[67] Although Said described his study of Orientalism as "the history of a strange, secret sharer of Western anti-Semitism," it would be more accurate to say that he subsumed Western antisemitism into Orientalism.[68] Before World War II, he suggested, antisemitism was simply the Jewish branch of Orientalism. After the war, "one Semite [the Jew] went the way of Orientalism, the other, the Arab, was forced to go the way of the Oriental."[69]

Subsequent scholarship has elaborated the application of Said's arguments to the history of the Jews in Europe. Heschel compared "Christian theological discussion of Judaism" to "European orientalism," arguing that "Judaism functions in Christian theology as the opposite, the other, whose negation confirms and even constitutes Christianity." Her study of the German-Jewish theologian Abraham Geiger presented his work as a "revolt of the colonized" and an early example of "postcolonialist writing."[70] Pasto described the Jews in Germany in similar terms as a "colonized population" or an "internal 'oriental' colony." He argued that German Bible scholars and political writers treated Jews implicitly or explicitly "as 'Orientals' and . . . represent[ed] Judaism with typical Orientalist characteristics, portraying it as degenerate, tyrannical, fanatical, anti-Western, and allochronic."[71] Likewise, historian Jonathan Hess emphasized how German thinkers in the late eighteenth and early nineteenth centuries counterposed modernity to an Oriental past purportedly embodied in Jewry and Judaism.[72] Following Said, sociologist Aziza Khazzoom argued that Jews have been Orientalizers as well as objects of Orientalism. Beginning with the Enlightenment, she pointed out, "Christians cast Jews in their countries as their eastern foils. . . . Jews in Western Europe were not simply constructed as being backward, but as backward because they were Oriental, Eastern, or Asian." According to Khazzoom, "the strategy Jews used to become western was to produce other groups as eastern." She described a "great chain of Orientalism" in which western European Jews distinguished themselves from their eastern European counterparts, who in turn distinguished themselves from Middle Eastern Jews, who later distinguished themselves from Arabs.[73]

Studies of the Orientalization of Jews within the European metropole remedy an oversight in the postcolonial critique of sociology, but they have a significant limitation of their own. The postcolonial critique usefully draws attention to the significance of the metropole's relationship to its colonies for the origins and development of sociology, but it is important not to lose sight of the inner workings of the metropole and its colonies. After all, the West was variegated, divided, and shot through with its own internal relations of power and cultural domination. Europeans and Americans therefore did not need to look beyond the civilization of the metropole to find an other against whom they could construct their own self-image. As Said suggested and as subsequent scholarship in Jewish history has confirmed, Jews in Europe served a comparable role *within* the civilization of the metropole. To make this point, however, both Said and subsequent scholars have assimilated the historical experience of Jews in Europe to that of Europe's colonies. They have brought Jews into their accounts of the construction of European identity, but the chief story remains the social logic of colonialism.[74]

My study challenges attempts to fold Jewish-gentile relations into the history of Orientalism in three ways. First, it offers a different way to understand what sociologist Steven Seidman calls the discourse of modernity. Seidman writes: "If it is plausible to interpret the modern/tradition dichotomy as a cultural code that classifies, organizes, and establishes hierarchies, then we need to ask: what are the social conditions that produced this code, and what is its moral-political significance?" Echoing Connell, he answers that "European imperialism formed an important 'background condition' for the production of the modern/tradition binary. . . . Europeans frequently interpreted the native other as the antithesis of the modern."[75] Without disputing Seidman's claim, I would like to suggest that it is too narrowly focused. However important, European imperialism was not the only background condition for the production of the modern/tradition binary. Sociologist Claus Offe and political scientist Andrei Markovits have shown that the meaning of European modernity was constructed not only by opposition to the Orient, but also by contrast to America.[76] Similarly, in this chapter I have suggested that the historical relationship between Jews and Christians constituted yet another background condition for the production of the modern/tradition binary. This background condition was chronologically primary and not reducible to European imperialism.

Second, as we have seen, a major element of the postcolonial critique is that sociology "attribute[d] agency and innovation in modernity to the metropole alone," occluding the role that colonial subjects and relationships played in constituting modernity. Sociologist Julian Go, for instance, criticizes what he calls internalist accounts of the French and Industrial Revolutions for neglecting the impact of the Haitian slave revolt of 1791 to 1804 on the former and India's contributions to the latter.[77] The Jews, too, were often regarded as a foreign and even Oriental presence rather than as an integral part of the metropole. However, in contrast to colonial subjects, Jews were far from invisible in modern social thought and on the contrary attracted considerable attention. Indeed, continuous mutual reference within the historical relationship between Jews and Christians made it difficult for Jews to keep a low profile even when they did not welcome heightened visibility. Jews were assigned a completely fabricated role as architects of the French Revolution, their part in capitalist development was emphasized and often exaggerated, and they were hailed for bold experiments in democratic reconstruction in the United States. To the extent that Jews were regarded as alien to the metropole yet agents of social change (for better or worse), they do not fit neatly or easily into the history of Orientalism.

Third, my findings provide only partial support for the thesis that social thinkers in Europe and America cast Jews or particular subsets of Jews as their Oriental foils. Durkheim's depiction of Jews may have been implicitly Orientalist in some respects, but this implicit Orientalism was moderated by his reluctance to distinguish the premodern from the modern too sharply.

Orientalist assumptions about Jews (derived in part from German idealist philosophy) also appeared in German social thought, most notably in Bruno Bauer's polemics. However, Marx and Simmel avoided characterizing Jews as an Oriental people, and Weber insisted that the Jewish ethic was "worlds apart from the paths of salvation offered by Asiatic religions."[78] As already noted, Park and his students in the United States attributed a creative dynamism to Jews that Orientalism typically reserved for the West. In sum, representations of Jews in modern social thought did not always fit neatly within an Orientalist framework because social thinkers could not agree on whether Jews signified (Eastern) tradition or (Western) modernity. This point stands out even more sharply when we take Occidentalism into consideration.

Occidentalism, "the dehumanizing picture of the West painted by its enemies," is the inverted counterpart to Said's Orientalism.[79] As Ian Buruma and Avishai Margalit conceived it, Occidentalism is not a discourse produced primarily by the East about the West. Rather, Occidentalism originated in Europe; they emphasized especially its roots in the German Romantic reaction to "Napoleon's army and the universalistic claims of French civilization."[80] Occidentalism was subsequently "transferred to other parts of the world," but even then, it continued at least partly to follow European models.[81] At its core is revulsion against the perceived destruction of a "unified spiritual culture" by the modern West, which is conversely envisioned as "a machine-like society without a human soul."[82] Buruma and Margalit identified several expressions of this Occidentalist revulsion: to the city, in contrast to the country; to capitalism and commercialism, in contrast to a warrior ethos of heroism and sacrifice; to a calculating, instrumental, atomistic rationalism, in contrast to organic unity; and to materialism, in contrast to spiritualism. Their study has important implications for the history of sociology insofar as it identifies Occidentalist elements in the work of Marx and especially Sombart.[83] It also has important implications for Jewish history, showing that European social thinkers associated Jews not only with a backward Orient but also with various aspects of a corrosive West: the metropolis, trade and finance, universalistic ideals, and so on.[84] My own study confirms and supports this finding with its examination of antisemitic discourse in Third Republic France; the work of Simmel, Marx, and Sombart in Germany; and the depiction of Jews in American sociology as a "city people" and as agents of social disorganization in Europe. A variety of groups and nations have been identified with the Orient, and others (most notably England, America, and France) with the Occident, but it is difficult to think of another group besides Jews who have figured so prominently in both Orientalist and Occidentalist discourses. Because modern social thought has represented Jews inconsistently as symbols of Eastern traditionalism *and* Western modernism, any body of scholarship that focuses on one of these two aspects at the expense of the other can produce only a partial and distorted understanding of how Jews have been represented and what they have been made to signify in the prevailing discourse on the social world.

Are Jews really exceptional in this respect? "Except in the most extreme and unusual situations," sociologist George Steinmetz has argued, "European representations of non-Europeans were much more layered and fragmentary than theories of 'Orientalism' have led us to believe." Drawing on the work of Homi Bhabha, he showed that European thought constructed non-Western others in multivocal, inconsistent, and ambiguous ways.[85] However, the variations that Steinmetz described were mostly evaluative: they concerned negative or positive views of colonial subjects (the vertical axis in table 5.1). The dominant European ethnographic discourse sometimes depicted colonial subjects as ignoble savages, and sometimes as noble savages, but savage in both versions. Far more rarely did colonizers question the assumption that non-Western was synonymous with backward, primitive, and premodern (the horizontal axis in table 5.1).[86] The major exception that Steinmetz found to this pattern was China, which Europeans initially viewed as "equal civilizationally to Europe and even superior in some respects." However, this view did not persist; in the nineteenth century, China lost "its status as Europe's civilizational equal" and instead came to be associated with stagnation and decay.[87] Steinmetz pointed to Max Weber's 1915 study of Chinese religion as an example of this discursive shift.[88] Jews, in contrast, continued to signify modernity as well as tradition into the twentieth century. Thus, while "Orientalist or ethnographic discourses" were rarely "seamless and uniform," they were not multivocal in the same way or to the same extent as the discourse about Jews.[89] The explanation for these differences lies in the peculiarities of the historical relationship between Jews and Christians, which as we have seen was not identical to the relationship between European colonizers and their non-Western subjects.

The discourse about Jews more closely resembles the European discourse about America than the Orientalist discourse about colonial subjects. European discourse about America has also been multivocal and inconsistent. Offe has shown that European thinkers like Alexis de Tocqueville, Max Weber, and Theodor Adorno could not agree on what America signified and sometimes even reversed their views over time.[90] Markovits reached similar conclusions: Europeans have represented America as "too religious, too secular; too idealistic, too materialistic; too elitist, too populist; too prudish, too pornographic; too individualistic, too conformist; too anarchic, too controlling; too obsessed with history, not having any history; too concerned with culture, not having any culture; too dominated by women, too controlling of women."[91] As we have seen, multivocality alone is not distinctive. More importantly, representations of Jews and representations of America varied along the same axes, including the horizontal axis in table 5.1 from the traditional to the modern. Like the Jews, America has been seen as both a "*latecomer* . . . standing at a stage of development that Europe has already paced out" and an "*advance guard* whose explorations allow Europeans to gaze into their own future."[92] In this respect, representations of America are similar to portrayals of Jews but differ from depictions of Europe's colonized subjects.

If Jews and America have been represented in similar ways, as both premodern and modern, it is because the relationship between Jews and Christians resembled in important respects the relationship between Europe and America. As previously noted, the relationship between Jews and Christians was characterized by "common historical origins, continuous mutual reference, and latent competition."[93] The relationship between Europe and America was analogous. As Offe pointed out, "Asia and, especially, Africa were felt by Europeans to be alien regions," but America's European settlement and shared religious traditions "gave it the status of a more or less distant relative whose independent destiny . . . inevitably irritated us—and challenged us to make comparative assessments—because of its evident deviation from European patterns." America has always been for Europeans "a branch on the same tree," yet one that bears "unfamiliar blossoms and fruits."[94] This resemblance between the two systems of difference—Jews and Christians on the one hand, Europe and America on the other hand—also helps to account for the linkage between antisemitism and anti-Americanism.[95] When Sombart declared that "Americanism is nothing else . . . than the Jewish spirit distilled," he was in effect using one opposition to signify the other.[96]

To conclude, Jews were not the only group, nation, or category that European and American social thinkers adduced to define what it meant to be modern, but social thinkers represented Jews in distinctive ways, and these differences were rooted in the peculiarities of the historical relationship between Jews and Christians. What distinguishes representations of Jews in European and American social thought is not simply that these representations were multivocal or inconsistent. A wide range of groups have elicited positive evaluations based on identification as well as negative interpretations rooted in repulsion. Jews were hardly the only group to be constructed as Oriental and therefore backward. Nor were Jews alone in becoming symbols of a corrosive Western modernity. But colonized subjects usually did not appear as objects of Occidentalist discourse, and prominent symbols of a soulless Occident such as England or France were rarely if ever identified with Oriental stagnation or underdevelopment. What sets representations of Jews apart is the way they have persistently appeared as objects of both Orientalism and Occidentalism. The image of the Jew constitutes a rare point at which these antithetical discourses converge, and in this way, it confounds their visions and divisions of the social world.[97]

New Jews and Old in the Twenty-First Century

Just as the upheavals of the long nineteenth century generated anxiety and conflict about what it meant to be French, German, or American in the modern era, profound changes since the fall of the Soviet Union and the close of the Cold War raise similar questions today. The end of the short twentieth century from 1914 to 1991 brought exuberant confidence in the apparent worldwide triumph of (neo)liberal capitalist democracy, the reunification of Germany, and the transformation of the European Common Market into the European Union.[98] However, the Islamist terrorist attack that destroyed the World Trade Center in 2001, the US invasions of Afghanistan in 2001 and Iraq in 2003, and further Islamist terrorist attacks in European cities from 2004 onward have fostered a more fearful and embattled mood. These developments seemed to lend credence to earlier predictions of a clash of civilizations, primarily between the West and the rest, though widespread European opposition to the Iraq War also indicated deep tensions between Europe and America.[99] At the same time, globalizing flows of capital and migrants have stoked anticapitalist, populist, and nativist countermovements in Western Europe and the United States on both the left and right ends of the political spectrum.

In this context, the Muslim population in Western Europe has become a new focal point for debates about the principles of 1789, the social exclusion generated by late capitalism, and the movement and mixing of peoples and cultures. Mainly comprised of colonial or postcolonial migrants and their offspring, this population grew from tens of thousands in the early 1960s to an estimated 15 to 20 million in the European Union by 2010.[100] The three largest sources of Muslim immigration have been North Africa for France, Turkey and Kurdistan for Germany, and South Asia for the United Kingdom.[101] First-generation Muslim migrants typically came from rural areas with little education or training, formed part of the manual working class in their countries of destination, and were "overrepresented in dirty, dangerous, unpleasant, ill-paid, and menial occupations."[102] Many of these guest workers stayed in Western Europe after its postwar economic boom subsided in the

1970s, bringing their fiancées and family members with the help of court rulings, and waves of refugees and asylum seekers since the 1980s have further augmented Western Europe's Muslim population.[103] Muslims now comprise nearly 8 percent of the population of France, almost 5 percent of the population in Germany, and just over 4 percent of the population of the United Kingdom, the three countries with the largest numbers of Muslims in Western Europe.[104] The members of these communities, including the younger generations who grew up in European societies, continue to experience socioeconomic marginalization and discrimination, and in recent years, they have become the targets of anti-immigrant or anti-Islamic political mobilization.[105] As Western Europe's largest ethnoreligious minority today, Muslims are at the center of ongoing social conflicts over the wearing of headscarves and other distinctive attire, ritual slaughter, circumcision, the use of religious law in family disputes, the building of mosques, immigration, schooling, and integration.[106]

The threat of Islamist terrorism has heightened the salience of Muslims in the United States as well, though the situation of American Muslims differs from that of their Western European counterparts in important respects. In demographic terms, Muslims comprise a much smaller share of the population in the United States: less than 1 percent, or fewer than three million people.[107] Roughly two-thirds of American Muslims are first-generation immigrants, originating mainly from the Middle East, North Africa, or South Asia. However, because the great majority of immigrants to the United States are Christians, Muslims comprise only a small portion (5 percent at most) of the country's foreign-born and their children. A sizable minority of Muslims in the United States (about one-fifth) is African American.[108] In socioeconomic terms, Muslims in the United States are generally better off than their counterparts in Western Europe. Indeed, although the percentage of American Muslims employed full-time lags behind that of the US general public, Muslims in the United States have levels of education and family income comparable to those of the country's population as a whole.[109] Last, notwithstanding popular antipathy since September 11, 2001, the constitutional-legal integration of Muslims in the United States has been facilitated by an exceptional religion-state constellation, which combines a formal separation of church and state, a much higher level of religiosity than in Western Europe, and a history of religious diversity.[110]

The rise of Muslims as a prominent ethnoreligious minority in Western Europe and the United States raises a pertinent question for this study: Have they taken the position formerly occupied by Jews as a foil for the construction of modern European and American identities? Numerous scholars have suggested such a displacement. "Today, the 'Jewish Question' in Europe has largely been 'solved,'" sociologist Krishan Kumar has declared, "mainly by getting rid of the Jews. But Muslims present a different problem. . . . Muslims are not only the most numerous of the new immigrant populations, but culturally they seem the most distinctive, and to many (in the host cultures, at least) they seem the most difficult to absorb. As such, they have become the new 'other' of Europe, replacing the Jews of an earlier era."[111] David Theo Goldberg has described a similar "shift in Europe's dominant fixation of concern and resentment" from Jews before World War II to Muslims today.[112] Likewise, Aziz Al-Azmeh has suggested that a negative stereotype of Muslims as homogeneous, "innocent of modernity," "obsessed with prayer, fasting, veiling, medieval social and penal arrangements," and incapable of reconstruction has "gathered force" in Europe "now that the previous internal enemy—the Jew—could no longer legitimately be conceived as such."[113] Political scientist Amikam Nachmani concurs: "Without doubt, a strong parallel can be drawn between Europe's 'Jewish question' and its mirror image, the 'Muslim migrant question.' In fact, the question 'Are Muslims the Jews of Europe Today?' is at the heart of an oft-heard debate nowadays argued by the three interested parties: the Muslim migrant minority, the European majority and the Jewish world." Staking out his own position in this debate, Nachmani has concluded: "In the past Europe's salient migratory grouping—one that has profoundly coloured its culture and civilization—was the Jew who was always branded the 'foreigner,' the 'other,' a threatening presence. . . . Today, the Wandering Jew is no longer the issue. . . . Now [Europe] is preparing to defend itself against . . . the immigrant, more specifically, the Muslim immigrant. . . . The Jew, Europe's prototypal 'other,' has now largely been replaced by the Muslim 'other.' . . . Prejudice and discrimination once directed at European Jewry is now aimed at European Muslims."[114] Jonathan Laurence has also drawn analogies between Jewish emancipation in the nineteenth century and the European integration of Muslims in the twenty-first century. He points out that contemporary European politicians themselves make such analogies, while the opponents of Muslim integration question the civic fitness of Muslims with arguments that resemble those previously used against Jews.[115] In sum, this scholarship suggests that Muslims are the new Israel, if by Israel is meant a pariah rather than a chosen people.

At the conclusion of this study, we are in a good position to assess these claims. At a high level of abstraction, the experiences of Jews and Muslims in the West may be seen as variations on a common process of civil incorporation.[116] Nevertheless, the suggestion that Muslims are the new Jews is open to three major criticisms.[117] First, comparisons of Jews and Muslims tend to overlook significant differences in the social and historical contexts of their incorporation. Second, these comparisons neglect important differences in the discursive representation of the two out-groups. Third, while Muslims have indeed emerged as an important other in contemporary European and American discourse, they have not superseded Jews as an object of concern, resentment, or antagonism. Let us consider each of these points in turn.

While Jews and Muslims have experienced similar processes of civil incorporation in the West, these processes have been shaped by different social and historical conditions. In demographic terms, the number of Muslims in Western Europe today far exceeds that of Western Europe's prewar Jewish population, which totaled fewer than two million.[118] Furthermore, though Jews and Muslims in the West can both be seen as strangers in Simmel's sense, the Jews had "no country where they could claim not to be visitors or strangers" before 1948. Thus, "their strangeness was not confined to any particular place; they were *universal* strangers."[119] In contrast, Muslim guest workers came to Western Europe from Muslim-majority countries, and the governments of their countries of origin continue to "keep a hand in European Muslim life" so that "the interaction of religious policies in Europe and the Muslim world has geopolitical resonance."[120] In this respect, Muslims in Western Europe are comparable not to Jews but to Italian emigrants between 1880 and 1915 and to Mexican emigrants in the first decade of the twenty-first century; in both cases, the Catholic Church and government officials in the countries of origin sought to maintain relations with these emigrants.[121] The socioeconomic contexts of Jewish and Muslim incorporation also differ. Most French and German Jews had joined the ranks of the bourgeoisie by the late nineteenth century, but alongside them arose a Jewish working class comprised mainly of recent immigrants from eastern Europe. The Jewish class structure was thus more differentiated in contrast to the economic disadvantage prevalent among Muslims in Western Europe today. Last, in terms of the political context, there was no analogue among Jews in nineteenth- and early twentieth-century Europe to the radical Islamist terrorism that has struck at European and American cities and stoked fear and suspicion of Muslims in the West.[122] Although Jews, too, were frequently viewed as a threatening presence in the late nineteenth and early twentieth centuries, bourgeois Jews were generally thought to menace by nonviolent and especially pecuniary means. To be sure, some Jews were involved in revolutionary movements, but such involvement, even when disproportionate, did not make these movements Jewish. Unlike Islamist terrorism, which is based upon an interpretation of Islam, revolutionary violence in Western Europe was not based upon an interpretation of Judaism.[123] In short, the civil incorporation of Muslims today and Jews in the past has proceeded under different conditions, which include the relative size, type of "strangeness," and socioeconomic status of the out-group, as well as the presence or absence of organized and religiously inspired political violence.[124]

The notion that Muslims are the Jews of the twenty-first century also neglects important differences in the collective representations of the two out-groups. Again, at a high level of abstraction, these representations will look similar: opponents of incorporation stigmatize out-groups as carriers of anticivil traits, while proponents of incorporation strive to counter the stigma of incivility with favorable representations that foster identification with out-groups and broaden the boundaries of solidarity.[125] These competing representations may be placed along the vertical axis in table 5.1, with polluting images at the bottom and purifying descriptions at the top. However, if we shift our attention to the table's horizontal axis, we find that representations of Jews and Muslims are linked in different ways to the opposition between tradition and modernity. As we have seen, Jews have appeared in modern social thought both as personifications of a backward Orient and as agents of Western modernity. In contrast, Muslims are rarely represented in contemporary European or American discourse as agents or symbols of modernity. Instead, contemporary representations of Muslims in Western Europe and the United States fall predominantly into the lower right-hand corner (B–) of table 5.1. This pattern is well documented in recent scholarship.

Although "Muslims have never been the sole 'others' of the West," political scientist Jocelyne Cesari contends, "the liberal modernist story at the heart of Western modern identity has adopted Islam as its foil in order to create itself." She traces this opposition back to a "European cultural crisis linked to the advent of modernity," which defined itself against the Ottoman Empire.[126] The West's "dominant meta-narratives about Islam" today, she adds, are rooted in these historic "perceptions . . . deposited over the centuries."[127] Her study of elite political discourse and public opinion surveys indicates that many contemporary Europeans view Muslims as bearers of obscurantist values—sexist, violent, fanatical, and intolerant—which are incompatible with Western, Christian, Enlightenment, or liberal values; they question Muslims' loyalty and ability to assimilate to national and Western values; and they fear that Muslims in large numbers may eventually alter prevailing cultural norms, impose *sharia* (Muslim religious law) or other unwanted changes on non-Muslims, and threaten national identities.[128] Likewise, social scientists Justus Uitermark, Paul Mepschen, and Jan Willem Duyvendak find that a Europe-wide "neoculturalist" discourse targets Muslims "in the name of progress and sexual emancipation" as "backward, intolerant, and incongruous with European secular modernity. . . . European identities and nationalisms have become reimagined as progressive and tolerant while Muslims have become framed as homophobic, sexually backward, and stuck in traditional family and religious values."[129] They add that "the central tropes of this discourse—individualism versus the lack thereof; 'tolerance' versus 'fundamentalism'—frame an imagined modern self against an imagined traditional (Muslim) other."[130] Although from a constitutional-legal perspective the integration of Muslims has been less problematic in the United States than in Western Europe, public depictions of Islam have been similarly negative. Viewed by many Americans as violent and disloyal, Muslims are associated in the US context with concerns about national security. Furthermore, opposition to the building of mosques, campaigns to ban *sharia*, and calls to curtail the constitutional rights of Muslim Americans provide evidence of a "movement . . . against the Islamization of the country, which is seen as a threat not only to national security but also to core American values."[131] In short, Muslims are widely viewed as antithetical to national, European, or Western identities that are in turn equated with civility and modernity.[132] This representation of Muslims only partly approximates historical representations of Jews. What Jews and Muslims have in common is that both groups have been the objects of Orientalist discourse, but as previously noted, only the first of these two groups has also figured prominently in Occidentalist discourse.[133]

There is a final reason to doubt that Muslims are the new Jews: The old Jews have not disappeared from the Western imaginary. While Muslims have surely emerged as an important and significant touchstone in their own right, they have not displaced Jews in contemporary discourse. On the contrary, the Jews—and now the Jewish state—continue to serve as a touchstone for defining the meaning of European or American modernity in the twenty-first century. The state of Israel is now home to more than six million Jews, a plurality of the fourteen million Jews worldwide.[134] This does not make criticism of Israel, its human rights violations, or the policies of its successive governments antisemitic, any more than criticism of Muslim states is inherently Islamophobic. However, when Israel is demonized in a selective, one-sided, essentialist, or paranoid fashion, or when demands are made for its outright elimination, it is important to recognize that the world's largest Jewish population is thereby targeted. Furthermore, while antisemitism and anti-Zionism are analytically distinguishable, Jews and Israel (or "Zionists") play analogous symbolic roles in these cultural structures or ideological formations.[135] For example, political scientist Mitchell Cohen has pointed out that the motifs of Jewish foreignness or alienness, exclusive particularism, power, and wickedness not only recur across different forms of antisemitism but also parallel or correspond to "anti-Zionist motifs repeated in the contemporary Arab and Muslim worlds, and also in many Western leftwing and intellectual circles."[136] In a similar fashion, we should expect to find that the Jewish state, like the Jews, can signify a superseded past or the most modern of tendencies, and that these meanings, depending on ideological orientation, can lead either to denunciation or praise. While a comprehensive overview of contemporary representations of Jews and Israel is beyond the scope of this study, this point can be illustrated with a few prominent examples.

Let us first consider contemporary variations on the theme of Jewish backwardness. Jewish solidarity in the form of Jewish nationalism (which today means Zionism) is frequently decried as atavistic and retrograde. This view is more than a diffuse prejudice; intellectual elites like the British-born historian Tony Judt and the Italian-born historian Enzo Traverso have given it elaborate theoretical expression.[137] Perhaps the best example can be found in the work of Alain Badiou, who describes himself as "the most widely read and translated French philosopher in the world."[138] Badiou's "Uses of the Word 'Jew'" reproduces all of the motifs that Cohen identified in classical antisemitic discourse and deploys them in the service of a new narrative of supersession. Badiou extols Paul's Christian universalism, which refuses to privilege anyone on the basis of "communitarian, religious, or national labels," in contrast to the exclusive particularism of the Jews, "the supposed bearers of the most radical election in the eyes of God."[139] Today, Badiou declares, the "privileging" of Jewish particularity takes a new form: The Shoah reconstituted the Jews as a "mythico-communitario-racial" totality and conferred upon them an "exceptional," "sacred" status "worthier . . . than all others" as the "incomparable victim."[140] This consecration, he contends, makes the Jews powerful; their name is now "a word one is bound to recognize and respect, and before which one must bow," a "word brandished" to claim "superior rights," "turn in a profit," and silence others.[141] Reviving the motif of Jewish usury, Badiou insists that it is Zionists, above all, who have "cashed in" on the Shoah and continue to "draw interest on it."[142] While they use the status and power of the Jewish name to raise Israel above all criticism, he claims, the Jewish state in a "perverse reversal" engages in Nazi-like "racial militarism," "chauvinism and unending war."[143] The perverse reversal is in fact Badiou's. He makes Israel the embodiment of Europe's criminal past and a "Jewish exception" to contemporary postnationalism. To him, Israel signifies "obsolete" colonial oppression and a "kind of archaism," not only because it occupies the West Bank, but because "Israel has called itself a 'Jewish state' with an 'Arab minority.'"[144] "Truly contemporary states or countries are always cosmopolitan," Badiou insists.[145] "The modern conception of a state is an open conception," a "creative patchwork" made up of "all the people who live and work there."[146] Holding up the European Union as a model, he asserts that "Israelis and Palestinians," like "France and Germany," are "fiancés by war" who must be "fused, pure and simple."[147] "Today's equivalent of Paul's religious rupture with established Judaism" is thus "a subjective rupture with the State of Israel," which is to say, with "its exclusive identitarian claim to be a 'Jewish state,' and with the way it draws incessant privileges from this claim." In Israel's place he proposes to create an abstract, "secular and democratic Palestine, one subtracted from all predicates, and which, in the school of Paul—who declared that, in his view of the universal, there is no longer 'Jew nor Greek' and that 'circumcision is nothing, and uncircumcision is nothing'—would show that it is perfectly possible to create a place in these lands where, from a political point of view . . . there is 'neither Arab not Jew.'"[148] The venerable opposition between backward Jewish particularism and progressive Christian universalism, familiar to us from chapter 3, is hence pressed into service again in the twenty-first century.

Allegedly holding more than others to an outdated history that must be abolished, the Jews, "Zionists," or the Jewish state appear as an obstacle to all of the contrary qualities required by modern progress. Such characterizations bring to mind earlier representations of Jews as backward Orientals, and indeed many of the same attributes that Orientalist discourse has assigned to Arabs and to Islam are now also often conferred upon the Jewish state. Israel, too, is described as dishonest, bloodthirsty, and sadistic, and the Orientalist "fear that Muslims (or Arabs) will take over the world" finds its echoes in the image of a fearsome Jewish lobby powerful enough to drive the world's only remaining superpower into a war against its national interests.[149] In the same way that contemporary Orientalists have explained Palestinian opposition to Israeli settlement and occupation as "merely the 'return of Islam,'" so Israeli policies are explained as simply the most recent expression of an essential racist ideology dating back to 1897.[150] What Said wrote regarding Orientalist discourse about Arabs applies as well to contemporary demonization of "Zionists" (a term now increasingly used as an epithet) and Israelis: "the result is to eradicate the plurality of differences among the Arabs . . . in the interest of one difference, that one setting Arabs off from everyone else."[151] Nevertheless, it would be a mistake to conclude that the contemporary denunciation of Israel as an anachronism is simply a revival of Orientalist thinking. In contemporary discourse, the Jewish state is not deemed to be backward because it is Oriental. Rather, in a cruel historical irony, the Jews who were once denigrated as an Oriental presence in Europe are now denounced as a European or Western presence in the Middle East.[152] But if the Jewish state is discursively constructed as an expression or manifestation of the West, it is not the purportedly progressive, postnationalist, and contemporary West extolled by Badiou and others, and hence not the West's collective ego ideal.[153] Through processes of projection and splitting well known to psychoanalysis, what the Jewish state really represents to the Western intellectuals who most vehemently detest it today is the West's polluted and polluting past: ethnic nationalism, racism, religious intolerance, colonialism, imperialism, militarism, and so on. When this process is taken to an extreme, Israel is equated with Nazi Germany and its treatment of the Palestinians with the Shoah.[154] The Jewish state is imagined to recapitulate the worst crimes of *old* Europe and to lack all of the virtues of the *new*, postwar, postnationalist Europe, or at least of Europe's most enlightened forces.[155]

What about the counterimage in which Jews do not represent a superseded past but the forward line of modernity? Although overshadowed in the twenty-first century by the castigation of a purportedly outmoded Jewish nationalism, it has not entirely disappeared. In a time of growing economic inequality, Jews continue to symbolize the forces of late capitalist modernization, for better or worse, and the Jewish state sometimes plays an equivalent role. For instance, when Song Lihong, the deputy director of Nanjing University's Institute of Jewish Studies, was asked in 2011 to explain growing Chinese interest in Judaism and Israel, he invoked the titles of popular Jewish-interest books in Chinese bookstores. These titles reportedly included *The Talmudic Wisdom in Conducting Business*, *Talmud: The Greatest Jewish Bible for Making Money*, and *Unveiling the Secrets of Jewish Success in World Economy: What's behind Jewish Excellence?* According to Song, these titles do not indicate Chinese hostility to Jews. On the contrary, he suggested, as China strives to further its economic and technological development, it looks upon Jews as a successful "model it can employ to modernize itself."[156] Contemporary American scholars also emphasize the role of Jews as social winners in the process of capitalist development. In a study that echoes earlier depictions of Jews as social carriers of a capitalist spirit, Amy Chua and Jed Rubenfeld attribute Jewish success in the United States to a "triple package" of cultural characteristics that include a sense of superiority, insecurity, and impulse control.[157] All of these examples characterize Jews in a positive light, falling into the upper left-hand corner (A+) of table 5.1.

Negative depictions of Jews as malevolent purveyors of disruptive and harmful forms of modernization (A–) also appear in contemporary discourse on the social world. In the Muslim and especially the Arab world, sinister representations of Jews, "Zionists," and Israel as agents of capitalist globalization are widespread.[158] Similarly negative images have reappeared in the West in conjunction with protests against capitalist globalization. Although the antiglobalization movement as a whole is not antisemitic, Jews and Israel have been identified on both the far left and the far right as agents and beneficiaries of globalization.[159] For instance, the celebrated French antiglobalization activist José Bové declared that Israel was "putting in place—with the support of the World Bank—a series of neoliberal measures intended to integrate the Middle East into globalized production circuits"; the German far-left-turned-far-right activist Horst Mahler declared that "what is generally meant by 'Democracy' is actually Jewish rule, which Jewish plutocrats exercise through their control of global finance, the monetary system and the media"; and the American white supremacist Matt Hale praised antiglobalization protests for helping to "shut down talks of the Jew World Order WTO."[160] From this perspective, Jews and Israel do not represent Europe's past but instead the Occidentalist fear of a judaized-Americanized future. In a particularly notorious moment at the 2003 World Economic Forum in Davos, protesters wore masks of the Israeli prime minister and the US defense secretary—the latter wearing a yellow Star of David—while carrying an effigy of a golden calf loaded with money. Going well beyond opposition to US and Israeli policies, this bit of agitprop signaled, according to one interpretation, that "America was in the hands of Israel and Mammon-worshipping Jews—the mercenary avant-garde of capitalist globalization."[161]

At this point, we have taken our discussion of contemporary social thought as far as this study allows. Our historical inquiry may be seen as a long detour meant to return us to the present with greater insight and understanding. We find ourselves separated from classical sociology by the intervening traumas, upheavals, and rebirths of the twentieth century. The Shoah, World War II, and the establishment of the state of Israel represent in this sense a historic break. Yet we find that old habits of thought reappear in the discourse on the social world that prevails today. The Jews or the Jewish state still serve as an intermediary for self-reflection in our own time. Social thinkers continue to invoke the Jews or draw analogies to them in order to make points about matters that are often only tangentially related to Jews. Whether as the chief threat to modern values or the personification of them, Jews are repeatedly placed at the sacred center of society. In reality, Jews are neither responsible for the problems of modernity nor have they resolved them. Yet by conferring symbolic centrality upon Jews, social thinkers encourage these perceptions. Nowhere is this more apparent than in the immense significance that some political elites attribute to the Jewish state. Not content to criticize the real injustices for which Israel is responsible, they make this tiny state the font of all troubles in the Middle East and even the world.[162] This "thrusting of Israelis to the centre of a worldview," as sociologist David Hirsh argues, "mirrors antisemitic traditions insofar as they have always constructed Jews as being central to what is wrong with the world." Antisemitism does indeed rest on the assumption of Jewish centrality, though Phoebe Maltz Bovy rightly notes that the assumption is more broadly shared and is not unique to antisemitic thought. The problem, as she points out, is not that it is always antisemitic to confer symbolic centrality upon the Jews. The problem is that repeatedly placing Jews at the sacred center renders them prime targets in ongoing conflicts over society's sacred ideals, images, and symbols, even when Jews may be peripheral to those conflicts or have little real influence over them.[163]

Does the persistence of old habits of thought mean that we are condemned always to repeat the past? A reflexive history of social thought gives us hope that such pessimism may be avoided; it seeks to bring problematic but recurring patterns of thought to light, trace their history, grasp the social logic that underlies them, show how they continue to inform the present, and ultimately emancipate us from their grip. The social thought of our time must let the dead bury their dead in order to arrive at its own content. This does not mean that we can disregard or dispense with the history of social thought, for it is only through critical reflection upon the categories, concepts, and principles we have inherited that we become aware of the otherwise hidden and unconscious influences in our own thought. The more aware we become of the social unconscious within us, the more we can reflexively master the tools of thought we apply to the social world, and the less likely we are to be weighed down by the tradition of all dead generations.

Notes

Chapter One

1. For a similar investigation that concentrates on nineteenth-century German literature, see Achinger, "Threats to Modernity." Throughout this study, I use the related terms *social thought*, *sociology* (or *sociological thought*), *classical sociology*, and *classical sociological theory*. These terms may be understood as nested categories. Social thought comprises the broadest and most general category: all sociologists are social thinkers, but not all social thinkers are sociologists. Classical sociology is a subset of sociology; it refers to the ideas and research that the discipline's founders (identified and canonized by their successors) produced in the discipline's formative years. The ideas of the disciplinary founders are now sometimes called classical sociological theory, a designation that unfortunately abstracts these ideas from the empirical and historical research in which many of the founders were engaged.

2. The notion of modernity elaborated in classical sociology has since been criticized, reworked, and sometimes rejected. See Alexander, "Modern, Anti, Post and Neo"; Eisenstadt, "Multiple Modernities in an Age of Globalization"; Eisenstadt, "Multiple Modernities"; Eisenstadt, "Pluralism and the Multiple Forms of Modernity." Taking a similar approach to that of Hess in *Germans, Jews and the Claims of Modernity*, this study treats the term *modernity* primarily as an object of study rather than a tool for sociological analysis. In other words, I attempt to understand what modernity meant for the intellectuals examined in this study and what role their reflections on Jews and Judaism played in constructing this category in the first place. Viewed from this perspective, modernity is not merely a historical period or a set of structural and cultural changes to which Jews and gentiles were subjected; it is also a discourse, a signifier that serves mythological and narrative functions (as Alexander pointed out), and an instrument of exclusion: "We call something (perhaps ourselves) modern in order to distance that of which we speak from some antecedent state of affairs. The antecedent is most unlikely to be of neutral effect in defining either what is to be called 'modern' or the 'modernity' attributed to it; and in understanding the uses of the whole family of words, it is usually important to understand what is being excluded from the 'modern,' to what past it is being relegated, and what structures of past and history are being imposed upon experience." Pocock, "Modernity and Anti-Modernity," 48. None of this is meant to suggest that social thinkers can or should discard the idea of modernity. As Adams, Clemens, and Orloff point out, "the concept does too much useful

work." Like them, I prefer to "remake modernity" through critical reflection upon the analytical categories we have inherited. Adams, Clemens, and Orloff, "Social Theory," 14.

3. Vogt, "Political Connections," 71–72. Lukes, *Émile Durkheim*, 354–60, 363–78. Durkheim, "Intellectual Elite and Democracy," 59. The growth of sociology in France at the end of the nineteenth century was closely connected to the nation's social conflicts: "In the latent civil war situation of the times (exemplified by the 'school war,' the Dreyfus Affair, and the separation of church and state dispute) the new science was entrusted with the impossible task of elaborating elements of a moral consensus and of providing it with scientific foundation." Karady, "Prehistory of Present-Day," 41. In this context, Durkheim became "a major political force, a leader of the New Sorbonne, a particularly effective Dreyfusard, and one of the foremost academic defenders of the Radical Republic," that is, the Third Republic after the Radical Party became the dominant group within the Chamber of Deputies at the turn of the century. Ringer, *Fields of Knowledge*, 284.

4. Ringer, *Decline of the German Mandarins*, 6, 117. Ringer describes German sociologists as heterodox mandarins. Stehr and Grundmann, "Introduction," xiii–xiv.

5. Bourdieu, *Language and Symbolic Power*, 106.

6. Bourdieu, *Political Interventions*, 267.

7. I do not hyphenate the term antisemitism because I do not consider the terms Semite or Semitism to have a meaningful referent in reality. On this point, see Almog, "What's in a Hyphen"; Y. Bauer, "Definition of Antisemitism"; Levy, "Forget Webster."

8. Schechter, *Obstinate Hebrews*, 105. Emphasis in the original.

9. Leff, *Sacred Bonds of Solidarity*.

10. Maltz Bovy, "'Embrasser les Juifs.'"

11. Hess, *Germans, Jews and the Claims of Modernity*, 6.

12. Yovel, *Dark Riddle*, xi.

13. Goldstein, *Price of Whiteness*, 40–41.

14. Nirenberg, *Anti-Judaism*, 2–3, 6.

15. Carlebach, *Karl Marx and the Radical Critique*. Pickering, "Enigma of Durkheim's Jewishness." Strenski, *Durkheim and the Jews*. Birnbaum, *Geography of Hope*, 36–168. Raphaël, *Judaïsme et capitalisme*. Abraham, *Max Weber and the Jewish Question*. Muller, *Capitalism and the Jews*, 33–61. Nirenberg, "Birth of the Pariah." Nirenberg, *Anti-Judaism*, 430–45. Hart, *Social Science and the Politics of Modern Jewish Identity*. Stoetzler, *Antisemitism and the Constitution of Sociology*. Eisenstadt, *Jewish Civilization*. Cahnman, *Jews & Gentiles*.

16. Nisbet, *Sociological Tradition*, 21. For the elaboration of this thesis, see 21–44.

17. Of course, the collapse of the old regime in Europe had a more direct effect upon sociology as well: it greatly facilitated the participation of Jews in the cultural life of the peoples among whom they lived, including their involvement in the new social sciences. The participation of Jewish intellectuals in public discussions about Jews and Judaism was not unprecedented in France or Germany, but the collapse of the old regime made it possible for Jews to speak more freely, and the social sciences provided a new basis on which Jewish and gentile intellectuals alike could legitimize their claims.

18. Connell, "Why Is Classical Theory Classical," 1516–17.

19. Heschel, *Abraham Geiger*. Heschel, "Revolt of the Colonized." Pasto, "Islam's 'Strange Secret Sharer.'" Hess, *Germans, Jews and the Claims of Modernity*. Khazzoom, "Great Chain of Orientalism."

20. Kant, *Anthropology from a Pragmatic Point of View*, 100.

21. Maurras quoted in Roudiez, *Maurras jusqu'à l'Action Française*, 304. My translation.

22. Buruma and Margalit, *Occidentalism*, 27–29, 33–35.

23. Bourdieu, *Political Interventions*, 224–25, 267. See Durkheim, *Elementary Forms*, on the categories of understanding. On culture and civilization, cf. Elias, *Civilizing Process*, 3–34.

24. This study emphasizes how assumptions about the Jews shaped social thought, but the reverse also holds. For instance, when social thinkers in one national context influenced thinkers in another context, their intellectual influence sometimes transmitted or reinforced implicit assumptions about the Jews. See, for instance, the remarks in chapter 4 about German influences on American thinkers.

25. Bourdieu, *Political Interventions*, 103. I have italicized the terms *past*, *future*, *traditional*, and *modern* for emphasis. Other italicized terms are Bourdieu's emphasis.

26. Alexander, *Civil Sphere*, 63, 65; see 53–67 on the discourse of civil society. On the sacred center, see Shils, "Center and Periphery." On the symbolism of right and left, see Hertz, "Pre-Eminence of the Right Hand."

27. Alexander, *Civil Sphere*, 8–9; see 459–502 for an elaboration of these points.

28. Alexander, *Civil Sphere*, 503–47. Alexander, *Remembering the Holocaust*, 3–102.

29. This table is modeled on Offe, *Reflections on America*, 5–6. He summarizes in a similar fashion four conceptions of the relationship between Europe and the United States.

30. Camic and Gross, "New Sociology of Ideas," 245–46.

31. Alexander, "Centrality of the Classics," 51–57. Quotation from 53.

32. Camic, "Classical Sociological Theory."

33. My attempt to transcend the division between historicist and presentist modes of analysis is similar in spirit to the approach that Camic advocated: "the embrace . . . of historicist means to accomplish objectives whose points of departure and return lie in the present." It is this synthesis, he argued, that makes classical sociological theory a field of research irreducible but equally relevant to the history of sociology and sociological theory. Where I differ from Camic is in regard to my main reason for studying the sociological classics. Three reasons may be distinguished. First, the presentist studies the classics to extract "'usable bits of lore' that may fit with our particular projects of the moment." Second, the historicist studies the classics in order to relativize contemporary thinking. This is the rationale that Camic favors. As he put it, the main benefit of such study is that it provides a "critical distance which frees us from the immediate present, exposes us to voices that do more than duplicate our own, and enlarges the horizon of theoretical alternatives beyond the finite bounds of current possibilities." Camic, "Classical Sociological Theory," 2–3, 6. Bourdieu suggested a third reason to study the sociological classics, historical anamnesis, which is the chief rationale for this study.

34. Levine, *Visions*, 3. Cf. Heilbron, *French Sociology*, especially 218–23.

35. This discussion draws on Tilly, *Big Structures*, 80–86. He distinguished universalizing, variation-finding, individualizing, and encompassing comparisons.

36. Levine also distinguished British and Italian traditions of sociology in *Visions*, but in my judgment they are more peripheral to the discipline. The individualistic premises of the British tradition, though increasingly influential in today's neoliberal context, have more typically served as a foil in efforts to define a distinctively sociological viewpoint. See, most notably, Parsons, *Structure of Social Action*. Although individualistic tendencies can also be found in the American tradition (neglected in *Structure of Social Action*), they are tempered there by the philosophical influence of pragmatism. Levine, *Visions*, 260–68. Italian social thinkers like Gaetano Mosca and Vilfredo Pareto made insightful contributions, but they are generally not considered foundational for the discipline of sociology.

37. Levine, *Visions*, 172.

38. Ringer, *Fields of Knowledge*, 284.

39. Nandan, "Editor's Introduction." Karady, "Prehistory of Present-Day."

40. Ringer, *Fields of Knowledge*, 284.

41. Levine, *Visions*, 212–30.

42. Levine, *Visions*, 194. Sombart is not as well known today as Marx, Simmel, or Weber, but in his own lifetime, he was one of Germany's most prominent and controversial social scientists, he was "held in high esteem by the grand old men of German sociology," and "there were countless major reviews of his books in core sociology journals." Grundmann and Stehr, "Why Is Werner Sombart Not Part of the Core of Classical Sociology," 259.

43. Tönnies, *Fundamental Concepts*, initially elaborated the famous dualism between *Gemeinschaft* (community) and *Gesellschaft* (society) without reference to the Jews. Later, in "Individual and the World," Tönnies associated the Jews with modern capitalism, individualism, and self-interest, though he also insisted that Jews formed a close-knit community among themselves.

44. Levine, *Visions*, 263. On American sociology and pragmatism, see 251–68.

45. As Durkheim conceived them, collective representations "express 'the way in which the group conceives itself in its relations with the objects that affect it.'" While they "result from the substratum of associated individuals," he argued that "they cannot be reduced to and wholly explained by features of individuals: they have *sui generis* characteristics." Accordingly, to "'investigate how *représentations collectives* are formed and combine'" is a task for sociology. Lukes, *Émile Durkheim*, 6–8.

46. This threefold division of the historical context is indebted to Camic and Gross, "New Sociology of Ideas."

47. Camic, "Classical Sociological Theory," 3. My emphasis.

48. Matthews, *Quest for an American Sociology*, 124–25.

Chapter Two

1. Wilson, *Ideology and Experience*, 613, 635. Nisbet, *Sociological Tradition*, 21–44.

2. Durkheim, *Textes*, vol. 2, 252–54. Pickering and Martins, *Debating Durkheim*, 174–79. C. A. Goldberg, "Introduction," 321–23.

3. On sociology and the French Revolution, see Nisbet, "French Revolution." On Durkheim and the two revolutions, see Nisbet, *Émile Durkheim*, 19–23. "After his review of Ferneuil's *Les Principes de 1789 et la science sociale* [in 1890], Durkheim provided a sociological interpretation of the French revolution and appraised its moral significance." Nandan, "Editor's Introduction," 9.

4. Jacobs, "Statistics," 531.

5. Hyman, *Jews of Modern France*, 1–15, 115–135.

6. Birnbaum, *Jews of the Republic.*

7. Jacobs, "Statistics," 531. Hyman, *Jews of Modern France*, 53–76. Gartner, *History of the Jews*, 152–53, 159, 216.

8. For other studies of Durkheim's ideas and context, see Alexander, "Durkheimian Sociology"; Birnbaum, "French Jewish Sociologists"; Clark, "Émile Durkheim"; Clark, *Prophets and Patrons*; Collins, "Durkheimian Movement"; Fournier, "Durkheim's Life and Context"; Fournier, *Émile Durkheim*; Giddens, *Capitalism and Modern Social Theory*, 65–118; Giddens, "Durkheim's Political Sociology"; Heilbron, *French Sociology*, 59–123; Jones, "Understanding a Sociological Classic"; Jones, "Durkheim, Frazer, and Smith"; Jones, "Positive Science of Ethics";

Jones, "Ambivalent Cartesians"; Jones, "Other Durkheim"; Jones, *Durkheim's Social Realism*; Jones and Kibbee, "Durkheim, Language, and History"; Karady, "Prehistory of Present-Day"; Lukes, *Émile Durkheim*; Mosbah-Natanson, "Facing Antisemitism"; Mosbah-Natanson, "La sociologie comme 'mode'"; Nandan, "Editor's Introduction"; Pickering, "Enigma of Durkheim's Jewishness"; Ringer, *Fields of Knowledge*, 282–99; Strenski, *Durkheim and the Jews*; Vogt, "Political Connections." My focus on the interplay of ideas is in keeping with Durkheim's own multidimensional approach: while he was careful to acknowledge "the social situatedness of symbolic formations" and to attend to "the bearers of symbols and the concrete circumstances of their struggles," he also insisted that symbolic forms had their own "internal logic and organization" and their own "causal significance." Emirbayer, "Useful Durkheim," 115.

9. Rémond, *Right Wing in France*, especially 184–90, 225–27, 247–52. Davies, *Extreme Right in France*, 9–25.

10. Wilson, *Ideology and Experience*. Benbassa, *Jews of France*, 137–38.

11. Vital, *People Apart*, 188.

12. Hyman, *Dreyfus to Vichy*, 19. Wilson, *Ideology and Experience*, 349–50.

13. Wilson, *Ideology and Experience*, 349. Benbassa, *Jews of France*, 138.

14. Maurras, *Les vergers sur la mer*, xi. This and subsequent translations from French are my own unless otherwise indicated.

15. Picard, *Synthèse de l'antisémitisme*, 85.

16. Drumont, *La France juive*, vol. 1, 323. Drumont, *La France juive*, vol. 2, 247, 329. The theme of social dissolution, which appears in both French antisemitism and Durkheim's sociology, pervaded nineteenth-century French social thought. Lukes, *Émile Durkheim*, 195–99.

17. Chabauty, *Les juifs*, 247–48. Lémann, *La prépondérance juive*, 62. Wilson, *Ideology and Experience*, 515. Sorlin, *"La Croix" et les Juifs*, 92; see also 164–67. Brustein, *Roots of Hate*, 60.

18. Lazare, *Antisemitism*, 182. Wilson notes in *Ideology and Experience* that Jews in fact "played very little part in the French Revolution; nor were Jews prominent in Republican, let alone revolutionary, politics in the later nineteenth century" (352–53). But see Birnbaum, *Jews of the Republic*, and Birnbaum, *Jewish Destinies* (45–63), on the rise of "state Jews" under the Third Republic.

19. Wilson, *Ideology and Experience*, 613, 615.

20. Drumont, *La fin d'un monde*, 37.

21. Drumont, *La France juive*, vol. 1, xii.

22. Brunetière, "Revue Littéraire," 693. Brunetière "did not see himself as an opponent of the French Revolution," but he equated Jews with modern individualism, which he saw as antithetical to a Catholic French soul. Jennings, "Anti-Semitic Discourse," 29. Brunetière accordingly praised Drumont's claims about the negative "influence of certain Jewish ideas, since the last hundred years or so, on the new orientation . . . of the modern mind" ("Revue Littéraire," 697).

23. Maurras, *Les vergers sur la mer*, 217–18.

24. Maurras quoted in Roudiez, *Maurras jusqu'à l'Action Française*, 304.

25. Brustein, *Roots of Hate*, 58–62, 117–30.

26. Wilson, *Ideology and Experience*, 560–61. "Not only did the equality of Jews challenge the special role that the Church had historically occupied in France; Jews also dissented from Catholic claims to a special role in education and in the definition of French culture more broadly." Hyman, *Jews of Modern France*, 96. Alfred Naquet's role in legalizing divorce, Léon Blum's questioning of traditional sexual mores, Paul Grunebaum-Ballin's support for separating church and state, and Camille Sée's involvement in educational reform made them prime targets of Catholic antisemitism. Brustein, *Roots of Hate*, 61–62.

27. Wilson, *Ideology and Experience*, 491–93. Cf. Brunetière, "Revue Littéraire," 697–98. Brustein argues in *Roots of Hate* (102–17, 338–41) that Jewish immigration from eastern Europe fueled racial antisemitism, but given the timing and sweeping nature of racial antisemitism, it is doubtful that its adherents had only immigrants in mind.

28. Noland, *Founding of the French Socialist Party*, 188–92. Judt, *Marxism and the French Left*, 95–99.

29. Noland, *Founding of the French Socialist Party*, 33. See also Silberner, "French Socialism and the Jewish Question," and Fournier, *Émile Durkheim: A Biography*, 209–10, 345–47.

30. Noland, *Founding of the French Socialist Party*, 40, 43, 187–202. Judt, *Marxism and the French Left*, 115–19. Wilson, *Ideology and Experience*, 330–31.

31. Vital, *People Apart*, 198; see also 199–205. See also Hyman, *Dreyfus to Vichy*, 10, 16–17.

32. Benbassa, *Jews of France*, 139. See also Szajkowski, "Jewish Saint-Simonians," 58.

33. Silberner, "French Socialism and the Jewish Question." Brustein, *Roots of Hate*, 82–85, 117, 191, 197–98. Brustein and Roberts, *Socialism of Fools*, 24–82.

34. H. Goldberg, "Jean Jaurès and the Jewish Question." Hyman, *Dreyfus to Vichy*, 17. Wilson, *Ideology and Experience*, 330–40. Hyman, *Jews of Modern France*, 98–99. Brustein, *Roots of Hate*, 84, 197–99. Syndicalist involvement in the Dreyfus Affair developed in a similar manner. Most French trade unions opposed involvement in the affair, and the CGT denounced "both Jesuit and Jewish speculators and exploiters" in 1898; when trade unions did back the Dreyfusard cause, their support generally came late. Wilson, *Ideology and Experience*, 74. The syndicalist Georges Sorel, initially a Dreyfusard but later an adherent of Action Française, published antisemitic views into the 1910s. Brustein, *Roots of Hate*, 62, 84.

35. Though reacting to modern capitalism, radical antisemites resorted to the language of 1789, much like the 1848 revolutionaries described by Marx: "Just when they seem engaged in revolutionising themselves and things, in creating something entirely new, precisely in such epochs of revolutionary crisis they anxiously conjure up the spirits of the past to their service and borrow from them names, battle slogans and costumes in order to present the new scene of world history in this time-honoured disguise and this borrowed language." Tucker, *Marx-Engels Reader*, 595.

36. Wilson, *Ideology and Experience*, 329; cf. 341.

37. Brustein, *Roots of Hate*, 84n112.

38. Hertzberg, *French Enlightenment and the Jews*; see 314–68 on Rewbell. Brustein, *Roots of Hate*, 77–85.

39. Vital, *People Apart*, 203–4.

40. Toussenel, *Les Juifs*, vol. 1, 256, 122.

41. Proudhon, *De la justice*, vol. 6, 277. Proudhon, *Résumé de la question sociale*, 36.

42. Silberner, "Charles Fourier on the Jewish Question." Silberner, "Proudhon's Judeophobia." Wilson, *Ideology and Experience*, 265.

43. Proudhon, *Césarisme et christianisme*, vol. 1, 139. See also Wilson, *Ideology and Experience*, 267–79.

44. Proudhon, "Si les traités de 1815," 423. Chirac, *Les rois de la république*.

45. The role of Jews well into the second half of the nineteenth century as creditors in Alsace and their prominence in banking, finance, and large-scale retailing fueled economic antisemitism. Hyman, *Jews of Modern France*, 95. Brustein, *Roots of Hate*, 189–205. However, "the role of Jewish bankers" was "greatly inflated by antisemitic opinion" (Hyman, *Jews of France*, 93). "Most Jews only secured a stable position in the low and middling ranks of the bourgeoisie

at the end of the [nineteenth] century" (Hyman, *Jews of France*, 62), and an immigrant Jewish working class grew between 1880 and 1914 (Hyman, *Dreyfus to Vichy*, 73–77).

46. Benbassa, *Jews of France*, 139.

47. Hertzberg, *French Enlightenment and the Jews*, 268–313. Hyman, *Jews of Modern France*, 32–33. Benbassa, *Jews of France*, 85.

48. Wilson, *Ideology and Experience*, 562–63. Brustein, *Roots of Hate*, 84.

49. Proudhon, *Carnets*, vol. 2, 23.

50. Hutton, *Cult of the Revolutionary Tradition*, 158–59; see also 47. Tridon, *Du molochisme juif*. Parisian Jews (particularly the wealthy elites among them) tended to be acculturated rather than religiously traditionalist. Proudhon and Tridon had provincial origins, so it is possible that provincial Jewish communities were the targets of their antireligious antisemitism. However, I have found no evidence that they had any personal experience with religious Jews, and they may have simply adopted stereotypes from other authors.

51. Fournier, *Marcel Mauss*, 14, 16.

52. Fournier, *Émile Durkheim: A Biography*, 645. The English translation includes the following sentence which is missing from the original French text: "The religious ceremony [for Émile Durkheim and Louise Julie Dreyfus] took place the next day [after the civil ceremony] in the great La Victoire synagogue, and the couple were blessed by Zadoc Kahn, the Chief Rabbi of Paris." Fournier, *Émile Durkheim: A Biography*, 93. Cf. Fournier, *Émile Durkheim*, 112.

53. Birnbaum, *Geography of Hope*, 90–91.

54. Coser, *Masters of Sociological Thought*, 162–63. Moore, "David Émile Durkheim," 288. Pickering, "Enigma of Durkheim's Jewishness," 15. Fournier, *Marcel Mauss*, 13.

55. Quotations are from Moore, "David Émile Durkheim," 288; and Pickering, "Enigma of Durkheim's Jewishness," 18. Cf. Birnbaum, *Geography of Hope*, 83–122.

56. Fournier, "Durkheim's Life and Context," 47.

57. Fournier, *Marcel Mauss*, 16. Birnbaum, "French Jewish Sociologists," 26–27. Birnbaum, *Geography of Hope*, 104–5, 121–22.

58. Quotation is from Birnbaum, *Geography of Hope*, 121. Pickering, "Enigma of Durkheim's Jewishness," 18.

59. Birnbaum, *Geography of Hope*, 95.

60. Fournier, "Durkheim's Life and Context," 47.

61. Birnbaum, *Geography of Hope*, 118. Fournier, *Émile Durkheim: A Biography*, 202.

62. Pickering, "Enigma of Durkheim's Jewishness," 17. Fournier, "Durkheim's Life and Context," 48. Hyman, *Dreyfus to Vichy*, 56–57.

63. Hyman, *Dreyfus to Vichy*, 127. Birnbaum, *Geography of Hope*, 118–20. Fournier, *Émile Durkheim: A Biography*, 687–91.

64. Hyman, *Dreyfus to Vichy*, 59. See also Fournier, *Émile Durkheim: A Biography*, 688.

65. Hyman, *Dreyfus to Vichy*, 128.

66. C. A. Goldberg, "Introduction."

67. Birnbaum, "French Jewish Sociologists," 24, 28.

68. Strenski, *Durkheim and the Jews*, 7, 113.

69. Hyman, *Dreyfus to Vichy*, 42–46; quotation is from 43.

70. Fournier, *Émile Durkheim: A Biography*, 688–89.

71. Pickering, "Enigma of Durkheim's Jewishness," 14; see also 19.

72. Birnbaum, *Geography of Hope*, 90–91. For instance: "Although a nonobservant Jew . . . [Marcel] Mauss never denied his place within Judaism"; he was "on the best of terms" (his

words) with the chief rabbi of Épinal, talked openly about his "rabbinical family," and in the 1930s served on the central committee of the Alliance Israélite Universelle (Fournier, *Marcel Mauss*, 16, 48 337). Isidore Lévy was a member of the Société des Études Juives (Strenski, *Durkheim and the Jews*, 95). Lucien Lévy-Bruhl was a "member of the Consistoire Central, the main Jewish religious assembly," and a regular participant in its meetings; he was a cousin by marriage to Alfred Dreyfus, for whom he testified at the latter's 1894 trial; and he was "in charge of the Comité d'Assistance aux Intellectuels Juifs" during World War II (Fournier, *Marcel Mauss*, 339; Birnbaum, "French Jewish Sociologists," 10). Robert Hertz sacrificed himself in World War I to defend the honor of French Jewry against antisemitic charges of self-interest and indifference (Strenski, *Durkheim and the Jews*, 50, 114).

73. Hyman, *Dreyfus to Vichy*, 8, 28; see also 30, 40–42.

74. Moore, "David Émile Durkheim," 290.

75. Wilson, *Ideology and Experience*, 171. Hyman, *Jews of Modern France*, 96. Brustein, *Roots of Hate*, 119. Brunetière reviewed Drumont in "Revue Littéraire." Durkheim criticized Brunetière in "Individualism and the Intellectuals" and *Textes*, vol. 2, 252–54.

76. Durkheim, "Lettres de Durkheim," 118. Durkheim, *Lettres à Marcel Mauss*, 495.

77. Lukes, *Émile Durkheim*, 514–17, 534–36. Fournier, *Émile Durkheim: A Biography*, 487–89, 655–57.

78. Lukes, *Émile Durkheim*, 354–60, 372–78.

79. Fournier, *Émile Durkheim*, 637. Fournier's remarks about Barrès, Maurras, Durkheim, and sociology appear in a section omitted from the English translation. For this reason I cite the original French version here. See also Lukes, *Émile Durkheim*, 375.

80. Wilson, *Ideology and Experience*, 611.

81. Maurras, *Les vergers sur la mer*, 113, 322–23.

82. Lukes, *Émile Durkheim*, 374–75; see also 354–60, 372–78.

83. Benbassa, *Jews of France*, 138.

84. Durkheim, *Rules of Sociological Method*, 108–18.

85. Durkheim, *Division of Labor*, 128, 134–35, 204–5.

86. Durkheim, *Division of Labor*, 129, 142, 106; on repressive law, see 24–29. When English translations of Durkheim's texts were available, I have cited them, altering the translations where necessary and indicating that I have done so.

87. Durkheim, *Division of Labor*, 49–50, 92–94. Durkheim may have been influenced by German philosopher Immanuel Kant's view of Judaism, which is discussed in chapter 3. However, Durkheim took a less negative view than Kant did. Durkheim rejected, for instance, assessments of Talmudic Judaism as desiccated and overly ritualistic. Strenski, *Durkheim and the Jews*, 82–115.

88. Durkheim, *Division of Labor*, 247, 249.

89. Birnbaum, *Geography of Hope*, 102.

90. Durkheim's *Suicide* characterized the army (in contrast to civilian society) in similar terms, which might be read as an implicit critique of French militarism. Elsewhere Durkheim argued that French militarism stanched demoralization and restored social solidarity (on the basis of a "truly superstitious cult to [France's] army"), but in a manner that was abnormal ("one cannot consider normal the manner in which war is still extolled, nor the fresh outbreak of militarism which we are currently witnessing"). Durkheim added that "there are other ideas, besides that one, in which all Frenchmen can be united, other ends to pursue jointly." Durkheim, *Textes*, vol. 3, 160–63. I am indebted to Jeff Weintraub for calling this similarity to my attention.

91. Durkheim, *Suicide*, 159–60.

92. Durkheim pointed out in a series of reviews published in *L'Année sociologique* from 1899 to 1907 that Jewish law and religious practices changed over time to fit new conditions of social life. Durkheim, *Emile Durkheim: Contributions to* L'Année Sociologique, 216–18, 244–46, 251–52, 269–71, 339–41. However, this awareness does not appear to inform his description of Jewish solidarity in *Suicide*.

93. Durkheim, *Suicide*, 162, 169.

94. Durkheim, "Individualism and the Intellectuals," 49.

95. Durkheim, *Socialism and Saint-Simon*, 215.

96. Durkheim, *Suicide*, 167–68. Nisbet noted in *Émile Durkheim* (18): "Far from hating tradition, convention, and the corporate unities in society, Durkheim repeatedly declared their necessity and lent the force of his entire scholarship to a demonstration that, without these elements of conservatism and integration, no society or social group is conceivable." But Durkheim's assessment of Jewish tradition, convention, and corporate unity seems more complicated than Nisbet suggests. Durkheim identified three possible relationships between rational reflection and Jewish solidarity: (1) rational reflection is superimposed upon Jewish solidarity without altering its archaic nature; (2) rational reflection replaces the "collective prejudices" of Jewish solidarity; or (3) Jewish solidarity is lost but not replaced. Durkheim described the third possibility in a posthumously published review in *L'Année sociologique* in which he traced a rising suicide rate among Jews to assimilation and urbanization: "To the degree that the Jewish population is further assimilated into the surrounding population, it loses its traditional virtues, without perhaps replacing them by others. It is a special case of a very general law. A social group that has a moral culture *sui generis* can hardly change without running the risk of becoming demoralized." Durkheim, *Emile Durkheim: Contributions to* L'Année Sociologique, 438. When Durkheim acknowledged changes in Jewish law and religious practices elsewhere, he did not equate them with demoralization. Here, however, he implies that Jewish culture can only be lost, not reconstructed in new and modern forms. Reconstruction would constitute a fourth possible relationship between rational reflection and Jewish solidarity that Durkheim never really explored. This possibility is discussed in chapter 4.

97. Durkheim, *Division of Labor*, 314. On the association of Jews with money and mobility, see Wilson, *Ideology and Experience*, 363–64, 408.

98. Durkheim, *Elementary Forms*, 213.

99. Durkheim, "Individualism and the Intellectuals," 50.

100. Durkheim, "Principles of 1789 and Sociology," 34–35. Cf. Alexis de Tocqueville: "[The French Revolution] created an atmosphere of missionary fervor and, indeed, assumed all the aspects of a religious revival—much to the consternation of contemporary observers. It would perhaps be truer to say that it developed into a species of religion, if a singularly imperfect one, since it was without a God, without a ritual or promise of future life. Nevertheless, this strange religion has, like Islam, overrun the whole world with its apostles, militants, and martyrs" (quoted in Nisbet, *Sociological Tradition*, 34–35).

101. Durkheim, *Elementary Forms*, 215, 430.

102. Durkheim, "Individualism and the Intellectuals," 50, 45, 53–56. Durkheim was careful to distinguish his conception of individualism as an essentially religious attitude from the utilitarianism or economic individualism that he criticized.

103. Durkheim, *Suicide*, 83.

104. Durkheim in C. A. Goldberg, "Introduction," 322. With this remark, Durkheim likely

had in mind the acculturation of French Jewry in the century that passed since their emancipation in 1790–91. Hyman, *Jews of Modern France*, 55–76.

105. Durkheim, *Division of Labor*, 246–68.

106. Durkheim, "Determination of the Moral Fact," 38. Cf. Bouglé, "Philosophie de l'antisémitisme." Bouglé was a prominent and influential member of the Durkheim group. He examined the idea of race upon which antisemitic thinking rested, questioned its scientific pretensions, stressed its incompatibility with the French conception of nationhood, and emphasized social over biological determinants of human behavior.

107. Lukes, *Émile Durkheim*, 245–53, 320–30. Fournier, *Émile Durkheim: A Biography*, 184–85, 209–14.

108. Lukes, *Émile Durkheim*, 347, 538n43, 542–46. Burns, *Dreyfus*, 328–31. Durkheim, *Lettres à Marcel Mauss*, 225. Fournier, *Émile Durkheim: A Biography*, 491–92. See also Fournier, *Émile Durkheim* (252, 271, 438), for remarks about Guesde that have been omitted from the English translation.

109. Durkheim, *Lettres à Marcel Mauss*, 78, 225, 286.

110. Lukes, *Émile Durkheim*, 327–28.

111. Lukes, *Émile Durkheim*, 350.

112. Lukes, *Émile Durkheim*, 247, including n11.

113. Lukes, *Émile Durkheim*, 317–19. Fournier, *Émile Durkheim: A Biography*, 184–85, 210.

114. Durkheim in Lukes, *Émile Durkheim*, 323–24; see also 320–30.

115. Durkheim, *Socialism and Saint-Simon*, 204.

116. Durkheim in Lukes, *Émile Durkheim*, 324. Of course, it is possible to advocate class warfare without equating the privileged classes with the Jews. The point here is not that radical antisemitism stemmed from the endorsement of class warfare, but that Durkheim opposed class warfare and radical antisemitism for similar reasons.

117. Birnbaum, "French Jewish Sociologists," 5. C. A. Goldberg, "Introduction." Durkheim mainly analyzed antisemitism in *fin de siècle* France and accordingly had in mind the scapegoating of native French Jews. Jewish immigration from eastern Europe fueled French antisemitism, but the challenge it presented "became apparent primarily after 1905" (Hyman, *Dreyfus to Vichy*, 64), after Durkheim formulated his analysis.

118. Durkheim, *Socialism and Saint-Simon*, 68–69. Lukes, *Émile Durkheim*, 545.

119. Durkheim, *Socialism and Saint-Simon*, 120.

120. Durkheim, *Socialism and Saint-Simon*, 122.

121. Durkheim, *Division of Labor*. Durkheim, *Professional Ethics and Civic Morals*. Durkheim, "Individualism and the Intellectuals."

122. Quotations are from Durkheim, "Individualism and the Intellectuals," 56. See also Lukes, *Émile Durkheim*, 326–27. The precept to which Durkheim refers has a Saint-Simonian origin: "Each man will be placed according to his capacity, and rewarded according to his work." Saint-Simon, *Selected Writings*, xxxv.

123. On the nation as an imagined community, see Anderson, *Imagined Communities*.

124. Szajkowski, "Jewish Saint-Simonians."

125. Benbassa, *Jews of France*, 120.

126. Moore, "David Émile Durkheim."

127. Bauman, "Exit Visas and Entry Tickets," 75.

128. Hyman, *Dreyfus to Vichy*, 6, 235.

129. Wilson, *Ideology and Experience*, 423.

130. On Protestants, see Durkheim, *Suicide*, 157–60.

131. Lehmann, *Durkheim and Women*, 4, 32–33.

132. Durkheim, *Suicide*, 213, 215. Durkheim used the same argument in 1906 to explain why women were less likely than men to commit crimes: "This is because the causes are social, and women, . . . by not participating as directly as men in the collective life, submit less to its influence and experience less of its various consequences." Durkheim, *Emile Durkheim: Contributions to* L'Année Sociologique, 409.

133. Lehmann, *Durkheim and Women*, 36. See also Durkheim, *Division of Labor*, 192, 194.

134. Lehmann, *Durkheim and Women*, 98–99.

135. Durkheim and Denis, *Qui a voulu la guerre?* Durkheim, *L'Allemagne au-dessus de tout.* Lukes, *Émile Durkheim*, 549–52, 557–58. Fournier, *Émile Durkheim: A Biography*, 665–66, 677–85, 703–7.

136. Durkheim, *Suicide*, 247. Durkheim, *Professional Ethics and Civic Morals*, 71–74.

137. Durkheim, *L'Allemagne au-dessus de tout*, 42, 44. Lukes, *Émile Durkheim*, 547–48, 552–54. Fournier, *Émile Durkheim: A Biography*, 667–68, 700–703, 708.

138. Durkheim, *Moral Education*, 121.

139. Birnbaum in *Geography of Hope* (113–14) suggests that Durkheim eventually substituted the religion of Australian aborigines for that of the Jews as the exemplar of primitiveness, which would make the Jew and the colonial subject functionally equivalent for Durkheim's thinking.

140. Kurasawa, "Durkheimian School and Colonialism," 200, 203. To be sure, Durkheim saw continuities between the premodern and the modern, especially in his later work, and in this sense the groups assigned to these categories were not entirely foreign to each other. However, this point should not be overstated. Acknowledgment of continuities did not mean that the premodern and modern were indistinguishable or that Durkheim abandoned his evolutionary assumptions. For instance, while Durkheim argued in *Elementary Forms* that elementary forms of religion gave birth to modern science, he also insisted that science is "a more perfected form of religious thought" which takes over its "cognitive and intellectual functions" with a "critical spirit that is unknown in religion" (431).

141. Kurasawa, "Durkheimian School and Colonialism," 191; see also 201, 204.

142. The notion of a French-Jewish symbiosis may have been implicitly directed against the views of antisemitic writers who drew explicit analogies between colonial subjects and Jews in order to justify discrimination against the latter. As noted in chapter 1, Maurras provided a notable example of such analogies in 1899.

143. Birnbaum, *Geography of Hope*, 99–113.

144. Nisbet, *Émile Durkheim*, 9.

145. Birnbaum, "French Jewish Sociologists." Strenski, *Durkheim and the Jews*; see especially 9, 84–85, 97, 100, 104, 113–14, 124–25, 127–29, 142. For an overview of the scholarship on Durkheim's relationship to Jews and Judaism, see Fournier, "Durkheim's Life and Context," 46–47. Studies that emphasize Durkheim's Jewish context include Birnbaum, "French Jewish Sociologists"; Pickering, "Enigma of Durkheim's Jewishness"; and Strenski, *Durkheim and the Jews.* Studies that emphasize his French context include Clark, "Émile Durkheim"; Clark, *Prophets and Patrons*; Heilbron, *French Sociology*, 59–123; Jones, "Other Durkheim"; Jones, *Durkheim's Social Realism*; and Vogt, "Political Connections."

146. Tucker, *Marx-Engels Reader*, 32.

147. Durkheim, *Elementary Forms*, 227.

Chapter Three

1. Naumann quoted in Muller, *Mind and the Market*, 229.

2. Nisbet, *Sociological Tradition*, 23–31. Landes, *Unbound Prometheus*, 1–39. Mayer, *Persistence of the Old Regime*, 49–53, 65–68, 71, 73–74. Muller, *Mind and the Market*, 231–33.

3. Ringer, *Decline of the German Mandarins*. Löwy, *Georg Lukács*, 15–67.

4. Ringer, *Decline of the German Mandarins*, 25–42. Mayer, *Persistence of the Old Regime*, 265–69.

5. Ringer, *Decline of the German Mandarins*, 6.

6. Quotations are from Ringer, *Decline of the German Mandarins*, 89, 117; see also 83–90. Elias, *Civilizing Process*, 3–34.

7. The antinomy between *Kultur* and *Zivilisation* is linked to the idea of a German *Sonderweg* (special path of historical development). Dating to the early nineteenth century, when the German path was contrasted to revolutionary and Napoleonic France, this idea has since structured much of the scholarship about modern German history. Before 1945 the German *Sonderweg* was usually endowed with a positive value, especially by German intellectuals. After the war, many historians turned the idea on its head, pointing to the aberration of the German path from English and French standards to explain the catastrophe of Nazism. "Thus the German *Sonderweg* was reinstated with all the moral signs reversed" (Blackbourn and Eley, *Peculiarities of German History*, 4). One version of this thesis holds that the roots of Nazi success lay in the peculiarities of German ideological development (Stern, *Politics of Cultural Despair*; G. L. Mosse, *Crisis of German Ideology*). Blackbourn summarizes it this way in "Discrete Charm of the Bourgeoisie" (211): "Germans of the educated class celebrated the peculiar virtues of their own culture by way of contrast to the mere civilizations of the superficial and degenerate French and the money-grubbing English. And the reaction against western modernity in its various forms has been viewed as culminating in the rejection of advanced industrial society from the last decades of the nineteenth century." For an important critique of the *Sonderweg* idea, see Blackbourn and Eley, *Peculiarities of German History*. Blackbourn argues in "Discrete Charm of the Bourgeoisie" (211–21) that the German educated class was characterized by ambivalence toward modernity rather than a blanket rejection of it. Löwy in *Georg Lukács* (49) similarly stressed the "profound ambivalence" of German romantic anticapitalism and insisted that it did not always or necessarily end in fascism.

8. Nirenberg, "Birth of the Pariah," 230n8. See also Lange, *Antisemitic Elements*; Muller, *Mind and the Market*, 234, 237–38, 253–55; Muller, *Capitalism and the Jews*, 33–61.

9. Ben-Sasson et al., "Germany," 527–29. Brenner, "Between Revolution and Legal Equality," 295–301. Gartner, *History of the Jews*, 218–28. Jacobs, "Statistics," 531. Jersch-Wenzel, "Population Shifts," 51, 55–59, 76–89. Pulzer, "Legal Equality and Public Life," 154–62. Richarz, "Demographic Developments," 7–13. Richarz, "Occupational Distribution," 35–37.

10. See Ringer, *Decline of the German Mandarins*, 143–62, on the historical school of economics. On Jewish engagement in commerce and moneylending, see Muller, *Mind and the Market*, 10–12; Muller, *Capitalism and the Jews*, 23–28. See also Baron et al., *Economic History of the Jews*; W. E. Mosse, *Jews in the German Economy*. On the interplay between the social perception and reality of the German-Jewish merchant, see Landes, "Jewish Merchant." See Penslar, *Shylock's Children*, on Jewish perceptions of their own economic activities and modern Jewish identity. For a discussion of Jews as social winners in the process of capitalist development, see Muller, *Capitalism and the Jews*, 72–132. Bodemann argues in "Ethnos, Race and Nation" and "Coldly Admiring the Jews" that with the exception of Sombart and some others, classical Ger-

man sociology dealt only minimally with the Jewish question and other ethnonational phenomena. I contend that sociological interest in Jews was far from cursory, but it was more likely to appear in discussions of capitalism than race or nationality.

11. Parsons, *Structure of Social Action*, 6–15, 41–42. Parsons, "Role of Theory."

12. On religious antagonism in Europe and the symbolic construction of Jews as threats, see Alexander, *Civil Sphere*, 8–9, 463–66; Nirenberg, "Birth of the Pariah"; Nirenberg, *Anti-Judaism*. Jews and Judaism were, of course, not the only reference point with which German social thinkers constructed their understanding of modernity and national identity. References to Jews occurred in the context of a struggle between Protestants and Catholics. Altgeld, "German Catholics." In this struggle, liberal Protestants worked to make Christianity more appealing to the educated middle class as part of a new German national identity "free of both Judaism and Catholicism." Pasto, "Islam's 'Strange Secret Sharer,'" 448. These linkages, though important, are beyond the scope of this chapter.

13. DiMaggio, "Culture and Cognition," 273–74. Cultural schemas include the "binary oppositions that make up a given society's fundamental tools of thought, but also the various conventions, recipes, scenarios, principles of action, and habits of speech and gesture built up with these fundamental tools"; they can be transposed to new situations; and they vary in depth, which is to say, the degree to which they are pervasive and unconscious (Sewell, "Theory of Structure," 7–8). As constraining frameworks, schemas make it possible to produce a range of practices that are neither completely predictable nor infinitely diverse. Cf. Bourdieu, *Logic of Practice*, 54–55. On schemas, see also Brubaker, Loveman, and Stamatov, "Ethnicity as Cognition," 41–44.

14. To say that Christian theological schemas formed part of the *doxa* of the German intellectual field (its taken-for-granted, widely shared, partly preconscious assumptions and organizing categories) does not imply that all German intellectuals described Jews in the same way. Because common dispositions and the shared *doxa* they establish are the product of similar socialization, intellectuals with atypical or aberrant educations would not fully share this *doxa*. Furthermore, even among the similarly educated, shared *doxa* does not preclude intellectual disputes. The *doxa* of a field includes "the major obligatory pairs of opposites which, paradoxically, unite those whom they divide, since agents have to share a common acceptance of them to be able to fight over them, or through them, and so to produce position-takings which are immediately recognized as pertinent and meaningful by the very agents whom they oppose and who are opposed to them." Bourdieu, *Pascalian Meditations*, 100–101. Judaism and Christianity formed one such pair of consecrated opposites for the German intellectual field. Last, *doxa* is not unbreakable; even "the most fundamental and most deeply buried oppositions" can be "subverted or destroyed" under certain conditions (Bourdieu, *Pascalian Meditations*, 101). Ultimately, the line that separates competing intellectual views, which can be explicitly questioned, from *doxa*, which is taken for granted, is itself one of the stakes of intellectual struggles.

15. Nirenberg, "Birth of the Pariah," 215–27. Nirenberg, *Anti-Judaism*, 59–60, 87–134, 246–68.

16. Marshall, "Christ and the Cultures." Vlach, *Church as a Replacement of Israel*.

17. To be clear, these cultural schemas were not peculiar to Protestantism but were part of Christianity more generally. I emphasize Protestantism because it was through this form of Christianity that the schemas were transmitted to Marx, Simmel, Sombart, and Weber.

18. Karl Marx's father converted to Protestantism circa 1819, Karl himself was baptized in 1824, and his mother accepted baptism in 1825 (Sperber, *Karl Marx*, 17, 23). Marx "learned liberal Protestant theology both in its original form," having "received a Protestant religious education"

at his *Gymnasium*, and "in its secularized Young Hegelian version" (Sperber, *Karl Marx*, 129; see also 29–31, 134; Birnbaum, *Geography of Hope*, 48–50). Some of Simmel's contemporaries described his thinking as Jewish, but later scholarship is rightly skeptical of such essentialism (Coser, "Georg Simmel's Style"; Salomon, "Georg Simmel Reconsidered"; Alexander, "Rethinking Strangeness," 98–102). Liebersohn in *Fate and Utopia* (152) notes that Simmel's "'subjective culture' was Protestant, and he and his family went to great lengths to win social recognition of this choice. Simmel was the baptized child of baptized parents; a liberal Protestant theologian, Hans von Soden, presided over his wedding to Gertrud Kinel, a Prussian Protestant. . . . Even though he had no use for religion as church or credo, he thoroughly shared the prejudices of other secularized *Kulturprotestanten*."

19. Ringer, *Decline of the German Mandarins*, 90–98. Löwy, *Georg Lukács*, 22n10. Sperber, *Karl Marx*, 61–63.

20. Tucker, *Marx-Engels Reader*, 53, 321.

21. Vital, *People Apart*, 66, 171–79. Gartner, *History of the Jews*, 121, 134–35. Wasserman, "Prussia," 655–56. Suppression of the 1848 revolutions forestalled Jewish emancipation, but civil equality for Jews was eventually legislated by the North German Confederation in 1869 and extended to the states united in the German Empire in 1871.

22. Hegel, *Introduction to the Philosophy of History*, 21.

23. Vital, *People Apart*, 192.

24. B. Bauer, *Jewish Problem*. Brustein and Roberts, *Socialism of Fools*, 92–96.

25. Tucker, *Marx-Engels Reader*, 44.

26. Avineri, "Marx and Jewish Emancipation." "I have just been visited by the chief of the Jewish community [in Cologne]," Marx wrote to the German political philosopher Arnold Ruge in March 1843, "who has asked me for a petition [on emancipation] for the Jews to the Provincial Assembly, and I am willing to do it. However much I dislike the Jewish faith, Bauer's view seems to me too abstract. The thing is to make as many breaches as possible in the Christian state and to smuggle in as much as we can of what is rational." Marx and Engels, *Collected Works*, vol. 1, 400.

27. Traverso, *Marxists and the Jewish Question*, 20. Wasserman, "Prussia," 656.

28. Tucker, *Marx-Engels Reader*, 52, emphasis added.

29. Tucker, *Marx-Engels Reader*, 48.

30. B. Bauer, *Jewish Problem*, 123.

31. Tucker, *Marx-Engels Reader*, 49–50.

32. Tucker, *Marx-Engels Reader*, 48–49. *Judentum*, the term used by Marx, "could mean Judaism (the religion), the Jews (as a group), or, like its English equivalent 'jewing,' a synonym for bargaining, fraught with negative connotations" (Muller, *Capitalism and the Jews*, 37). Marx's essay relied on two variants of the economic Jewish stereotype without clearly distinguishing them: "the financial-plutocrat model" and "the poor-huckster model" (Draper, "Marx and the Economic-Jew," 605; cf. Penslar, *Shylock's Children*, 11–49, on the Jew as master and pauper). Marx and Engels expected the assimilation of the Jews (ideally with political emancipation) into what they called the "historic nations," which in turn would provide a stepping stone to universal human emancipation in a world community (C. A. Goldberg, "Two Marxes," 421–22). The supersessionism of Marx's later work was thus already present *in nuce* in his early work, though there it stood in tension with his insistence that the Christians had become Jews. As shown below, he would resolve this tension by redefining the Jewish role in capitalist development. For a different interpretation, see Fine, "Rereading Marx"; he argues that Marx understood human emancipation not as emancipation from particularity but from "the dominance of abstractions

over individual lives" (154). My objections to this interpretation are first, the abstraction to which Marx refers is citizenship; second, it is not the dominance of this abstraction that bothers Marx but its separation from "the real, individual man," which makes the "abstract citizen" unreal; and last, the alienation for which citizenship provides only an illusory solution cannot be overcome except in a universalistic manner.

33. Marx and Engels, *Collected Works*, vol. 4, 87–90, 94–99, 106–18.

34. Marx and Engels, *Collected Works*, vol. 5, 3. I have slightly altered the translation of *schmutzig-jüdisch* here to express the plain meaning. According to Feuerbach's *Essence of Christianity* (112–19), the Jewish doctrine of creation implied a practical relation to nature that made it an object of egoistic use, in contrast to the theoretic relation of heathenism that made nature an object of reverential contemplation. While Hegel maintained that Jews could only take what they needed from nature through the mediation of its divine master, Feuerbach insisted that the Jewish God was the "personified selfishness of the Israelitish people" themselves. Marx rejected the privileging of theory over practice, but instead of giving Judaism's practical relation to nature a positive interpretation, he argued that practice need not take the "dirty-Jewish" form that Feuerbach described. On Feuerbach and Marx, see Carlebach, *Karl Marx and the Radical Critique*, 104–10; Arkush, "Judaism as Egoism"; Geller, *Other Jewish Question*, 150–211. The influence of Moses Hess on Marx's early views about Jews and capitalism remains subject to debate and is beyond the scope of this chapter. However, it is worth noting that both Hess and Marx were influenced via German idealist philosophy (and in Hess's case via the Bible scholar Friedrich Wilhelm Ghillany) by the same Protestant religious traditions.

35. Marx and Engels, *Collected Works*, vol. 5, 369; see also 180.

36. Marx and Engels, *Collected Works*, vol. 11, 44; vol. 12, 9; vol. 18, 64, 305.

37. Marx and Engels, *Collected Works*, vol. 4, 109–10, emphasis in the original.

38. Marx and Engels, *Collected Works*, vol. 11, 512, 522–23. On disqualification of Jews and the election of Rothschild, see Gartner, *History of the Jews*, 133, 160.

39. Tucker, *Marx-Engels Reader*, 432.

40. Marx, *Grundrisse*, 504.

41. Marx, *Grundrisse*, 487, 505. Marx and Engels, *Collected Works*, vol. 37, 329–30.

42. Marx and Engels, *Collected Works*, vol. 34, 118–19.

43. Marx, *Grundrisse*, 859. Marx and Engels, *Collected Works*, vol. 35, 174–75. Marx and Engels, *Collected Works*, vol. 37, 327–30.

44. Marx, *Grundrisse*, 233, 505–12, 856, 859. Marx and Engels, *Collected Works*, vol. 32, 464; vol. 37, 323, 325, 332–35, 588, 592–93.

45. Marx and Engels, *Collected Works*, vol. 32, 396–97, 464–65, 541; vol. 35, 165, 173; vol. 37, 328, 414, 592, 606–7. Marx also linked the "cult of money" to Protestantism in *Grundrisse* (232): "The cult of money has its asceticism, its self-denial, its self-sacrifice—economy and frugality, contempt for mundane, temporal and fleeting pleasures; the chase after the *eternal* treasure. Hence the connection between English Puritanism, or also Dutch Protestantism, and money-making." Although this passage emphasizes asceticism rather than hucksterism, it seems more consistent with Marx's earlier claim that "the Christians have become Jews" (Tucker, *Marx-Engels Reader*, 49) than with his later narrative of supersession. This may reflect the transitional nature of the *Grundrisse*, which Marx drafted in the late 1850s.

46. B. Bauer, *Jewish Problem*, 10. Marx, *Grundrisse*, 487, 858. Marx and Engels, *Collected Works*, vol. 35, 90; vol. 37, 328.

47. Marx and Engels, *Collected Works*, vol. 34, 119; cf. vol. 37, 593.

48. Marx, *Grundrisse*, 507–12, 858–59. Marx and Engels, *Collected Works*, vol. 35, 90; vol. 37,

325, 328, 330, 334, 589, 592, 605. Quotation about a new society taking shape is from Marx and Engels, *Collected Works*, vol. 6, 327–28.

49. Marx and Engels, *Collected Works*, vol. 37, 325, 328. Cf. Marx, *Grundrisse*, 858.

50. Marx and Engels, *Collected Works*, vol. 37, 334–35.

51. Marx and Engels, *Collected Works*, vol. 32, 465.

52. Marx and Engels, *Collected Works*, vol. 32, 541; vol. 37, 592.

53. Marx and Engels, *Collected Works*, vol. 32, 465; see also vol. 37, 594–95, 598. Here Marx identified the money system with Catholicism rather than Judaism. His 1844 manuscripts previously invoked the categories of Catholicism and Protestantism, comparing Adam Smith to Martin Luther (Marx and Engels, *Collected Works*, vol. 3, 290–91). Simmel later argued in *Philosophy of Money* (191) that money, no less than credit, depends on faith. Weber also stressed the importance of trust in economic transactions and linked it to Protestantism.

54. Marx and Engels, *Collected Works*, vol. 35, 165.

55. Romans 2:29. Cf. Deuteronomy 30:6.

56. Tucker, *Marx-Engels Reader*, 49, 52.

57. Engels eventually adopted this new view of the Jews and modern capitalism in his own writings. In a letter on antisemitism published in the *Arbeiter-Zeitung* in 1890, he suggested that the Christian nations were ruled by industry, not money, once capitalism was fully developed. Only in the economically backward regions of Europe, Engels wrote, "where capital is not yet strong enough to gain control of national production as a whole, so that its activities are mainly confined to the Stock Exchange . . . there, and there alone, is capital mainly Jewish" (Marx and Engels, *Collected Works*, vol. 27, 50–51). Here, as in Marx's writings in the late 1850s and 1860s, Jews appeared primarily as usurers and merchants who helped to bring the capitalist mode of production into existence only to be superseded within it later.

58. Weber, *Protestant Ethic*, 185n2. All references to Weber's *Protestant Ethic* are from the translation made by Talcott Parsons in 1930 unless otherwise indicated; the Parsons translation was based on the expanded German edition of 1920. Frisby, *Georg Simmel*, 93–94, 139–45. Poggi, *Money and the Modern Mind*, 57, 60. A slightly expanded version of *Philosophie des Geldes* was published in 1907; it is this second edition on which the English translation is based (Frisby, *Georg Simmel*, 93–94, 139–45; Poggi, *Money and the Modern Mind*, 57, 60). For useful secondary sources on Simmel, see Spykman, *Social Theory of Georg Simmel*; Frisby, *Georg Simmel*; Poggi, *Money and the Modern Mind*; Salomon, "Georg Simmel Reconsidered"; Muller, *Mind and the Market*, 242–52; Morris-Reich, "Three Paradigms"; Morris-Reich, "Assimilationist Antiracism"; Muller, *Capitalism and the Jews*, 46–53, 59–60. For a sociological challenge to Simmel's conception of money, see Zelizer, *Social Meaning of Money*. On social discrimination and organized antisemitism, see Pulzer, *Rise of Political Anti-Semitism*; Vital, *People Apart*, 248–77; Gartner, *History of the Jews*, 218–28; Brustein and Roberts, *Socialism of Fools*, 109–37. The prolonged worldwide economic depression from 1873 to 1896 and the westward migration of eastern European Jews after 1881 provided fertile ground for expressions of antisemitism.

59. Simmel, *Philosophy of Money*, 138; see also 85–107. Frisby, *Georg Simmel*, 97–102. Poggi, *Money and the Modern Mind*, 95–101, 134–36.

60. Poggi, *Money and the Modern Mind*, 136–48, 175–84.

61. Simmel, *Philosophy of Money*, 228, 226.

62. Simmel, *Philosophy of Money*, 157, 241, 315, 417, 464, 478, 479.

63. Simmel, *Philosophy of Money*, 233–35. Poggi, *Money and the Modern Mind*, 144. Muller, *Mind and the Market*, 251.

64. Simmel, *Philosophy of Money*, 162.

65. Simmel alluded to the impersonality of money when he wrote that his intellectual legacy would be distributed "like cash . . . among many heirs, each of whom puts his share to use in some trade that is compatible with *his* nature" but which could no longer be recognized as coming from Simmel's estate (quoted in Coser, "Introduction," 24; Frisby, *Georg Simmel*, 150). The impersonality of money is related to its mobility, which is to say, its capacity to transfer values rapidly and over long distances (Simmel, *Philosophy of Money*, 157, 380–83). The mobility of value, in turn, facilitates social mobility: insofar as money allows "every property" to be "transferred into a value," it eliminates traditional "limits to the ambition of outsiders" (Simmel, *Philosophy of Money*, 479). What was once a closed status monopoly is now thrown upon the open market, available to anyone—including the Jewish *parvenu*—with the cash to buy it (Arendt, *Origins of Totalitarianism*, 56–68).

66. Simmel, "Money in Modern Culture," 249. Cf. Simmel, *Philosophy of Money*, 279–80; see also 298–302, 481–83.

67. Simmel, "Money in Modern Culture," 252.

68. Simmel, "Psychology of Money," 233–35. Simmel, *Philosophy of Money*, 222–24, 390, 465–68. Poggi, *Money and the Modern Mind*, 190, 201–2. Muller, *Mind and the Market*, 244–45, 249–52.

69. Simmel, "Money in Modern Culture," 250–51. Cf. Simmel, *Philosophy of Money*, 245–50, 266.

70. Simmel, *Philosophy of Money*, 491.

71. The common starting point of Marx's and Simmel's accounts of alienation was the premise, drawn from German idealist philosophy, that consciousness does not just passively perceive the objective world but instead actively constructs its object. Marx, though reformulating this insight in materialist terms, retained the assumption that human beings objectified themselves in the products of their life activity: Human subjects were producers and hence "living labor," while the objects they created were "accumulated," "past," or "dead" labor. The accumulated or objectified labor of human subjects was normally expected "to widen, to enrich, to promote" their existence, a process of cultivation which, as Marx described it, sounded like and was probably inspired by the ideal of *Bildung* extolled by the German educated middle class from which he sprang. Tucker, *Marx-Engels Reader*, 485. For the influence of this ideal on the young Marx, see Sperber, *Karl Marx*, 31–32. For Marx, as for Simmel, alienation meant an inversion of this normal relationship between subject and object: living labor was instead degraded to a mere "means to increase accumulated labour," and in this way the object came to dominate the laboring subjects who produced it. For further comparison of Marx and Simmel, see Frisby, *Georg Simmel*, 145–48.

72. Simmel, "Concept and Tragedy of Culture," 66–67, 72. Cf. Weber, "Religious Rejections of the World," on diverging value spheres. Cf. Durkheim, *Elementary Forms* (426) on the autonomy of culture.

73. Quotation from Simmel, *Philosophy of Money*, 507. Simmel, *Philosophy of Money*, 492–502, 504–7. Simmel, "Concept and Tragedy of Culture," 68–75. Weingartner, "Theory and Tragedy of Culture." Ringer, *Decline of the German Mandarins*, 263–65. Simmel described a division of labor within consumption as well as production, and he subsumed under this heading the separation of the producer from the means of production, the specialization of production, and the specialization of products. While Simmel initially suggested in *Philosophy of Money* (237, 507–10) that money could equally facilitate the development of individuals or foster their domination by an objective world they created, he later seemed to embrace a more pessimistic view in "Concept and Tragedy of Culture."

74. Poggi, *Money and the Modern Mind*, 142.

75. Simmel, "Money in Modern Culture," 252.

76. Simmel, "Psychology of Money," 243. Simmel, "Money in Modern Culture," 252. Simmel, *Philosophy of Money*, 254–56.

77. Simmel, *Philosophy of Money*, 255.

78. Simmel, *Philosophy of Money*, 238–40. Cf. Simmel, "Psychology of Money," 241. "Aware of this overriding power of money, [British statesman Thomas] Macaulay defended the emancipation of the Jews on the grounds that it would be nonsense to withhold political rights from them, because money already gave them the substance of power. They could buy voters or control kings; as creditors they could dominate their debtors, so that political rights would be nothing but the formal acknowledgment of what they already possessed." Simmel, *Philosophy of Money*, 240. As the example of Macaulay demonstrates, Bruno Bauer's view that money made the Jews powerful was not peculiar to German thinkers.

79. Simmel, "Stranger," 143–44.

80. Simmel, *Philosophy of Money*, 241–44; see also 188.

81. Simmel, *Philosophy of Money*, 241, 244. Cf. Salomon, "Georg Simmel Reconsidered" (373): "There is a passage in *The Philosophy of Money* which recalls a statement by Marx in '*Zur Judenfrage*'—that the emancipation of the Jews means that all men have become Jews under and through the modern economic system." Because Simmel identified the Jews as merely one of several groups with an interest in money, this equation of the stranger with the Jews may appear overstated. However, insofar as the Jews constituted his example par excellence, and insofar as he traced this exemplary status to Judaism and not merely to a social position that Jews shared with others, it may at least be said that Simmel reinforced the cultural association of Jews with modern capitalism.

82. Simmel, "Money in Modern Culture," 244–47. Simmel, *Philosophy of Money*, 371–75. Muller, *Mind and the Market*, 246.

83. Simmel, *Philosophy of Money*, 305–83.

84. Simmel, *Philosophy of Money*, 318–27, 361–69. Quotation is from Simmel, "Money in Modern Culture," 246–48. Cf. Simmel, *Philosophy of Money*, 306–14. On Simmel's ambivalent attitude toward modernity, see Coser, "Introduction," 18–23; Poggi, *Money and the Modern Mind*, 52–54, 165, 167, 211–12. On the individuating and liberating consequences of money, see Levine, "Some Key Problems," 113–15; Frisby, *Georg Simmel*, 104–5; Poggi, *Money and the Modern Mind*, 62–68, 153–56, 179; Muller, *Mind and the Market*, 245–49; and Muller, *Capitalism and the Jews*, 48–50.

85. The *Kathedersozialisten* arose in the late 1860s and early 1870s to challenge the ahistorical and abstract character of classical liberal economics, but by the time Sombart studied under them, the erstwhile dissenters formed the academic orthodoxy of their disciplines in German universities and exerted an important influence on German politics. Repp, *Reformers, Critics*, 29–39. For useful secondary sources on Sombart, see Lebovics, *Social Conservatism and the Middle Classes*, 49–78; Ringer, *Decline of the German Mandarins*; Sharlin, "Werner Sombart"; Mitzman, *Sociology and Estrangement*, 133–264; Mendes-Flohr, "Werner Sombart's 'The Jews and Modern Capitalism'"; Herf, *Reactionary Modernism*, 130–51; Backhaus, *Werner Sombart*; Repp, *Reformers, Critics*, 148–214; Grundmann and Stehr, "Why Is Werner Sombart Not Part of the Core of Classical Sociology"; Stehr and Grundmann, "Introduction"; Muller, *Mind and the Market*, 253–57; Muller, *Capitalism and the Jews*, 56–61. For critical assessments of Sombart's arguments about the Jews, see Oelsner, "Place of the Jews"; W. Mosse, "Judaism, Jews and Capitalism"; Davis, "Religion and Capitalism."

86. There is no published English translation of *Der moderne Kapitalismus* in its entirety. Karl F. Geiser completed a translation of a later edition, but Princeton University Press rescinded an agreement to publish it because of expense. See Geiser's faculty file, RG 28/3, Oberlin College Archives, Oberlin, Ohio. For useful summaries, see Parsons, "'Capitalism' in Recent German Literature"; Nussbaum, *History of the Economic Institutions*; and Backhaus, "Sombart's Modern Capitalism." For a partial translation of a later edition, see Sombart, *Economic Life in the Modern Age*, 247–62.

87. Sombart, *Quintessence of Capitalism*, 22, 357–59.

88. Sombart, *Quintessence of Capitalism*, 213–15, 217, 283.

89. Sombart, *Quintessence of Capitalism*, 272–75, 356–57. Mendes-Flohr, "Werner Sombart's 'The Jews and Modern Capitalism,'" 92–93.

90. On the reception of Sombart's work by Jewish intellectuals, see Davis, "Religion and Capitalism," 58–60; Grundmann and Stehr, "Why Is Werner Sombart Not Part of the Core of Classical Sociology," 270–71; Loader, "Werner Sombart's *The Jews and Modern Capitalism*," 75–77; Stehr and Grundmann, "Introduction," xl; Hart, "Jews, Race, and Capitalism." French sociologist Maurice Halbwachs, writing in Durkheim's journal *L'Année sociologique*, argued that Jewish dispositions were variable products of the social and economic conditions in which Jews were placed and to which they adapted. Halbwachs, who came from a Catholic family but married a Jewish woman, later died in the Buchenwald concentration camp at the hands of the Nazis whom Sombart would come to support. Halbwachs, "Review of *Die Juden und das Wirtschaftsleben*." Paul Wander, who received a bachelor of philosophy degree from the University of Chicago in 1908 for his thesis on "The Americanization of the Russian Jew," criticized the book on similar grounds in the *American Journal of Sociology*. Wander, "Review of *Die Juden und das Wirtschaftsleben*." The American Jewish lawyer Max Kohler, writing in the flagship journal of the American Economic Association, pointed out that the history of Russia, which then contained more than half of the world's Jewish population, failed to confirm Sombart's ideas about the economic influence of the Jews. Kohler, "Review of *Die Juden und das Wirtschaftsleben*."

91. Sombart, *Jews and Modern Capitalism*, 21, 115.

92. Sombart, *Jews and Modern Capitalism*, 109–10. Hilferding, *Finance Capital*.

93. Sombart, *Jews and Modern Capitalism*, 120–27; quotation from 127.

94. Sombart, *Jews and Modern Capitalism*, 133–54.

95. Sombart, *Jews and Modern Capitalism*, 152–53. Sombart in *Quintessence of Capitalism* (272–75, 295) similarly described the development of modern capitalism as the triumph of Jewish over Christian influences. Conceding that it would be "too much to ascribe the characteristics of modern man in his economic life to the influence of Jewish ethics," he nevertheless affirmed "the vast importance [*entscheidend wichtige Rolle*] of the Jews in the story of modern capitalism."

96. Sombart, *Jews and Modern Capitalism*, 257.

97. Sombart's *Halbbürger* brings to mind Simmel's *Fremde*, although Sombart did not refer to Simmel's 1908 essay. Sombart pointed to similar circumstances in *Quintessence of Capitalism* (287, 292–307, 335–36), again emphasizing Jewish migration and the resulting status of Jews as strangers and semicitizens. By effecting a break with "old ways of life and all old social relationships," he argued, migration allowed the stranger to develop an attitude of instrumental rationality in his transactions with other people and things (304–6). Cf. Nussbaum, *History of the Economic Institutions*, 134, 138, 140–41.

98. Sombart, *Jews and Modern Capitalism*, 209, 223–24.

99. Sombart, *Jews and Modern Capitalism*, 225–26, 236–38, 292n482; quotation is from 238.

In the original German, Sombart's imagery is more violent (he refers to the breaking of all bones in the natural man's body) and more sweeping (he refers to the reversal of all life valuation, not merely economic values). Sombart, *Die Juden und das Wirtschaftsleben*, 281.

100. Sombart, *Jews and Modern Capitalism*, 175–77, 242–43.

101. Sombart, *Jews and Modern Capitalism*, 246. Sombart reaffirmed many of these claims about the Jewish religion in *Quintessence of Capitalism* (263–66). While that book treated Judaism as one of several philosophical and religious influences upon the capitalist spirit, and it acknowledged that Judaism shared some elements with medieval scholastic morality, it continued to lay a heavy emphasis upon the Jewish character of modern capitalism. "What is especially peculiar to Judaism," Sombart wrote, "is that it perfected and carried to their logical conclusions all those teachings that were beneficial to the capitalist spirit" (264). On Kant and Hegel, see Rotenstreich, *Recurring Pattern*; Rotenstreich, *Jews and German Philosophy*; Yovel, *Dark Riddle*; Mack, *German Idealism and the Jew*. Nietzsche also denounced a Jewish break with nature (Yovel, *Dark Riddle*, 154–60). Freud's first published reference to sublimation appeared in *Three Essays on the Theory of Sexuality* (22n2), originally published in German in 1905. On the contested interpretation and application of the Deuteronomic commandment on usury in European economic history, see Nelson, *Idea of Usury*.

102. Sombart, *Jews and Modern Capitalism*, 322.

103. Sombart, *Jews and Modern Capitalism*, 284–85, 329. Contrast Weber, *Economy and Society* (1202): "The Israelites were probably never a 'desert people' in the sense that . . . they were shaped by desert conditions, as Sombart believed." Weber described them as "a sworn confederacy of mountain tribes" that "defended its independence against the urban patriciate of the Canaanite and Philistine cities."

104. Sombart, *Jews and Modern Capitalism*, 258–68, 293–94, 339–42.

105. Sombart, *Jews and Modern Capitalism*, 334; see also 340.

106. Sombart, *Jews and Modern Capitalism*, 347–51.

107. Sombart, *Jews and Modern Capitalism*, 322. English economist Mordechai Epstein translates loosely here, but Sombart clearly emphasized the role of blood (*Blut*) in the formation of Jewish nature (*jüdische Wesen*). Cf. Sombart, *Die Juden und das Wirtschaftsleben*, 402. Sombart reaffirmed in *Quintessence of Capitalism* (263–66) that the supposed Jewish aptitude for capitalism stemmed from racial characteristics and not merely objective circumstances. The Jews, he wrote, were a trading people by blood (*die Juden sind ein händlervolk von Geblüt*). "Place a negro in a new environment," he added; "will he build railways and invent labour-saving machines? Hardly. There must be a certain fitness; it must be in the blood [*Blutsveranlagung*]." Sombart, *Quintessence of Capitalism*, 217, 307. Cf. Sombart, *Der Bourgeois*, 276, 397–98.

108. Sombart, *Jews and Modern Capitalism*, 323, 334–36.

109. Sombart, *Jews and Modern Capitalism*, 342–43.

110. Sombart, *Jews and Modern Capitalism*, 256, 394n506.

111. Sombart, *Why Is There No Socialism in the United States*, 4. Cf. Sombart, *Quintessence of Capitalism*, 151–52, 301–2.

112. Sombart, *Why Is There No Socialism in the United States*, 10–14, 27.

113. Sombart, *Quintessence of Capitalism*, 304.

114. Sombart, *Jews and Modern Capitalism*, 37–38, 44.

115. Sombart, *Jews and Modern Capitalism*, 249, emphasis in the original.

116. Sombart, *Quintessence of Capitalism*, 251, 255–56.

117. Lebovics, *Social Conservatism and the Middle Classes*, 62–63. Stehr and Grundmann, "Introduction," xxix. There is no English translation of *Händler und Helden*, but see Edgeworth,

"Economists on War," for a review. Ringer, *Decline of the German Mandarins*, 183–88. On the Occidentalist aspects of *Händler und Helden*, see Buruma and Margalit, *Occidentalism*, 52–54. Sombart continued to invoke the distinction between heroic and trading peoples after World War I in *New Social Philosophy* (71–72).

118. *Die Zukunft der Juden* does not primarily address the historical relationship of the Jews to modern capitalism but rather how to resolve the Jewish question. While Sombart advocated the migration of eastern European Jews to Palestine, he argued that the Jews in western Europe should remain there without assimilating and acquiesce to discrimination in the officer corps, academic appointments, and the civil service. There is no English translation of *Die Zukunft der Juden*, but see Clapham, "Review of *Die Zukunft*," and Goldenweiser, "Review of *Die Zukunft*." I am grateful to Anna Paretskaya for reading the Russian translation of the book and preparing a summary for me.

119. Sombart, *New Social Philosophy*, 178–79. I have modified Karl Geiser's translation, which is euphemistic and inaccurate here. Geiser, the political scientist who translated Sombart's *Deutscher Sozialismus*, was pressured to retire from Oberlin College in 1934 because of his support for Hitler. In 1938, a year after the translation was published, Hitler awarded Geiser the Order of the German Eagle, First Degree. See Geiser's faculty file, RG 28/3, Oberlin College Archives, Oberlin, Ohio. "I do not see the book as improving Sombart's own reputation," Horace Kallen wrote in a scathing review, "or doing anything better than adding just one more volume to the current debate between those who insist that human life is best when so organized that most are bond and few are free, and those who insist that it is best when all are free." Kallen, "Review of *A New Social Philosophy*."

120. Weber, *Protestant Ethic*, 17–19. All quotations from Weber's *Protestant Ethic* are from the Parsons translation, but in all instances I have compared them to the more recent translation by Stephen Kalberg. Both the Parsons and Kalberg translations of Weber's *Protestant Ethic* include Weber's introduction to the first volume of his *Collected Essays in the Sociology of Religion*. Weber's notion of adventurers' capitalism may have been inspired by Simmel's essay "The Adventure." The social type that Simmel called the adventurer stands in opposition to the calculating nature of modern times: he relies partly on luck and thus "considers that which is uncertain and incalculable" to be "the premises of his conduct, while others consider only the calculable" (227–28). Weber largely agreed in *Protestant Ethic* with Sombart that economic rationalism was "the salient feature of modern economic life as a whole" (75), but he added that one may "rationalize life from fundamentally different basic points of view and in very different directions" (78). Hence, "what is rational from one point of view may well be irrational from another" (26). Modern capitalism is highly rational in the sense that profit-making becomes more calculable, but from another point of view—as an iron cage in which one lives to work rather than works to live—it does not appear rational at all.

121. This threefold categorization follows Collins, "Weber's Last Theory of Capitalism"; Collins, *Max Weber*, 83–94; and Swedberg, *Max Weber and the Idea of Economic Sociology*, 17–20. My summary of economic and political preconditions relies on Weber, *Protestant Ethic*, 21–28; Weber, *Economy and Society*, 161–64; Weber, *General Economic History*, 275–78, 286, 312–14, 354. For biographical and historical perspectives on Weber, see Mitzman, *Iron Cage*; Marianne Weber, *Max Weber*; Mommsen, *Max Weber and German Politics*; Ringer, *Max Weber*; Radkau, *Max Weber*.

122. Weber, *Protestant Ethic*, 26–27. Weber, *General Economic History*, 313–14, 354.

123. Weber, *Protestant Ethic*, 26–27.

124. Weber, "Science as a Vocation," 139.

125. Weber, *General Economic History*, 355.

126. Weber, *General Economic History*, 322–23.

127. On the double economic ethic, see Weber, *Protestant Ethic*, 57–58; Weber, *General Economic History*, 356, 359–60. On the importance of trust for continuous and regular economic relations, see Weber, "Protestant Sects and the Spirit of Capitalism." Cf. Weber, *General Economic History* (366): "Acceptance into a sect was conditioned upon a strict inquiry into one's ethical conduct. Membership in a sect which did not recognize the Jewish distinction between internal and external moral codes guaranteed one's business honor and reliability and this in turn guaranteed success."

128. Weber, *General Economic History*, 364–66.

129. On Weber's *Ancient Judaism*, see Fahey, "Max Weber's *Ancient Judaism*"; Camic, "Weber and the Judaic Economic Ethic"; Schluchter, "Approach of Max Weber's Sociology of Religion." For critical assessments of Weber's views on the Jews, see Shmueli, "'Pariah People' and Its 'Charismatic Leadership'"; Eisenstadt, "Format of Jewish History"; Momigliano, "Note on Max Weber's Definition of Judaism"; Barbalet, *Max Weber, Passion and Profits*, 183–213. For comparisons of Weber to Simmel and Sombart, see Raphaël, "Les Juifs"; Raphaël, *Judaïsme et capitalisme*; Raphaël, "L'Étranger et le paria." Other useful sources on Weber and the Jews include Abraham, "Max Weber on 'Jewish Rationalism'"; Abraham, *Max Weber and the Jewish Question*; Roth, "Max Weber's Views on Jewish Integration"; Nirenberg, "Birth of the Pariah"; Nirenberg, *Anti-Judaism*, 423–59.

130. Weber, *Ancient Judaism*, 3–5, 219–25, 245, 254–55, 262–63, 311, 394, 400. Weber, *Protestant Ethic*, 105, 117, 222n19. Weber, *Economy and Society*, 618–19. Weber, *General Economic History*, 322, 360–64. The exile and concomitant demilitarization of the Jewish people was significant in Weber's view because they transformed Judaism from a military cult into a religion that "exalted inner, moral conditions." Collins, "Max Weber's Last Theory of Capitalism," 110.

131. Weber, *Ancient Judaism*, 4.

132. Weber, *General Economic History*, 360–61.

133. Weber, *Ancient Judaism*, 4–5.

134. Weber, *Ancient Judaism*, 50–51, 343–55. For Weber, as for Sombart, the Jewish double ethic was exemplified by Deuteronomy 23:21. Weber, *Protestant Ethic*, 271n58. Weber, *Economy and Society*, 498, 615. Weber, *General Economic History*, 267–68, 359–60. Weber, *Ancient Judaism*, 51, 64. Of course, religious prophecy created a new community without regard to clan membership; this was one reason that tribal divisions disappeared among the Jews, and in this respect Jewish prophecy anticipated Christian universalism. Weber, *Ancient Judaism*, 75–81. Weber, *General Economic History*, 45–46. Nevertheless, in Weber's view, universalism failed to develop fully within the confines of Judaism.

135. Weber, *General Economic History*, 322–23. Weber, *Economy and Society*, 622–23.

136. Weber, "Protestants Sects and the Spirit of Capitalism," 305. Weber, *General Economic History*, 366.

137. Weber, *General Economic History*, 271, 356. Weber notes in *Economy and Society* (1200): "Judaism must be formally classified as a church, since it is an institution into which a person is born, not an association of persons with specific religious qualifications." Presumably, in addition to its double ethic, the organization of Judaism as a church also thwarted the development within it of the kind of moral certification that characterized the Protestant sect, but Weber's emphasis was upon the double ethic.

138. Weber, *Protestant Ethic*, 271n58. Weber, *Economy and Society*, 617.

139. Weber, *General Economic History*, 196.

140. Weber, *Protestant Ethic*, 117.

141. Weber, *Economy and Society*, 620–21.

142. Weber, *Protestant Ethic*, 117, 120–21, 153. Weber, *General Economic History*, 365–66.

143. Weber, *Protestant Ethic*, 181.

144. Weber, *Economy and Society*, 497–98. There is one instance in which Weber seems to reconsider his claim that Judaism lacked the notion of a calling: "With the Puritans the Jews have in common the purposive legitimation of formally legal profit, which is considered a sign of Divine blessings, *and the idea of the calling*, although it does not have as strong a religious foundation as in Puritanism." Weber, *Economy and Society*, 1203–4, emphasis added. However, the claim that Jews and Puritans shared the idea of a calling was immediately qualified in this instance and contravened by statements that Weber made elsewhere.

145. Weber, *Ancient Judaism*, 254, 401, 403, 405. Weber, *Economy and Society*, 497–98, 611–12, 619–21, 1201–2.

146. Weber, *Protestant Ethic*, 120–21.

147. Weber, *Protestant Ethic*, 172, 176–79.

148. Weber, *Protestant Ethic*, 165–66.

149. Weber, *Economy and Society*, 1203; see also 612–14, 826–27, 1203–4.

150. Weber, *Ancient Judaism*, 3–5, 336–55, 417–18; Weber, *Economy and Society*, 492–500, 617–18. Weber, *General Economic History*, 196, 358–60. Weber defined a pariah people as "a distinctive hereditary social group lacking autonomous political organization and characterized by internal prohibitions against commensality and intermarriage originally founded upon magical, tabooistic, and ritual injunctions. Two additional traits of a pariah people are political and social disprivilege and a far-reaching distinctiveness in economic functioning." Weber, *Economy and Society*, 493. The Jews were distinguished from other guest peoples in medieval Europe by their inability to enter into *commercium* (legal contract under Roman law) or *conubium* (marriage) with Christians, and their inability to take part in communion excluded them from the *coniuratio* (sworn union) on which urban citizenship was based. Weber, *General Economic History*, 322, 358–59. On the external conditions that fostered pariah capitalism, see Weber, *Protestant Ethic*, 39; Weber, *Economy and Society*, 614.

151. Weber, *Economy and Society*, 1203; cf. 613–14.

152. Weber, *General Economic History*, 360.

153. Weber, *Protestant Ethic*, 166. The Puritans were Calvinists. Weber associated the Puritan roots of modern rational capitalism not with his own Lutheran Germany, but with Britain and the United States. Liebersohn, *Fate and Utopia*, 104. Roth, "Weber the Would-Be Englishman." On the contrast between Jewish pariah capitalism and Puritan rational capitalism, see also Weber, *Protestant Ethic*, 180, 186n.6, 271n58; Weber, *Economy and Society*, 615–23; Weber, *General Economic History*, 367. Weber suggested in *Protestant Ethic* that capitalist rationality eventually dissolves the religious roots that give rise to it; in this sense, one might say that Protestantism itself is superseded by a meaningless iron cage. However, this is to take Weber's supersessionism too literally; Christianity may be superseded, but modern economic rationalism endures.

154. Weber, *Protestant Ethic*, 166. Weber, *Economy and Society*, 623, 1204.

155. Weber, *Economy and Society*, 492–500. Weber suggested that "Puritan nations, especially the Americans," welcomed and completely absorbed those Jews "who had abandoned orthodoxy," in contrast to Germany, "where the Jews remain—even after long generations—'assimilated Jews.'" The "absorption of Jewish proselytes," he noted, "was not accomplished by nations with other than Puritan orientations." He attributed this difference to the "inner similarity" or "kinship" that Puritanism felt to Judaism, on the one hand, and the Christian

breakthrough against the "Jewish taboos and messianic promises" that set Jews apart as a pariah people, on the other hand. Weber, *Economy and Society*, 622–23. For Weber's views on Jewish assimilation and Zionism, see Roth, "Max Weber's Views on Jewish Integration." Nirenberg also notes in "Birth of the Pariah" (204) and in *Anti-Judaism* (574n26) the supersessionist character of Weber's argument. However, insofar as supersession entails the absorption of Jewish elements, Nirenberg errs in claiming that Weber sought to "quarantine" the spirit of capitalism from Jewish influence ("Birth of the Pariah," 205; *Anti-Judaism*, 443–44). Another reason to think that Weber did not intend to quarantine the spirit of capitalism entirely from Jewish influence is his assertion that "politically oriented adventurers' capitalism" and "rational bourgeois capitalism" do not differ in "absolute terms" but rather "shade off into each other" (Weber, *Protestant Ethic*, 186n6). See Wax, "Ancient Judaism and the Protestant Ethic," on developments in ancient Judaism that were precursive to the Protestant ethic and rational bourgeois capitalism.

156. Tucker, *Marx-Engels Reader*, 49.

157. Cf. Geller, *Other Jewish Question* (169–211); he shows "how several key signifiers associated with *Judentum* [continue to] play out in [Marx's] writings during his lifetime" (172), even where explicit references to *Judentum* are absent.

158. Camic and Gross, "New Sociology of Ideas."

159. Coser, "Georg Simmel's Style."

160. Epstein, "Teaching of Economics in Germany," 433–34.

161. For descriptions of Sombart as a reactionary modernist or antimodernist, see Herf, *Reactionary Modernism*, 130–51. Mendes-Flohr, "Werner Sombart's 'The Jews and Modern Capitalism.'" Grundmann and Stehr, "Why Is Werner Sombart Not Part of the Core of Classical Sociology." Stehr and Grundmann, "Introduction."

162. Ringer, *Decline of the German Mandarins*, 135–39, 224.

163. Mommsen, *Max Weber and German Politics*. Abraham, "Max Weber on 'Jewish Rationalism.'" Abraham, *Max Weber and the Jewish Question*. Quotation is from Derks, "Nomads, Jews, and Pariahs," 43.

164. Some commentators have underscored the antisemitic aspects of Marx's writings: Bloom, "Karl Marx and the Jews." Silberner, "Was Marx an Anti-Semite?" Carlebach, *Karl Marx and the Radical Critique*, 344–58. Gilman, "Karl Marx and the Secret Language of Jews." Birnbaum, *Geography of Hope*, 36–82. Others have denied or minimized antisemitism in Marx's work: Avineri, "Marx and Jewish Emancipation." Draper, "Marx and the Economic-Jew," 591–608. Peled, "From Theology to Sociology." Fine, "Rereading Marx." Similarly, Sombart has been described as an antisemite and Nazi sympathizer: Harris, "Sombart and German (National) Socialism." Mitzman, *Sociology and Estrangement*, 340. Mendes-Flohr, "Werner Sombart's 'The Jews and Modern Capitalism.'" Herf, *Reactionary Modernism*. However, others have qualified or downplayed his hostility to Jews and his relationship to Nazism: Brocke, "Werner Sombart," 76–82. Ludwig, "Sombart and the Jews." Rieß, "Werner Sombart under National Socialism." Loader, "Werner Sombart's *The Jews and Modern Capitalism*."

165. Fischer, *Socialist Response to Antisemitism*, xii–xiii. On stereotypes, see Brubaker, Loveman, and Stamatov, "Ethnicity as Cognition," 38–40. As they point out, "stereotypes are no longer defined in terms of cognitive deficiencies—in terms of false or exaggerated or unwarranted belief—but more neutrally as cognitive structures that contain knowledge, beliefs, and expectations about social groups. Nor are stereotypes seen as the distinctive and pathological propensity of particular kinds of personalities . . . but rather as rooted in normal and ubiquitous cognitive processes. . . . Because they are not the products of individual pathology but of cogni-

tive regularities and shared culture, stereotypes . . . are not individual attitudinal predilections, but deeply embedded, shared mental representations of social objects" (38–40).

166. Arendt, *Origins of Totalitarianism*, 3–120. Draper, "Marx and the Economic-Jew," 597–600. Peled, "From Theology to Sociology." For criticism of this approach, see Fischer, *Socialist Response to Antisemitism*, 6–12, and Nirenberg, *Anti-Judaism*, 462–64.

167. For psychological interpretations of Marx, see Blanchard, "Karl Marx and the Jewish Question"; Gilman, "Karl Marx and the Secret Language of Jews." For psychological interpretations of Sombart and Weber, see Mitzman, *Iron Cage*; Mitzman, *Sociology and Estrangement*; Radkau, *Max Weber*. Past scholarship has emphasized the philosophical influences of German idealism and (on Sombart and Weber) Marx and Nietzsche.

168. This chapter extends Durkheim's thesis in *Elementary Forms* about the religious origin of mental categories to modern European social thought. Herberg compared Judeo-Christian religion and Marxian socialism in "Christian Mythology of Socialism," but in contrast I do not treat Judaism and Christianity as elements of a unified religious heritage. Carlebach suggested in *Karl Marx and the Radical Critique* that Marx "transmitted many of Luther's ideas on the Jewish religion in secular form" (352), but he mainly emphasized German idealism as the source of Marx's images of Jews and Judaism, and he confined his study to Marx's early work. Carlebach also compared Marx, Weber, and Sombart (214–34), but aside from a passing reference to Sombart's transformation of "traditional religious and political polemic into respectable pseudo-scientific theses" (233), he said nothing about the influence of Christian theology on Weber and Sombart. Swatos and Kivisto emphasized in "Max Weber as 'Christian Sociologist'" the importance of Protestant Christianity for Weber's life and work, and Liebersohn showed in *Fate and Utopia* how Protestantism informed the utopian elements in the thinking of Simmel and Weber, but they said nothing about how Protestantism informed their views of the relationship between Jews and modern capitalism. Boer's *Criticism of Earth* related the engagement of Marx and Engels with biblical criticism and theology to features of their historical context, but aside from a discussion of Marx's essay "On the Jewish Question" (86–95)—which Boer rightly says turns "Christian supersession of Judaism . . . on its head" (93)—he had little to say about their views of Jews or Judaism, and later German sociologists fall entirely outside the scope of his study. Nirenberg's discussion of Marx in *Anti-Judaism* is limited to "On the Jewish Question" and *The Holy Family* on the grounds that "similar views are reflected in his mature published and unpublished work" (573n17). In contrast, I argue that Marx's views changed significantly; my analysis extends to Simmel, whom Nirenberg does not discuss; and I make a sharper distinction than Nirenberg between the discourses of judaization and supersession.

169. Cf. Bourdieu, *Logic of Practice* (56): "The *habitus*—embodied history, internalized as a second nature and so forgotten as history—is the active presence of the whole past of which it is the product."

Chapter Four

1. For a wider discussion of how American social scientists dealt with the Jewish question in the first two-thirds of the twentieth century, see King, "Rise of Sociology." This chapter challenges his conclusion that American sociology exhibited little concern with Jews before World War II.

2. Quotation from D. Smith, *Chicago School*, 5. The pragmatist influence is well documented: Rucker, *Chicago Pragmatists*, 132–57. Carey, *Sociology and Public Affairs*, 163–67. Rock,

Making of Symbolic Interactionism, 59–101. Lewis and Smith, *American Sociology and Pragmatism*. Joas, *Pragmatism and Social Theory*, 14–51. Levine, *Visions*, 251–68. Plummer, *Chicago School*, vol. 2, 113–96.

3. Matthews, *Quest for an American Sociology*, 89. Faris, *Chicago Sociology*, x, xiii. Persons, *Ethnic Studies at Chicago*, 33, 131, 146. Abbott, *Department & Discipline*, 4–33, 80–192. Rucker, *Chicago Pragmatists*, 133. Morris in *Scholar Denied* challenges the claim that the Chicago school was the first school of American scientific or empirical sociology, and I make no such assertion here. Nevertheless, as Morris acknowledges (111–12, 184–85), the Chicago school played a central, prestigious, and dominant role in the history of American sociology. The rise of the first Chicago school coincided with the professionalization of American sociology as an academic discipline and its separation from social work and social reform. Deegan, *Jane Addams and the Men*.

4. Faris, *Chicago Sociology*, x. Matthews, *Quest for an American Sociology*, 179, 182–83. Abbott, *Department & Discipline*, 9–10.

5. Abbott and Egloff, "Polish Peasant," 220.

6. Janowitz, "Introduction," viii, lii–lviii. Persons, *Ethnic Studies at Chicago*, 33, 44–45.

7. Quotation from Gartner, *History of the Jews*, 217; see also 201–12, 217, 258–66, 276–80, 322–33. Atkin et al., "United States of America."

8. Morris in *Scholar Denied* (112–18) argues that two main theoretical principles guided Park and the Chicago school: social Darwinism and a conception of sociology as an objective and nomothetic science. According to Morris, these principles, reinforced by Booker T. Washington's influence on Park, led Park to conceive races mainly in biological and essentialist terms, to take for granted the existence of a racial hierarchy, and to assume black inferiority; in addition, they encouraged the Chicago school to downplay human agency in the maintenance of racial inequality (100–48). Morris concludes that Park "clearly imported racist views into his science" (222). Morris and I interpret Park differently. In contrast to Morris, I emphasize the influence of pragmatism on Park and the Chicago school, I stress the nonessentialist and democratic elements in Park's thinking, and I underscore how Park and his students viewed marginal men as potentially efficacious agents of social change. Admittedly, Park's thinking was not entirely consistent and changed over time. Readers will have to assess my interpretation of Park for themselves on the basis of the textual evidence I provide in this chapter.

9. Park, "Culture and Cultural Trends." Park, "Problem of Cultural Differences," 12–13. Park, "Culture and Civilization," 16. Matthews, *Quest for an American Sociology*, 132–33. Persons, *Ethnic Studies at Chicago*, 34–36, 88.

10. Cooley, *Social Organization*.

11. Wirth, "Urbanism as a Way of Life." Persons, *Ethnic Studies at Chicago*, 36–37.

12. Matthews, *Quest for an American Sociology*, 104; see also 112. I do not mean to suggest that the Chicago sociologists embraced a simplistic notion of unilinear evolution; they presumed that at least some premodern categories would persist even in modern societies. Thomas defined primary groups as "those societies which through kinship, isolation, voluntary adhesion to certain systems of definitions, secure an emotional unanimity among their members." Thomas, "Analytical Types," 168. Although the primary group was "found in all societies," he believed that social evolution produced new forms of social organization "based upon rational co-operation." Thomas and Znaniecki, *Polish Peasant*, 1117–18. Cf. Park and Miller, *Old World Traits*, 41–42.

13. Quotation from Persons, *Ethnic Studies at Chicago*, 34. Park, "Problem of Cultural Differences," 10–13.

14. Quotations from Park, "Human Migration," 885, 887–88. Matthews, *Quest for an American Sociology*, 144. Thomas and Znaniecki in *Polish Peasant* had similarly argued before Park that the contact and collision of cultures resulted in social disorganization (see, e.g., 1120–21, 1139, 1173, 1304). Stonequist characterized the effects of migration in similar terms in *Marginal Man* (218).

15. Park in Stonequist, *Marginal Man*, xvii–xviii.

16. Quotations from Park, "Human Migration," 890. See also: Park and Burgess, *Introduction to the Science*, 867. Persons, *Ethnic Studies at Chicago*, 89. The Chicago school's signature concepts of social organization and disorganization derived from Cooley, *Social Organization*. They were elaborated in modified form by Thomas and Znaniecki in *Polish Peasant* and subsequently used to interpret a variety of phenomena in the 1920s and 1930s. Faris, *Chicago Sociology*, 87. Matthews, *Quest for an American Sociology*, 100. "The rules of behavior, and the actions viewed as conforming or not conforming with these rules, constitute . . . *social institutions*, and the totality of institutions found in a concrete social group constitutes the *social organization* of this group." Thomas and Znaniecki, *Polish Peasant*, 32–33. Conversely, *social disorganization* refers to a "decrease of the influence of existing social rules of behavior upon individual members of the group. . . . It is not . . . the preservation or dissolution of any particular rule of behavior which is indicative of the status of a given community, but the question whether there are common rules and how well they are observed." Thomas and Znaniecki, *Polish Peasant*, 1128, 1171.

17. Simmel, "Stranger." Thomas, "Analytical Types," on the creative man. Veblen, "Intellectual Pre-Eminence." Park, "Human Migration." "The individual, who participates in a number of social circles and stands at their intersection, feels their contradictory pulls within himself." Simmel, quoted in Muller, *Mind and the Market*, 248. Simmel discusses intersecting social circles in "Web of Group Affiliations." Park and Miller, *Old World Traits* (143–44), and Park, *Immigrant Press* (43–44), suggested the basic idea of the marginal man, though without using the name; the latter text credits William James as a source of inspiration for the idea. The concept anticipated later discussions of hybridity in Bhabha, *Location of Culture*; Gilroy, *Black Atlantic*; Hall, "Cultural Identity and Diaspora"; Hall, "When Was 'the Post-Colonial'?"

18. Park, "Human Migration," 892.

19. Park in Stonequist, *Marginal Man*, xiv–xv, xviii.

20. Park, "Human Migration," 892.

21. Stonequist, *Marginal Man*, 4–5.

22. Green, "Re-Examination of the Marginal Man," 167. Golovensky, "Marginal Man Concept," 333.

23. Simmel, "Stranger," 144. Although Park equated the stranger and the marginal man, Levine et al. argue in "Simmel's Influence" (829–35) that Park in fact altered Simmel's original concept; they add that Stonequist did not see the stranger and the marginal man as identical, but other sociologists continued to confuse them. Cf. Levine, "Simmel at a Distance." What matters for my argument is not whether Park and others understood Simmel's concept of the stranger correctly; what matters is that they continued to invoke Jews to elucidate the concept even as they put it to work for new purposes in different circumstances (transforming it in the process).

24. Park, "Human Migration," 891–92. Park's interest in the Jews dates at least as far back as his trip to Europe in 1910–11. The two notebooks he wrote during this trip record his observations about Jewish life in Poland and Russia. His decision to hire a Jewish guide in Kraków and his remark that "the Cracow Jew is the most interesting and enigmatical figure we have yet met" indicate his curiosity about them. Some of his observations anticipate the way that he later described the Jews in published works. Robert Ezra Park Collection, Box 16, Folder 4. Park

and Burgess cited the Russian-born Jewish-American anthropologist Maurice Fishberg to support their claim about the social isolation of the Jews; their thesis that the breakdown of social isolation transformed Jews (and others) dovetailed with Fishberg's view, similar to that of his German-born Jewish-American colleague Franz Boas, that environment, not biology, defined Jews. Fishberg concluded that in the absence of racial differences, Jews would ultimately assimilate completely through intermarriage. Wirth's *Ghetto* (65, 70–73) also drew upon Fishberg's research.

25. Park and Burgess, *Introduction to the Science*, 271; quotations from 230. Cf. Park, *Immigrant Press*, 105. One hears echoes here of Max Weber's pariah-people thesis and what Karl Marx called "the idiocy of rural life" (Tucker, *Marx-Engels Reader*, 477).

26. Sombart, *Quintessence of Capitalism*, 292–307. Park and Burgess, *Introduction to the Science*, 317–22. The second migration noted by Sombart was the movement of Protestants fleeing religious persecution, and the third was European colonization, especially of America.

27. Thomas and Znaniecki, *Polish Peasant*, 130, 133, 156, 1200. Thomas and Znaniecki repeatedly stressed that Polish peasants learned economic individualism from contact with Jews and other outsiders (184–86, 292, 1203–4). On the peasant's contemptuous association of money making with Jews, see 292, 448n1, 501n1. Thomas and Znaniecki also attributed another form of disorganization to Jewish influence: crime and deviance. "The Jewish shopkeeper in a peasant village is usually also a liquor-dealer without license, a banker lending money at usury, often also a receiver of stolen goods and (near the border) a contrabandist. . . . We have seen in the documents [excerpts from Polish newspapers published between 1892 and 1913] the methods by which the shopkeeper teaches the peasant boy smoking, drinking, and finally stealing" (1200–1201; see also 1241–43 for a Polish priest's portrayal of Jews as moral and sexual corrupters of the peasant). This view dovetailed with the traditional prejudices of the Polish noble and gentry classes, who found it useful to blame Jews for the poverty and drunkenness of their own peasants (Vital, *People Apart*, 88, 90). "That Jews were no more than *lessors* of the nobility's established monopoly of the right to distill alcohol and trade in it and that there was no reason to suppose that if the Jews were eliminated from the chain others would not take their place were aspects of the problem that were, as usual, ignored" (Vital, *People Apart*, 95). The traditional prejudices of the Polish nobility probably found their way into *The Polish Peasant* via Znaniecki, who was born into a noble family. It should be noted that Jews were not only a disorganizing influence for Thomas and Znaniecki; they also competed with the peasant cooperative institutions that Thomas and Znaniecki saw as the basis for the social reorganization and reconstruction of peasant life in Poland. On Jewish competition with peasant cooperative institutions, see 369, 428, 1216–17, 1409–10. On cooperative institutions as a basis for social reorganization and reconstruction, see 1174, 1400–1402, 1423–24, 1431, 1442, 1826–27. See Abbott and Egloff, "Polish Peasant," regarding the book's influence on early American sociology.

28. Park and Miller, *Old World Traits*, 145.

29. Wirth, *Ghetto*, 36, 75–78, 83.

30. Park, "Problem of Cultural Differences," 13.

31. Park, *Immigrant Press*, 94–95.

32. Park, "Human Migration," 892.

33. Park, "Behind Our Masks," 247–48. Park, "Race Relations and Certain Frontiers," 132, 137. Park, "Etiquette of Race Relations in the South," 186. Park, "Race Relations Cycle in Hawaii," 189.

34. Quotations from Wirth, *Ghetto*, 279, 73, 265; see also 78, 110, 280–81, 289–90. Wirth already anticipated this view in his master's thesis, "Culture Conflicts in the Immigrant Family,"

which described the Jewish immigrant family as a site of culture conflicts between parents and children (18, 20–21, 26–27, 125–26). "The immigrant may continue to live for the rest of his life in a social world which is more akin to the Old World than it is a product of the new. This is made possible by the circumstance that in our large cities the immigrants live in colonies of their own which are more or less isolated from the American cultural influences. With the second generation, however, it is quite different. The child often lives in a dual world—that of his parents and that of his playmates and schoolchums. Not only are the sanctions of each of these groups less absolute and compelling for him than for individuals living in only one of these social worlds, but there is room for confusion and finally of conflict." Wirth, "Culture Conflicts in the Immigrant Family," 126. In his doctoral dissertation, "The Ghetto: A Study in Isolation," Wirth wrote that the Jew "stands on the map of two worlds, not at home in either. His self is divided between the world that he has deserted, and the world that will have none of him" (289). He added that "the 'Jewish problem' is a problem of divided consciousness that is experienced by the partly assimilated Jews on the frontier of the Gentile world, not by the inhabitants of the ghetto itself" (306). Wirth has often been described as an assimilationist who expected Jews to disappear into American society. Etzioni, "Ghetto." Sklare, "Sociology of Contemporary Jewish Studies," 13–15, 18–19. Porter, "Jewish Presence in Sociology," 74–79. Diner, "Introduction." Berman, *Speaking of Jews*, 40–43, 45, 51–52. However, Birnbaum in *Geography of Hope* (152–58) rightly notes Wirth's ambivalence about assimilation and his uncertainty about the disappearance of the ghetto. On the one hand, in the 1940s, Wirth continued to stress the vacillation of Jews between assimilation and cultural pluralism, he insisted that pluralism was compatible with the need for consensus in democratic societies, he noted that Jewish education as an important factor of Jewish cohesion was changing rather than disappearing in America, and he expressed his own commitment to pluralism through his involvement in Jewish organizations and his exhortation to his children to "stand up and be counted whenever there were questions that we were Jews." The quotation is from Wirth's daughter (Salerno, *Louis Wirth*, 13; see also 29). Wirth, "Education for Survival." Wirth, "Problem of Minority Groups," 259, 269. Wirth, "Consensus and Mass Communication," 34, 40. Diner, "Introduction," xxxiv, xxxix–xl. On the other hand, in "Problem of Minority Groups," Wirth described pluralism as a "way station" to assimilation, which he understood as the formation of a "new culture" from the blending of "cultural elements derived from all the ethnic groups constituting the American people" (256–60, 263).

35. Stonequist, "Problem of the Marginal Man," 9. Miller, "Social Contribution," 349. See also Stonequist, "Marginal Man: A Study in the Subjective Aspects," 67–69, 85–94, 112–17. Stonequist, "Marginal Character of the Jews." Stonequist, "Marginal Man: A Study in Personality," 334.

36. Quotation from Hughes, "Social Change and Status Protest," 59. See also Hughes, "Dilemmas and Contradictions of Status." When discussing Jews in America, Thomas, Park, and their students were mainly concerned with the recent immigrants from eastern Europe and their children. However, they recognized that in neither Europe nor America was the Jewish population monolithic. Thomas wrote about the prejudices that Jews sometimes held against other Jews on the basis of differences in national origins, and Park and Wirth distinguished the Sephardic, German, and eastern European waves of Jewish immigrants. Bressler, "Jewish Behavior Patterns," 184, 221. Park, *Immigrant Press*, 294. Wirth, *Ghetto*, 131–51.

37. Heinze, *Jews and the American Soul*, 29–36; quotation from 36.

38. Berman, *Speaking of Jews.*

39. M. M. Goldberg, "Qualification of the Marginal Man." Green, "Re-Examination of the Marginal Man." Golovensky, "Marginal Man Concept." Persons, *Ethnic Studies at Chicago*, 110n24.

40. Greifer, "Attitudes to the Stranger." Riesman, "Some Observations." Riesman, "Marginality, Conformity, and Insight."

41. Golovensky, "Marginal Man Concept," 334.

42. Raushenbush, *Robert E. Park*, 75. Morris, *Scholar Denied*, 145–47.

43. Du Bois, *Souls of Black Folk*, 3.

44. Park, "Negro Race Consciousness," 291–92. Before beginning his career in sociology, Park had worked as Washington's secretary, a position that was initially offered to and declined by Du Bois. Much later, in 1936, Park hosted a luncheon at which he met Du Bois in person. Raushenbush, *Robert E. Park*, 39, 152. Morris, *Scholar Denied*, 100–108. Raushenbush in *Robert E. Park* (74–75, 152) and Wacker in *Ethnicity, Pluralism, and Race* (53–54) suggest that Park's view of Du Bois was on the whole favorable despite some criticism, but see Morris, *Scholar Denied*, for a different view.

45. Wirth Marvick, "Louis Wirth," 336. Stonequist, "Problem of the Marginal Man," 6–7. Stonequist, "Marginal Man: A Study in Personality," 338.

46. Park, "Human Migration," 893. Park, "Mentality of Racial Hybrids," 382. Stonequist, "Problem of the Marginal Man," 7. See Park's handwritten notes on "The Mulatto Mind" (undated) and the "Marginal Man" (undated) in the Robert Ezra Park Collection, Box 3, Folder 3. The first set of notes refers to Du Bois's *Souls of Black Folk*. The second set of notes outlines what would become "Human Migration," but according to a prefatory note written by Everett Hughes in 1971, it was "evidently written well before the publication of the article" in 1928. The original title for the article was to be "The Marginal Man: A Study of the Mulatto Mind," which suggests that the emphasis Park placed upon Jews in his discussions of the marginal man was a later development.

47. Park, "Negro and His Plantation Heritage," 67–69. Wirth and Goldhamer, "Hybrid and the Problem of Miscegenation," 340. Stonequist, "Marginal Man: A Study in Personality," 336. In *American Dilemma*, Myrdal dissented from the application of the marginal man concept to African Americans: "The theory of the 'marginal man' was originally developed for Jews and other white immigrants in America, and for them it probably has validity and a strong empirical basis. It was transferred uncritically to the Negro situation where its validity is questionable" (1385n28). Myrdal also objected to the attempt to distinguish "mulattoes" or "fair-skinned Negroes" from other African Americans (699–700).

48. Park, "Human Migration," 889.

49. Park similarly contrasted Jews and blacks in a 1918 article in which he infamously described African Americans as "the lady among the races." Park, "Education in Its Relation to the Conflict," 280–81. The article was later reprinted in Park and Burgess, *Introduction to the Science* (see 139–40 for this phrase). As Reed points out in *W. E. B. Du Bois and American Political Thought* (107–25), the primitive was often identified with the feminine in Park's Progressive-era intellectual milieu. For a similar though later contrast, see Wirth, "Education for Survival" (691): "The [Jews] have long been sophisticated, urbanized, and literate. . . . The Negroes in these respects are virtually exactly opposite. The Jews, for instance, have no need for an urban league as do the Negroes, for the Jews, having grown up with the city, find urban life their natural milieu. . . . The fact that the Jews, through the centuries of their dispersion and their struggle for recognition and survival, acquired certain unmistakable successes within the framework of Western civilization no doubt gives them an advantage over the Negroes, who have had to traverse the road from African folk culture to Western civilization more recently and in a much shorter time." According to Reed in *W. E. B. Du Bois and American Political Thought* (122–23), Du Bois also "defined blacks as comparatively primitive and undeveloped as a race" in *The Souls*

of Black Folk, but Du Bois gave this seemingly deficient status a positive interpretation insofar as "the traits and talents of the Negro" became a salve for American fears of overcivilization.

50. US Bureau of the Census, *Historical Statistics*, 11–12.

51. Park, "Assimilation, Social," 282. Park, "Negro and His Plantation Heritage," 67–69. Park, "Politics and 'The Man Farthest Down.'" Raushenbush, *Robert E. Park*, 68–69. Persons, *Ethnic Studies at Chicago*, 34, 67, 80–81, 85. Kivisto, "What Is the Canonical Theory," 157.

52. Park, "Education in Its Relation to the Conflict," 267–69. Persons, *Ethnic Studies at Chicago*, 81, 85–86, 105, 107. Lal, *Romance of Culture*, 151. Cf. Wirth, "Education for Survival," 690–91.

53. Park, "Racial Assimilation in Secondary Groups," 214–15.

54. On the transformation of African Americans from caste to racial minority group, see Park, "Racial Assimilation in Secondary Groups," 217–20. Park, "Bases of Race Prejudice," 234–37, 243. Park, "Etiquette of Race Relations in the South." Park, "Race Ideologies," 308–11. Park's claim that slavery obliterated any African heritage among American blacks was a controversial one; it was later debated by the African-American sociologist E. Franklin Frazier, a student of Park who upheld his teacher's position, and the Jewish-American anthropologist Melville Herskovits, who challenged Park's view. Morris suggests in *Scholar Denied* that Du Bois anticipated Herskovits (201).

55. Park, "Mentality of Racial Hybrids," 382. Stonequist, "Problem of the Marginal Man," 3. On miscegenation, see Park and Burgess, *Introduction to the Science* (52–53): "The Negro, particularly in the southern states, is a constant theme of popular discussion. Every time a Negro finds himself in a new situation, or one in which the white population is unaccustomed to see him, the thing provokes comment in both races. On the other hand, when a southerner asks the question: 'Would you want your daughter to marry a Negro?' it is time for discussion to cease. Any question of relations between the races can always be immediately disposed of as soon as it is seen to come, directly or indirectly, under the intolerable formula. Political questions are matters of compromise and expediency. Miscegenation, on the other hand, is contrary to the mores. As such the rule against it is absolute." Perhaps for this reason Park and Burgess (737) took pains to distinguish assimilation from racial amalgamation. One of Park's students, E. B. Reuter, did focus on mixed-race individuals in America, but he too recast the discussion increasingly in terms of culture rather than heredity. Wacker, *Ethnicity, Pluralism, and Race*, 54–55. Persons, *Ethnic Studies at Chicago*, 111–30. This turn from race to culture was facilitated in the 1920s by the demise in American social science of the neo-Lamarckian view that acquired traits could be inherited. Wacker, *Ethnicity, Pluralism, and Race*, 31–33. In the 1950s, Park's student E. Franklin Frazier reversed the turn, in a sense, when he argued in "Theoretical Structure of Sociology" (302) that complete assimilation depended not only upon acculturation but also upon freedom of association in its most intimate forms: "The marginal man may be thoroughly acculturated from the standpoint of the dominant racial or cultural group but he cannot identify himself with the dominant racial or cultural group. This is because there are still barriers to intimate association with members of the dominant group especially in regard to intermarriage."

56. Highham, *Strangers in the Land*, 265, 283–99, 327. Gartner, *History of the Jews*, 322–25. Thomas and Znaniecki described the Jews in *Polish Peasant* as "the most unassimilable of races" (85), at least in the Polish context. Cf. Park, "Race Relations and Certain Frontiers," 132; Stonequist, "Problem of the Marginal Man," 9. In *Old World Traits*, Park and Miller described the Jewish situation in America in similar terms: "The Jew may wish to lose his identity as Jew because of the popular prejudice against his race. But this effort usually fails because the individual cannot completely lose the marks of identity with his native group; he is betrayed by some

sign—his speech or gestures, or sentiments" (143). Yet later in the same book they suggested that "in general the Jew [in America] is losing the marks of his identity as fast as possible, and to the degree that he does this the prejudice disappears" (306). In *Immigrant Press,* Park wrote that no people, "with the exception of the Chinese and the Japanese," had been better able than the Jews to "adapt their culture to America and still preserve it against the disintegrating effects of the American environment" (292). In "Behind Our Masks," Park wrote: "In the vast tide of cosmopolitan life the Jewish racial type does not so much disappear as become invisible. When he is no longer seen, anti-Semitism declines. For race prejudice is a function of visibility" (247). In this last passage it is unclear whether Park thought that Jews were becoming invisible by virtue of their assimilation or because society was becoming, like the Jew, cosmopolitan. In notes probably dating from the early 1940s, Wirth observed: "Whereas the Jews on many occasions faced their supreme problem in resisting assimilation, the Negro only rarely has been permitted to assimilate." Louis Wirth Papers, Box 51, Folder 7.

57. Park, "Race Relations Survey," 159–60. Park, "Behind Our Masks," 246–47, 252. Park, "Assimilation, Social," 282. Wirth, "Education for Survival," 691. Matthews, *Quest for an American Sociology,* 169–70. Wacker, *Ethnicity, Pluralism, and Race,* 44, 46–47. Lal, *Romance of Culture,* 124.

58. Park, "Negro and His Plantation Heritage," 76–77.

59. Park, "Racial Assimilation in Secondary Groups," 217–20.

60. Park, "Career of the Africans in Brazil," 202. Park, "Race Relations Cycle in Hawaii," 194.

61. Park and Miller, *Old World Traits,* 138, 143–44, 282–96, 308. Park, "Negro Race Consciousness." Park, "Personality and Cultural Conflict," 366–69. Wacker, *Ethnicity, Pluralism, and Race,* 45–46, 49. Lal, *Romance of Culture,* 124, 144, 151. See also Wirth, "Types of Nationalism" (113), and Stonequist, *Marginal Man* (160), on Jewish and black nationalism.

62. Aho, *German Realpolitik,* 231–32.

63. Park, "Politics and 'The Man Farthest Down,'" 176.

64. Park, "Etiquette of Race Relations in the South," 186. Cf. Park, "Career of the Africans in Brazil," 197; Park, "Race Ideologies," 311.

65. Wirth, "Education for Survival," 691.

66. Park and Miller, *Old World Traits,* 195.

67. Park, *Immigrant Press,* 290.

68. Wirth, *Ghetto,* 76, 95.

69. Wirth, "Education for Survival," 691.

70. Quotations from Park, "Immigrant Community and Immigrant Press," 152, 155. Park and Miller, *Old World Traits,* 195–98. Gartner, *History of the Jews,* 216–17, 277. Jews also concentrated in Paris and Berlin, but New York City was truly exceptional. A comparison of the three cities in 1900–1901 is instructive: There were 58,000 Jews in Paris at that time, comprising 2.18 percent of the city's total population of 2,660,000; there were 86,152 Jews in Berlin, comprising 4.56 percent of the city's total population of 1,844,151; and there were 672,776 Jews in New York City, comprising 19.56 percent of the city's total population of 3,437,202. Chicago resembled Berlin in this respect more than New York City; it was home to an estimated 60,000 Jews in 1900–1901, comprising 3.53 percent of the city's total population of 1,698,575. Jacobs, "Statistics," 531–532.

71. Park, "The City: Suggestions for the Investigation of Human Behavior in the City Environment," 589–90.

72. Park, "Human Migration," 892.

73. Park, "Race Relations and Certain Frontiers," 136–37.

74. Park, *Immigrant Press*, 93.

75. Quotations from Park, "The City: Suggestions for the Investigation of Human Behavior in the Urban Environment," 2; Park in Stonequist, *Marginal Man*, xvii–xviii. Park also stressed the connection between civilization and the Jews in his notes for a 1934 lecture on the marginal man: "It is safe to say also that the more civilized people are the people of the most mixed origin. The Jew, for example, who has wondered [sic] farthest and widest, and who has had the most varied experience, is the man who has in his veins the blood of every people he has come in contact with, and he is undoubtedly our most civilized man." Later in the same lecture notes, Park denied that "the Jew" can be "identified as a mixed blood," but he added that "he has been the permanent and classical minority, and he has been almost everywhere the man who was a middle man, who was an interpreter. He is the man who knows several languages, and he plays a very necessary role in society." "The Marginal Man: Personality and Culture" in the Robert Ezra Park Collection, Box 17, Folder 10.

76. On the city as melting pot, see Park, "Human Migration," 890; Wirth, "Urbanism as a Way of Life," 10. For Park and his colleagues, America was not exceptional in this respect; they believed that the social processes and conflicts remaking the nation were coming to typify the rest of the world as well. Matthews, *Quest for an American Sociology*, 121, 160. Persons, *Ethnic Studies at Chicago*, 11, 35. "A survey of the world today [1921] shows that vast changes are everywhere in progress. Not only in Europe but in Asia and Africa new cultural contacts have undermined and broken down the old cultures." Park and Burgess, *Introduction to the Science*, 867. From this perspective, the urban melting pot exemplified global as well as national tendencies.

77. Lal, *Romance of Culture*, 14.

78. Park, "Politics and 'The Man Farthest Down,'" 167.

79. Tucker, *Marx-Engels Reader*, 49.

80. Higham, *Strangers in the Land*. Nearly two and a half million Jews crossed international frontiers between 1881 and 1914, moving from eastern Europe to western Europe and the Americas. Approximately 80 percent of these Jewish migrants ended up in the United States, constituting a net proportion of about 11 percent of European immigrants between 1880 and 1914 and swelling the Jewish population in the United States from 260,000 in 1880 to more than three million in 1915. Gartner, *History of the Jews*, 213, 215, 238, 258–59, 277.

81. Lippmann, "Causes of Political Indifference." Leuchtenburg, *Perils of Prosperity*. Rourke, "Urbanism and American Democracy." Burner, *Politics of Provincialism*. Eagles, *Democracy Delayed*. Gusfield, *Symbolic Crusade*. Compare Gusfield to Hofstadter, "Pseudo-Conservative Revolt."

82. Grant, *Passing of the Great Race*, 81.

83. Zangwill, *Melting-Pot*. Higham, *Strangers in the Land*, 21–22, 124. Gerstle, *American Crucible*, 21–22, 50–51. Alexander, *Civil Sphere*, 432.

84. R. Smith, *Civic Ideals*. Gerstle, *American Crucible*. Higham, *Strangers in the Land*, 131–57, 165–75, 270–77, 316–24. "Of all the European groups that lay outside of the charmed Nordic circle none was subjected to quite so much hatred as the Jews. . . . [T]he Jews faced a sustained agitation that singled them out from the other immigrant groups blanketed by racial nativism—an agitation that reckoned them the most dangerous force undermining the nation." Higham, *Strangers in the Land*, 277–78. In addition to Henry Ford's antisemitic propaganda from 1919 to 1926 and the growth of the Ku Klux Klan, antisemitic agitation also took the form of discrimination against Jews in employment, education, and social clubs. Highham, *Strangers in the Land*, 265, 283–99, 327. Gartner, *History of the Jews*, 322–25. Albert Johnson, the chairman of the House Committee on Immigration after the Republican party gained control of Congress

in 1919, had close ties to Grant and other antisemitic nativists, and a committee report that he shaped to emphasize the undesirability of Jewish immigration "left a conviction in various quarters that the chief purpose of the immigration law of 1921 was to keep out the Jews." Highham, *Strangers in the Land,* 309–10; see also 313–14.

85. Matthews, *Quest for an American Sociology,* 157, 163. Wacker, *Ethnicity, Pluralism, and Race,* 13–40. Lal, *Romance of Culture,* 108, 153–54. "It is not apparent," wrote Thomas, Park, and Miller in *Old World Traits* (301, 303), "that even the most distinct races, the black, white, and yellow," were "specialized by heredity"; they ascribed the "peculiarities" of immigrant groups, including non-European immigrants, "to a long train of common experiences, not to inborn and ineradicable traits."

86. Higham, *Strangers in the Land,* 234–63. Wacker, *Ethnicity, Pluralism, and Race,* 7–8, 19–21, 25, 44. Persons, *Ethnic Studies at Chicago,* 17–18. The Americanization movement was assimilationist and therefore potentially more inclusive than the ethnic nationalism of the Anglo-Saxon restrictionists, but it aimed to incorporate immigrants on the basis of what they might become rather than what they were. In this respect, it was analogous to earlier proposals for the "civil improvement" (*bürgerliche Verbesserung*) of Jews in the German context.

87. Kallen, "Democracy versus the Melting-Pot." Bourne, "Jew and Trans-National America." Wacker, *Ethnicity, Pluralism, and Race,* 27–36. Persons, *Ethnic Studies at Chicago,* 18–20. Westbrook, *John Dewey and American Democracy,* 197–98, 205, 212–14. "In . . . restricting assimilation to the public and political realm Park left room for cultural pluralism and perhaps even some forms of ethnic nationalism." Persons, *Ethnic Studies at Chicago,* 87. See also Lal, *Romance of Culture,* 108–10.

88. Grant, *Passing of the Great Race.* Ross, *Old World in the New,* 144–45, 164. Stoddard, *Rising Tide of Color.* Gould, *America.*

89. Fairchild, *Melting Pot Mistake,* 136–54, 247. Grant, *Conquest of a Continent,* 347–48.

90. Commons, *Races and Immigrants,* 133, 153. Davenport, *Heredity in Relation to Eugenics,* 216. Ross, *Old World in the New,* 150, 154.

91. Grant, *Passing of the Great Race,* 81.

92. Stoddard, *Rising Tide of Color,* 166.

93. Burr, *America's Race Heritage,* 27, 121, 172. Fairchild, *Melting Pot Mistake,* 110–12. Grant, *Conquest of a Continent,* 225, 227.

94. Grant, *Passing of the Great Race,* 15–16. Burr, *America's Race Heritage,* 213–14. Fairchild, *Melting Pot Mistake,* 120–25.

95. Thomas and Park saw World War I itself as another expression, albeit one of unprecedented devastation and destructiveness, of the breakdown of social isolation and the clash of races, nationalities, and cultures in the modern era. Thomas and Znaniecki, *Polish Peasant,* 85. Park and Burgess, *Introduction to the Science,* 866–67. The national quotas legislation of 1921 and 1924, which privileged immigration from northwestern Europe over the purportedly inferior new immigration from southern and eastern Europe, remained in effect until 1965. On congressional refusal to reapportion seats in the House of Representatives, see Eagles, *Democracy Delayed.*

96. Bourne, "Jew and Trans-National America."

97. Persons, *Ethnic Studies at Chicago,* 107, 109.

98. Wyndham, "Review of *The Marginal Man,*" 831.

99. Wirth, "Consensus and Mass Communication," 39–40.

100. Green, "Re-Examination of the Marginal Man." Green, "Why Americans Feel Insecure."

101. Hughes, "Dilemmas and Contradictions." Hughes, "Social Change and Status Protest."

Turning the marginal man into an everyman made the concept less useful for analyzing the specificities of the Jewish experience with the gentile world. This may help to explain why attention shifted away from Jews in sociological discussions of marginality after World War II. Deegan's critique and reformulation of the marginal man concept provides a recent illustration of this shift; in an entire chapter devoted to this topic, she scarcely mentioned Jews. Deegan, *Race, Hull-House, and the University*, 93–111. While generalization of the concept may have fostered identification with Jews, it also rendered them less salient.

102. Golovensky, "Marginal Man Concept," 337–38.

103. This aim lay behind the "cult of synthesis" in American Jewish culture. Sarna, "Cult of Synthesis," 53, 57, 72–73. Heinze suggests in *Jews and the American Soul* that Jews played an important role in the development and popularization of psychology in the United States and shaped American views about the psyche to achieve similar ends.

104. Lasch, *New Radicalism in America*, 100–101. Lears, *No Place of Grace*, 35–39, 220–25. Conn, *Divided Mind*. Reed, *W. E. B. Du Bois and American Political Thought*, 107–25. Kaufmann, *Rise and Fall of Anglo-America*, 37–57. Heinze, *Jews and the American Soul*, 24–29.

105. Alexander, *Civil Sphere*, 520–43. Alexander, *Remembering the Holocaust*, 3–102. King, "Rise of Sociology," 193–200.

106. Wirth, "Culture Conflict and Misconduct," 235–36. Wirth, "Culture Conflicts in the Immigrant Family."

107. Miller, "Social Contribution," 350. Miller's characterization of the marginal man may have reflected his changing attitudes toward immigrants and minorities. Once sympathetic to immigrant nationalism, he began in the mid-1920s to view class, national, and racial consciousness as pathological. Wacker, *Ethnicity, Pluralism, and Race*, 24–25, 50–51.

108. Persons, *Ethnic Studies at Chicago*, 89–90. See also Park, "Missions and the Modern World," 338.

109. Wacker, *Ethnicity, Pluralism, and Race*, 87. See also Park, "Race Ideologies"; Park, "Missions and the Modern World."

110. Park, "Culture and Civilization," 20. See also Park, "Culture and Cultural Trends," 30; Park, "Assimilation, Social"; Matthews, *Quest for an American Sociology*, 167–68; Wacker, *Ethnicity, Pluralism, and Race*, 67–68, 87.

111. This view of conflict had roots not only in American pragmatism but also in the Austro-German conflict sociology of Ludwig Gumplowicz, Franz Oppenheimer, and Gustav Ratzenhofer; they emphasized the "constructive" and "civilizing aspects" of social conflict, which in their view gave rise to the state, legal systems, and class stratification. Aho, *German Realpolitik*, 20. Their influence is particularly evident in Park's "catastrophic theory of progress" and his race relations cycle. Park, "Human Migration," 882. Aho, *German Realpolitik*, 203–40. Like Simmel (another important influence on Park), Gumplowicz and Oppenheimer were both Jewish.

112. Stonequist made the analogy explicitly in *Marginal Man*, noting that the marginal man's "life history recapitulates something of the processes described in the race-relations cycle" (221).

113. Veblen, "Intellectual Pre-Eminence." Cf. Stonequist, *Marginal Man*, 81, 155–56. Veblen's years at the University of Chicago overlapped with those of Thomas, who enrolled as a graduate student in 1893 and joined the faculty in 1896, and those of Dewey, who was on the faculty from 1894 to 1904. On Veblen's relationship to the Chicago pragmatists, see Rucker, *Chicago Pragmatists*, 142–46. As Park did explicitly in his 1915 article "The City" (590), Veblen implicitly linked mobility as a metaphor for modernity with the Christian legend of the Wandering Jew: "[The Jew] becomes a disturber of the intellectual peace, but only at the cost of becoming an intellectual wayfaring man, a wanderer in the intellectual no-man's-land, seeking another place to rest,

farther along the road, somewhere over the horizon." Veblen, "Intellectual Pre-Eminence," 39. Unlike Park, Veblen feared that Zionism would isolate Jews, turn them inward upon themselves, and result in their cultural stagnation.

114. Park, "Personality and Cultural Conflict," 366–69. Aho, *German Realpolitik*, 223–32.

115. Wirth, "Culture Conflict and Misconduct," 241.

116. Stonequist, *Marginal Man*, 121–22.

117. Stonequist, *Marginal Man*, 220–21. In an undated manuscript on the "activities of the Jews in radical movements," Wirth traced "the great number of radicals" among Jews to the social disorganization that ensued from "the breakdown of the Ghetto," and he equated one type of radical with what Thomas in "Analytical Types" called the creative man. Louis Wirth Papers, Box 52, Folder 2. On mass movements as vehicles for social reconstruction, see Park and Burgess, *Introduction to the Science*, 766, 866–67, 874, 924–26. On immigrant nationalism (including Zionism) as an effort to participate in American life, see Park and Miller, *Old World Traits*, 138, 143–44, 290.

118. Park and Miller, *Old World Traits*, 61.

119. Thomas and Znaniecki, *Polish Peasant*, 1130.

120. Park, "Human Migration," 888.

121. John Dewey quoted in Westbrook, *John Dewey and American Democracy*, 290.

122. "By 1937, Park had so far modified his theory of the ethnic cycle as to concede that any of three configurations could prevail when the cycle was concluded: a caste system as in India; complete assimilation as in China; or a permanent unassimilated racial minority as with the Jews of Europe." Persons, *Ethnic Studies at Chicago*, 72–73. See Park, "Race Relations Cycle in Hawaii." Furthermore, social reorganization, as an alternative to either segregation or assimilation, was another means of creative adjustment. Last, Stonequist's notion of the marginal man as a potential cultural intermediary—a role that is "not necessarily inconsistent with Zionistic sentiments"—indicated yet another form that creative adjustment could take. Stonequist, *Marginal Man*, 175, 177–79, 182; quotation from 177. Stonequist suggested in "Marginal Character of the Jews" (309–10) that the victory of liberal, democratic, and internationalist forces in World War II would enable the Jewish marginal man to assume the role of the cultural intermediary; "this need not mean the end of distinctive peoples and cultures," he added, "but rather their interaction on a level where the forces of cooperation can hold in check the forces of competition and conflict in the interests of a common humanity." Stonequist later noted in "Marginal Man: A Study in Personality" that "the ideal of a culturally pluralistic society is reconcilable with the requirements of an effective democracy and more in keeping with the need for intercultural understanding beyond national frontiers" (343). Cf. Park, "Missions and the Modern World" (338–39), on Christian missions as the "intermediaries and the interpreters of the peoples in the Great Society to one another."

123. Thomas developed an early and enduring interest in the Jews. In a letter to Dorothy Thomas, dated January 1935, William Thomas noted that in 1896 he already had the idea to study a European immigrant group in its country of origin and in the United States. When he began to look for a suitable group for this study in 1908, Thomas wrote, "the choice was between the Italians, the Jews and the Poles." In another letter dated 1912, Thomas noted his plans to publish a series of volumes on "the cultural and social life of European peasants," adding that "the Eastern European Jews should also be brought in." William I. Thomas Papers, Box 1, Folder 1. In 1914 he began teaching a course on "The Jew" at the University of Chicago. Bressler, "Jewish Behavior Patterns," 2. Abbott and Egloff, "Polish Peasant," 232. In 1918, as the first volume of *The Polish*

Peasant went to press, he started work on his study of the Jews. Thomas learned Yiddish in order to conduct the study, received a grant from the Social Science Research Council to finish it, and by the mid-1930s had begun to negotiate with publishers. Bressler, "Selected Family Patterns," 563. Janowitz, "Introduction," xxviii.

124. Park and Miller, *Old World Traits*, 225.

125. Park and Miller, *Old World Traits*, 241.

126. Park and Miller, *Old World Traits*, 227–29, 232–34. Cf. Thomas and Znaniecki, *Polish Peasant*, 1533–38; they note that "as compared, for instance with the Jewish charitable institutions, the Poles in America have little to show in this line" (1533–34).

127. Park and Miller, *Old World Traits*, 235–36.

128. Park and Miller, *Old World Traits*, 236. Goren, *New York Jews*.

129. Goren, *New York Jews*, 119–25, 283n47.

130. Thomas and Znaniecki, *Polish Peasant*, 1121–22, 1215.

131. Park, "Immigrant Community and Immigrant Press," 155. For his assertion about Jews and crime, see Bingham, "Foreign Criminals in New York," 383. For Bingham's retraction, see "Wrong about Jews, Bingham Admits," *New York Times*, September 17, 1908, 16. The capacity of Jews for creative reorganization stands in contrast to Chicago pragmatist George Herbert Mead's negative appraisal of Judaism as a "cult," that is, an "instituted social habit" that "holds on to its imaginary objects in a fixed fashion." Rucker, *Chicago Pragmatists*, 124–25.

132. Bressler, "Jewish Behavior Patterns," 2, 4, 15–16, 78, 82, 398–400, 418.

133. Park, "The City: Suggestions for the Investigation of Human Behavior in the City Environment," 605. Park, *Immigrant Press*, 330, 466.

134. Janowitz, "Sociological Theory and Social Control"; Mead quoted on 83. Westbrook, *John Dewey and American Democracy*, 188–89. Joas, *Pragmatism and Social Theory*, 25.

135. Bressler, "Jewish Behavior Patterns," 440.

136. Park, "Crowd and the Public," 48, 78–79.

137. Park, *Immigrant Press*, 89.

138. Park, *Immigrant Press*, 294.

139. Park, *Immigrant Press*, 466–67.

140. Park and Miller, *Old World Traits*, 307.

141. Park and Miller, *Old World Traits*, 237–38.

142. Park and Miller, *Old World Traits*, 307.

143. Park and Miller, *Old World Traits*, 143–44. See also Lal, *Romance of Culture*, 96–107.

144. In *Polish Peasant*, Thomas and Znaniecki described the Jews as "the most unassimilable of races" (85); they repeatedly noted the strong connection that Poles made between Polish nationality and Catholicism (1383, 1394, 1446–48, 1460), which implied the exclusion of Jews, though they added that where the identification of "Catholicism and Polonism" was inexpedient, as with "Polish Protestants or Polonized Jews," nationalist appeals were made on "more general principles" (1460); and they noted that Poland's city population was less suited than its peasant class to provide an economic basis for national unity, in part because of "the large proportion of Jewish population in cities" (1441). The Polish republic was proclaimed at the end of World War I, in 1918, the same year that the first volume of *Polish Peasant* was published. All Polish parties preferred a Polish national state, even though a third of the country's population, including more than two and a half million Jews in 1921, were members of a national or religious minority, making Poland the chief target of postwar demands for national minority rights. Polish chauvinists resisted these demands, and "a series of pogroms and attacks which the new gov-

ernment did nothing to halt" signaled that "full Jewish equality in the Polish state was deemed unacceptable, much less minority rights." Gartner, *History of the Jews*, 282–83. Cf. Mendelsohn, *Jews of East Central Europe*, 32–83.

145. Park and Miller, *Old World Traits*, 261–62.

146. Park and Miller, *Old World Traits*, 270–71. Cf. Park and Burgess, *Science of Sociology*, 765–66. Thomas, Park, and Miller thought this learning process would proceed best according to Dewey's pragmatist pedagogy: "In education it is valuable to let the child, as far as possible, make his own discoveries and follow his own interests. He should have the opportunity of seeking new experiences which have a meaning for him when connected with his old experiences. A wise policy of assimilation, like a wise educational policy, does not seek to destroy the attitudes and memories that are there, but to build on them." They contrasted this pragmatist method to the "ordering and forbidding" approach which demanded from the immigrant "a quick and complete Americanization through the suppression and repudiation of all the signs that distinguish him from us." The latter was an anti-democratic method in conflict with the aim of organizing a democratic public. Park and Miller, *Old World Traits Transplanted*, 280–81. On Dewey's pragmatist pedagogy, see Westbrook, *John Dewey and American Democracy*, 96–111, 505–6. For a critical discussion of the search for a democratic public, see Fink, "Progressive Reformers."

147. Park and Miller, *Old World Traits*, 271.

148. Park, *Immigrant Press*, 88. Park's memorandum "Americanization as Participation," prepared in connection with the Americanization Study for which *Old World Traits Transplanted* was commissioned, made it clear that he construed participation broadly to include "social participation" and not only "political participation." Robert Ezra Park Collection, Box 3, Folder 3. This interpretation of assimilation is consistent with Park's other formulations. Recognizing that the public involved diversity of opinion, he criticized prevailing notions of assimilation for exaggerating the degree to which national solidarity required homogeneity and like-mindedness. Park, "Crowd and the Public," 80. Park, "Racial Assimilation in Secondary Groups," 204–5. In pragmatist fashion, Park suggested that the solutions to problems of collective concern were not prescribed beforehand by custom and tradition but instead required creativity and communication: "America . . . lies in the future rather than the past. . . . So far as Americanization is undertaken by the schools, effort should be directed, it would seem, toward maintaining and creating a mutual understanding among our peoples rather than toward perpetrating . . . a sentimental and ceremonial patriotism based on a reverent and uncritical contemplation of our national heritages which, as compared with those of other peoples, the Jews, for example, are not likely to impress the unbiased outsider as having great value." Park, "Education in Its Relation to the Conflict," 283. In calling for the creation of a common "fund of knowledge, experience, sentiments, and ideals," Thomas, Park, and Miller echoed Dewey: "The way to deal with hyphenism . . . is to welcome it . . . in the sense of extracting from each people its special good, so that it shall surrender into a common fund of wisdom and experience what it especially has to contribute." Dewey, "Nationalizing Education," 205. Likewise, Park and Burgess argued in *Introduction to the Science* that assimilation achieves a unity that is "not necessarily or even normally like-mindedness; it is rather a unity of experience and of orientation, out of which may develop a community of purpose and action" (737). Park later summarized the purpose of assimilation this way: in order for human beings to "meet the common crises of life with a common will," "there must be such a consciousness of common interest that differences can be discussed, and out of the conflict of interests a genuine public opinion may be formed. Where racial, religious or other cultural differences are so great that they provoke a racial, caste,

or class consciousness which makes full and free discussion impossible, assimilation does not take place." Park, "Assimilation, Social," 283.

149. Park and Miller, *Old World Traits*, 307.

150. This identification dovetailed with what Sarna has called the "cult of synthesis" in American Jewish culture, but remarkably it was three gentile sociologists who made it. Sarna, "Cult of Synthesis."

151. Park, "Community Organization and the Romantic Temper," 675, 677.

152. Park, "Review of *Jews in a Gentile World*," 711.

153. Stonequist, *Marginal Man*, 209.

154. Abbott, *Department & Discipline*.

155. Abbott, *Department & Discipline*, 16.

156. Deegan, *Jane Addams and the Men*. Deegan, *Race, Hull-House, and the University*. D. Smith, *Chicago School*. Lindner, *Reportage of Urban Culture*.

157. Alexander, *Civil Sphere*, 503–47.

158. Aho, *German Realpolitik*, 18.

159. Portes and Zhou, "New Second Generation." Alba and Nee, "Rethinking Assimilation Theory." Alba and Nee, *Remaking the American Mainstream*. Brubaker, "Return of Assimilation?" Kivisto, "What Is the Canonical Theory." Alexander, *Civil Sphere*, 425–57. Bloemraad, Korteweg, and Yurdakul, "Citizenship and Immigration."

160. Calhoun, "Nationalism, Political Community, and the Representation."

161. These were the terms set by Amitai Etzioni when he complained that Wirth's *Ghetto* allowed "no third alternative between community and 'society,' between segregation and assimilation." Etzioni, "Ghetto," 259. Nearly half a century later, Birnbaum described the Chicago school as oscillating between essentially the same terms: "to preserve a collective identity or to become assimilated as an individual within a new reference group." Birnbaum, *Geography of Hope*, 147–62; quotation from 162.

Chapter Five

1. The last two images (A– and B–) have been a major element in antisemitism since the nineteenth century in France, Germany, and the United States. Most of the social thinkers examined in this study, for all the ambivalence of their portrayals and characterization of Jews, also fall into these same two cells (A– and B–) in table 5.1. Although troubling, this does not necessarily make them antisemites. Rather, it demonstrates how widely these stereotypes were shared among antisemites and non-antisemites alike. The lower half of table 5.1 is consistent with Nirenberg's argument that Judaism is primarily "a category, a set of ideas and attributes with which non-Jews can . . . criticize their world." Nirenberg, *Anti-Judaism*, 3. Nirenberg showed with impressive erudition the wide range of critical work to which ideas about Judaism have been put in the history of Western thought, but his work is less helpful for understanding the invocation of Jews or Judaism by gentiles to praise or inspire hope (the upper half of the table). The most prominent example discussed in this study is the work of Thomas and Park, who called for gentiles to emulate the example of Jewish immigrants (see chapter 4).

2. Birnbaum, *Geography of Hope*, 99–113.

3. Thomas and Park's praise for the New York Jewish Kehillah brings to mind Weber's suggestion that America's Puritan heritage made it more welcoming of Jews and open to absorbing them. Weber, *Economy and Society*, 623. However, Thomas and Park do not necessarily reflect

an exceptional American philosemitism. As chapter 4 shows, their views were probably not representative of American public opinion.

4. Tucker, *Marx-Engels Reader*, 629.

5. Tucker, *Marx-Engels Reader*, 475.

6. According to Hobsbawm, *Age of Extremes*, the short twentieth century began in 1914 and ended in 1991.

7. Simmel, "Stranger." Marx, *Grundrisse*, 223. Tucker, *Marx-Engels Reader*, 327.

8. Bauman, *Modernity and Ambivalence*, 85. Cf. Bauman, "'Antisemitism' Reassessed."

9. Cahnman, *Jews & Gentiles*, 223–24.

10. Slezkine, *Jewish Century*, 4, 8, 40–41.

11. Slezkine, *Jewish Century*, 104. Sombart, *Jews and Modern Capitalism*, 49.

12. Anticipating these studies, Cuddihy argued in *Ordeal of Civility* that the integration of Jews into the modern world entailed their accommodation to norms of civility derived from Protestant Christianity. According to him, Jewish intellectuals like Marx, Freud, and Lévi-Strauss produced their ideas as a response to the "trauma of this cultural shock" (4). "The Jewish intellectual placed himself between his people, 'backward' and premodern, and their modern, Gentile status-audience" (6). On the one hand, the ideas of the Jewish intellectual expressed shame toward unassimilated Jews, whom he sought to enlighten or reform, and on the other hand, resentment toward gentiles, in whom he sought to uncover the same incivility that Jews exhibited. The internalized clash between Jewish culture and Protestant civility thus divided the Jewish self, and the Jewish experience in turn illuminated the broader costs and difficulties of "socialization into modernity" (234–35).

13. Mendes-Flohr, *Divided Passions*, 14.

14. Birnbaum, *Geography of Hope*, 31; see also 375.

15. Yovel, *Other Within.*

16. Cahnman, *Jews & Gentiles*, is a notable exception: "It is our initial thesis that theology comes first in the chain of causations that shape Jewish-Gentile relations as we know them today, and that the socio-economic reality that ensues bears the indelible stamp of its origin in theology. . . . By the fourteenth century, the economic conditions of the Jews had been molded in the image of theology" (11, 29). My discussion about the relationship between Jews and Christians is indebted to Cahnman.

17. Alexander, *Dark Side of Modernity*, 81, 83, 85, 98.

18. Nisbet, *Sociological Tradition*, 21–44.

19. Jones, "Ambivalent Cartesians," 36. Emphasis in the original.

20. Bourdieu, "Les conditions sociales." Bourdieu, *Political Interventions*, 222–27, 267.

21. Muller, *Capitalism and the Jews*, 15–71; quotation from 17.

22. Nirenberg, *Anti-Judaism*, 439.

23. Quotation from Bourdieu, *Political Interventions*, 224. Bourdieu uses the term *habitus* to refer to a system or set of enduring dispositions, formed through past experience, which generate and structure subsequent perception, action, and appreciation. Bourdieu, *Logic of Practice*, 52–65.

24. On national sociological traditions, see Levine, *Visions*; Heilbron, *French Sociology*, especially 218–23. On the transnational networks through which social politics was diffused, see Rodgers, *Atlantic Crossings.*

25. Cf. Ringer, *Decline of the German Mandarins*, who traces the long-term transmission of "unconscious mental habit[s]" in part to "their persistent usefulness as ideological tools" (394).

26. Bourdieu, *Logic of Practice*, 64.

27. Hobsbawm, *Age of Revolution*. Hobsbawm, *Age of Capital*. Hobsbawm, *Age of Empire*.

28. Tocqueville, *Old Regime*, 13.

29. Tucker, *Marx-Engels Reader*, 477, 296.

30. Park, "Our Racial Frontier on the Pacific," 149.

31. DiMaggio and Powell, "Iron Cage Revisited."

32. Meyer and Rowan, "Institutionalized Organizations."

33. Nisbet, *Sociological Tradition*, 221.

34. Alexander, "Durkheimian Sociology and Cultural Studies Today."

35. Durkheim, *Elementary Forms*.

36. The "novelty" of Levi-Strauss's structural anthropology was "the introduction into the social sciences of . . . the relational mode of thought which, by breaking with the substantialist mode of thought, leads one to characterize each element by the relationships which unite it with all the others in a system and from which it derives its meaning and function." Bourdieu, *Logic of Practice*, 4. On the advantages of conceiving social life in terms of relations rather than in terms of things or substances, see also Emirbayer, "Manifesto for a Relational Sociology." He notes that Saussurean linguistics and structural anthropology "stress in eminently relational terms that meaning derives not from the intrinsic properties of signs . . . but rather from their differences from all other signs within a semiological system" (300).

37. Quotations from Lévi-Strauss, *Totemism*, 77, 89 (emphasis in the original); see also 31. Wilcken, *Claude Lévi-Strauss*, 249–57.

38. Pasto, "Islam's 'Strange Secret Sharer,'" 449, 458.

39. Schechter, *Obstinate Hebrews*, 7.

40. Cahnman, *Jews & Gentiles*.

41. On Jews as a nation of priests, see Exodus 19:6.

42. Durkheim, *Elementary Forms*, 412–17. According to Durkheim, the hallmark of religious phenomena is their division of the universe into the mutually exclusive and antagonistic categories of sacred things, which are "set apart and forbidden" (44), and profane things, which "must keep at a distance from what is sacred" (38). He argued that the division between sacred and profane had a social origin in the contrast between intense periods of collective effervescence, on the one hand, and routine, ordinary periods of social life, on the other hand. Ritualized times of collective effervescence stimulated the individual's awareness of a reality external to him that constrained and uplifted him, namely, society. Durkheim added that the sacred was itself subdivided into the categories of the pure and the impure: pure forces are "benevolent, guardians of physical and moral order, . . . dispensers of life, health, and all the qualities that men value," while "impure powers" are "bringers of disorder, causes of death and sickness, instigators of sacrilege." He traced these two faces of the sacred to society in one or another of its aspects: pure forces represent society "when it confidently affirms itself and zealously presses things into the service of the ends it is pursuing," while it is the experience of collective mourning, distress, or anger that "man is interpreting when he imagines evil beings outside him whose hostility . . . can be disarmed only through human suffering" (412). Durkheim suggested that the common origin of pure and impure forces in society explains how a "holy thing" can be transformed into an "impure thing or an evil power" and vice versa: "Since they reflect the emotional state in which the group finds itself, a change in that state is sufficient to make the forces themselves change direction" (413, 416). Christianity's ambiguous consecration of Jews, and the close connection between the sacred and society, made Jews especially "good to think" about social questions.

Cf. Bauman, "'Antisemitism' Reassessed," which maintains that antisemitism and philosemitism are both rooted in allosemitism, "the practice of setting the Jews apart as people radically different from all others" (207–8).

43. Eisenstadt, *Jewish Civilization*, 8–9, 51, 83. This ambivalence brings to mind Simmel's description of the stranger as both socially close and distant. On ambivalence toward Jews, see also Bauman, "'Antisemitism' Reassessed"; Haynes, *Reluctant Witnesses*. Pasto, in "Islam's 'Strange Secret Sharer,'" also remarks on similarities in Christian and Muslim attitudes toward Jews: "Both Christians and Muslims have articulated foundational histories based on a succession to Jewish status as the primary people of a universal divinity; and both have applied this secessionist ideology to the conquest of other people. . . . In this context, Islam's 'strange secret sharer' is Christianity, since both share a representation of Jews as a subordinate people, both assume the authority to define Jewish past and presence, and both transfer this triumphalist ideology to other peoples" (469). Eisenstadt's reference to "continuous Jewish existence" does not mean a static or unhistorical existence. On the contrary, he showed that it involved periodic reconstructions of what he called Jewish civilization. To borrow a term from the title of Theodor Herzl's *Old-New Land*, Jews were in this sense an *altneu* group in relation to Christians: older yet repeatedly renewed. This may have contributed to the association of Jews with both premodernity and modernity.

44. Pocock, "Modernity and Anti-Modernity." Alexander, "Modern, Anti, Post and Neo." Gillespie, *Theological Origins of Modernity*, 1–18.

45. Emirbayer, "Useful Durkheim," 114–17, 121–23.

46. Alexander, *Dark Side of Modernity*, 5–28.

47. Ringer, *Decline of the German Mandarins*.

48. Nisbet, *Sociological Tradition*, 17. One need not accept Nisbet's thesis in its entirety or without qualification to acknowledge the ambivalence of classical sociology toward modernity. Cf. Blackbourn, "Discrete Charm of the Bourgeoisie" (211–21), on the ambivalence of German intellectuals at the end of the nineteenth century; Goldstein, *Price of Whiteness*, on white Americans' ambivalence about both Jews and modernity; and Alexander, *Dark Side of Modernity* (5–28), which traces the ambivalence of early twentieth-century social thinkers to historical experiences with world war and totalitarianism that upended their early faith in rational progress.

49. Lazare, *Antisemitism*, 43.

50. Ezekiel 37:1–14. The primary meaning of messianic redemption was not, as Weber thought, the elevation of the Jews over their persecutors. Rather, it signified the possibility of and hope for Jewish reconstruction: The house of Israel is dispersed, its land desolate, its cities laid waste (Leviticus 26:32–33), but its captivity will be turned, "the plowman shall overtake the reaper," and the people "shall build the waste cities, and inhabit them" (Amos 9:13–15). Exile and dispersion were understood as collective expiation to purify and prepare the people for a new collective life. On expiatory rites, see Durkheim, *Elementary Forms*, 392–412. Another source of the ambivalence that some Jewish intellectuals felt toward other Jews may have been their own status as marginal men, unable or unwilling to break with their past and traditions, and not fully accepted, because of antisemitism, in the broader society in which they sought to find a place. Park, "Human Migration," 892.

51. Fournier, *Émile Durkheim: A Biography*, 24. Birnbaum, *Geography of Hope*, 153.

52. Torpey, "A (Post-) Secular Age," 280–81.

53. Heschel, *Abraham Geiger*, 19.

54. Schechter, *Obstinate Hebrews*, 7–8.

55. Said, *Orientalism*; quotations from 208, 206, 309.

56. Go, "For a Postcolonial Sociology," 32–34. Steinmetz, "Sociology of Empires," 94.

57. Connell, "Why is Classical Theory Classical," 1516–17.

58. Alatas and Sinha, "Teaching Classical Sociological Theory." Magubane, "Overlapping Territories." Steinmetz, "Decolonizing German Theory." Zimmerman, "Decolonizing Weber." Bhambra, "Sociology and Postcolonialism." Chua, "Orientalism as Cultural Practices." Kemple and Mawani, "Sociological Imagination." Go, "For a Postcolonial Sociology." Go, *Postcolonial Sociology*. Seidman, "Colonial Unconscious."

59. Go, "For a Postcolonial Sociology," 32.

60. Magubane, "Overlapping Territories," 108, 94.

61. Go, "For a Postcolonial Sociology," 32.

62. Go, "For a Postcolonial Sociology," 33–34. Hertzberg showed in *French Enlightenment and the Jews* that the Enlightenment was complicit with antisemitism as well as imperialism. However, his assessment was more nuanced: two roads led from the French Revolution, he pointed out, one leading to Jewish emancipation and the other to modern antisemitism.

63. Said, *Orientalism*, 27–28.

64. Said, *Orientalism*, 99.

65. Said, *Orientalism*, 231, 234.

66. Said, *Orientalism*, 262.

67. Said, *Orientalism*, 286, 306–7.

68. Said, *Orientalism*, 27–28.

69. Said, *Orientalism*, 307.

70. Heschel, *Abraham Geiger*, 21–22, 2–3. Cf. Heschel, "Revolt of the Colonized."

71. Pasto, "Islam's 'Strange Secret Sharer,'" 449, 456, 466–67. "The idea of internal colonialism," Steinmetz argues in "Sociology of Empires," "seems to make a useful distinction only where the ancestors of current ruling elites arrived as colonial conquerors and where the internal colony is descended from the natives conquered by the original colonizers" (84). Because the Roman Empire (that is, Europeans) conquered the Jews in Palestine, but Jews migrated to Europe, it is not entirely clear whether this definition is meant to deny a colonized status to Jews in Europe. In *Devil's Handwriting*, Steinmetz noted that European colonizers sometimes compared their colonial subjects to Jews in the metropole (108, 118, 120, 183, 401, 427n303).

72. Hess, *Germans, Jews and the Claims of Modernity*.

73. Khazzoom, "Great Chain of Orientalism," 489, 491, 486.

74. Another limitation of this scholarship is that the interpretation of Jews as an "internal 'oriental' colony" within the European metropole excludes America from consideration. Does this silence imply that America is exceptional in regard to its treatment of Jews, or is the interpretation presumed to apply by extension to Jews in America?

75. Seidman, "Colonial Unconscious," 50. Cf. Connell, "Why Is Classical Theory Classical."

76. Offe, *Reflections on America*. Markovits, *Uncouth Nation*, 201–23. To be sure, it is possible to fold the relationship between Europe and America into an Orientalist frame of reference: America was initially colonized by European powers, which sometimes continued to regard it as immature and uncivilized. Heins, "Orientalising America?" However, the historical emergence of America as a Western imperial power in its own right strains the plausibility of this interpretation. While Offe and Markovits confined their studies to European views of America, it should be added that the process of identity construction was reciprocal: European anti-Americanism finds its parallel in Americans' long-standing conception of their own society as a new Promised Land, offering redemption from the corruption, rottenness, and spiritual slavery of old Europe.

77. Go, "For a Postcolonial Sociology"; quotation from 43.

78. Weber, *Ancient Judaism*, 4.

79. Buruma and Margalit, *Occidentalism*, 5.

80. Buruma and Margalit, *Occidentalism*, 51.

81. Buruma and Margalit, *Occidentalism*, 6; see also 8, 144–45, 149.

82. Buruma and Margalit, *Occidentalism*, 6, 9.

83. Buruma and Margalit, *Occidentalism*, 28, 52–54, 102–3, 109–110.

84. Buruma and Margalit, *Occidentalism*, 27–29, 33–35.

85. Steinmetz, *Devil's Handwriting*; quotation from 517. Cf. Bhabha, *Location of Culture*.

86. Steinmetz notes in *Devil's Handwriting* that alternative interpretive frames appeared in European discourse about colonized subjects, but none of them was "able to hold its own. . . . Any attempt to deviate from the dominant paradigm was subjected to the pressure of European assumptions about race, religion, and evolution" and constrained by "the preexisting formations of ethnographic conventions" (51, 90, 100, 356). Steinmetz also emphasized the "ambiguous identifications that take place across the colonizer-colonized boundary" (55). European colonizers recognized that their own activity transformed their colonial subjects into cultural hybrids who partly came to resemble or imitate the colonizers. However, such identification did not overcome the opposition between non-Western "archaism" and "Europeanized modernity"; it merely internalized the opposition, transposing it to the "divided souls" of colonial subjects (80, 121).

87. Steinmetz, *Devil's Handwriting*, 371, 389; see also 393–95.

88. Steinmetz, *Devil's Handwriting*, 415–16. Weber, *Religion of China*. Western countries (and the Chinese government itself) continue to classify China as a developing country, despite calls for a reconsideration of this status. Fish, "Is China Still a 'Developing' Country?" Analogies between Jews and Chinese were common in European social thought (Geller, *Other Jewish Question*, 50–87), but they do not obviate the important difference noted here.

89. Quotation from Steinmetz, *Devil's Handwriting*, 45–46.

90. Offe, *Reflections on America*.

91. Markovits, *Uncouth Nation*, 24.

92. Offe, *Reflections on America*, 5.

93. Eisenstadt, *Jewish Civilization*, 83.

94. Offe, *Reflections on America*, 3.

95. Markovits, *Uncouth Nation*, 150–200.

96. Quotation from Sombart, *Jews and Modern Capitalism*, 44.

97. Cf. Bauman, "'Antisemitism' Reassessed." Bauman argued that attitudes toward Jews were not so much *heterophobic* (resentful of the different) as *proteophobic*, which is to say, apprehensive about whatever "does not fit the structure of the orderly world, does not fall easily into any of the established categories" (208). For the classic study of proteophobia, see Douglas, *Purity and Danger*.

98. Fukuyama, "End of History?" Fukuyama, *End of History*.

99. Huntington, "Clash of Civilizations?" Huntington, *Clash of Civilizations*. Kagan, "Power and Weakness." Kagan, *Paradise and Power*. Habermas and Derrida, "February 15, or What Binds Europeans Together." Offe, *Reflections on America*, 93–105. Heins, "Orientalising America?" Markovits, *Uncouth Nation*.

100. Laurence, *Emancipation of Europe's Muslims*, 1, 9. Jikeli, *European Muslim Antisemitism*, 8–15. Pew Research Center, *Future of the Global Muslim Population* (125), provides a more conservative estimate of 11.3 million Muslims in Western Europe in 2010, but it expects the Muslim population of Western Europe to rise to 16.4 million or 8.6% of the total population by 2030.

101. Peach and Glebe, "Muslim Minorities," 29–31. Jikeli, *European Muslim Antisemitism*, 4, 8–15.

102. Brubaker, *Citizenship and Nationhood*, 76.

103. Peach and Glebe, "Muslim Minorities," 38–39. Buijs and Rath, "Muslims in Europe," 4–8. Laurence, *Emancipation of Europe's Muslims*, 8–11. Cesari, *When Islam and Democracy Meet*, 11–16. Jikeli, *European Muslim Antisemitism*, 8–15.

104. Laurence, *Emancipation of Europe's Muslims*, 2. For slightly different estimates of the Muslim proportion of the populations in France, Germany, and the United Kingdom, see Pew Research Center, *Future of the Global Muslim Population*, 210. In 2010 the populations of Austria, Belgium, the Netherlands, and Switzerland included slightly higher percentages of Muslims than the populations of Germany or the United Kingdom, but France, Germany, and the United Kingdom ranked highest among Western European countries in absolute numbers of Muslims. Jikeli, *European Muslim Antisemitism* (4), estimates that France, Germany, and the United Kingdom are together home to about 70 percent of Western Europe's Muslims.

105. Foner and Alba, "Immigrant Religion," 370–71. Alexander, "Struggling Over the Mode of Incorporation." Cesari, *When Islam and Democracy Meet*, 22–25, 29–37. Jikeli, *European Muslim Antisemitism*, 15–21.

106. Bowen, *Why the French Don't Like Headscarves*. Foner and Alba, "Immigrant Religion," 371–75. Joppke and Torpey, *Legal Integration of Islam*.

107. The Muslim population of the United States is smaller both proportionally and in absolute numbers than that of France, Germany, or the United Kingdom. However, if current trends continue, the Muslim population in the United States is expected to rise to 6.2 million (1.7% of the total US population) by 2030, larger in absolute numbers than the Muslim population of any European country other than Russia and France. Pew Research Center, *Future of the Global Muslim Population*, 137, 141.

108. Pew Research Center, *Muslim Americans*, 9–16. Foner and Alba, "Immigrant Religion," 374–76. Pew Research Center, *Future of the Global Muslim Population*, 141, 149.

109. Niebuhr, "All Need Toleration." Pew Research Center, *Muslim Americans*, 18–20. Foner and Alba, "Immigrant Religion," 376. Joppke and Torpey, *Legal Integration of Islam*, 129.

110. Niebuhr, "All Need Toleration." Foner and Alba, "Immigrant Religion." Joppke and Torpey, *Legal Integration of Islam*, 114–38. Klausen, *Islamic Challenge* (136–70), and Foner and Alba, "Immigrant Religion" (374), suggest that higher levels of secularism in Western European countries obscure the extent to which their state-church arrangements privilege Christianity over Islam, but this is a matter of scholarly debate. For a different view, see Laurence, *Emancipation of Europe's Muslims*, and Joppke and Torpey, *Legal Integration of Islam* (140–45). A systematic examination of how the European and American contexts of civil incorporation have differed is beyond the scope of this chapter. However, given the divergent historical experiences of European and American Jews, one might reasonably expect differences between the European and American contexts to be as consequential for the civil incorporation of Muslims as they were for the civil incorporation of Jews. This hypothesis need not entail a lachrymose view of ethnoreligious minorities in European societies, nor does it imply that America is devoid of anti-Jewish or anti-Muslim bigotry.

111. Kumar, "Nation-State, the European Union," 54.

112. D. T. Goldberg, "Racial Europeanization," 349.

113. Al-Azmeh, "Afterword," 209.

114. Nachmani, *Europe and Its Muslim Minorities*, 9, 140–41.

115. Laurence, *Emancipation of Europe's Muslims*, 8, 121–26, 130–31.

116. Alexander, *Civil Sphere*. For Jews and Muslims, civil incorporation has raised similar questions about religious reform (calls for a Euro-Islam, for instance, which parallel earlier calls for a Franco-Judaism) and the best mode of incorporation (assimilation, multiculturalism, etc.).

117. Others have also questioned the notion that Muslims are the new Jews. See Cesarani, "Why Muslims are Not the New Jews," on why a comparison between Jews in the Britain of the 1890s and Muslims in contemporary Britain is inapt. Walzer argues in "Islamism and the Left" that an analogy between Jews of the past and Muslims today is misleading because "Muslims in today's Western Europe have never been attacked by Christian crusaders, expelled from one country after another, forced to wear distinctive dress, barred from many professions, and slaughtered by Nazis. In fact, right now, some Muslim militants are among the chief purveyors of anti-Semitism in Europe (they get a lot of help from neo-fascists in France and Germany and other countries, too). In America, the 'new Jews' label clearly doesn't work. According to FBI statistics, between 2002 and 2011, there were 1,388 hate crimes committed against American Muslims and 9,198 against American Jews—and 25,130 against black Americans. We should defend all victims of hatred, but it isn't wrong to recognize where the greatest dangers lie." The notion that Muslims are the new Jews often arises in comparisons between Islamophobia and antisemitism. For a critical and insightful discussion of these comparisons, see Jikeli, *European Muslim Antisemitism*, 25–31.

118. Laqueur, *Changing Face of Antisemitism*, 126. Wasserstein, *On the Eve*, 1–2. The United States differs from Western Europe in this respect. As previously noted in this chapter, there are fewer than three million Muslims in the United States, comprising less than 1 percent of the country's total population. As noted in chapter 4, there were an estimated 3.25 million Jews in the United States in 1915, comprising 3.2 percent of the country's total population at that time. By 1925, the number of Jews in the United States had risen to 4.5 million, comprising nearly 4 percent of the country's total population. Thus, Jews were historically a bigger minority group in the United States than Muslims are today.

119. Bauman, *Modernity and Ambivalence*, 85.

120. Laurence, *Emancipation of Europe's Muslims*, 5.

121. Choate, *Emigrant Nation*. Fitzgerald, *Nation of Emigrants*. Before Italy's unification, Italian nationalists explicitly compared their nation to the dispersed and exiled Jews. Liberal Italian politicians insisted after unification that Italian emigration was not a diaspora, but their opponents explicitly compared it to the Jewish Diaspora in order to discredit the Liberals. Choate, *Emigrant Nation*, 6–7, 165.

122. Of course, not all Muslims subscribe to an Islamist political ideology, and only a small minority of Muslims are involved in terrorism. See Pew Research Center, *Muslim Americans* (49–56), on Muslim attitudes in Europe and America regarding Islamic extremism and terrorism. Majorities of Muslims in France (73%), Germany (58%), Great Britain (77%), and the United States (76%) reported in 2007 that they were very or somewhat concerned about the rise of Islamic extremism around the world. In addition, majorities of Muslims in France (64%), Germany (83%), Great Britain (70%), and the United States (78%) said that the use of suicide bombing against civilian targets to defend Islam from its enemies was never justified. However, only minorities of Muslims in France (48%), Germany (35%), Great Britain (17%), and the United States (40%) were prepared to believe that Arabs carried out the terrorist attacks against the United States on September 11, 2001.

123. Traverso asserts in *La fin de la modernité juive* (123, my translation) that "the specter of Islamist terrorism has replaced that of Judeo-Bolshevism," but the analogy is misleading be-

cause the former is quite real while the latter was an invention of antisemitic propaganda. Prominent Bolsheviks were Jews, but Bolshevism was never based upon an interpretation of Judaism.

124. I do not mean to suggest that Islam is uniquely capable of inspiring violence. It would not be difficult to adduce examples of contemporary violence inspired by extremist interpretations of other religions.

125. Alexander, *Civil Sphere.* Alexander, "Struggling Over the Mode of Incorporation."

126. Cesari, *Why the West Fears Islam*, 4–5.

127. Cesari, "Muslim Identities in Europe," 52–53.

128. Cesari, *Why the West Fears Islam*, 1–20. The manner in which Western Europeans portray Muslims today overlaps with historical and contemporary portrayals of other groups. Just as many Europeans perceive Islam as antithetical to Enlightenment values, secular Europeans and Americans often adopt a similar perspective on culturally conservative fundamentalist or evangelical Christians. Likewise, doubts about Muslim loyalty are comparable to historical and contemporary allegations of Jewish disloyalty and to Protestant claims (once commonplace in the United States) that loyalty to the pope precluded the inclusion of Catholics in a republic. These commonalities underscore Cesari's point that "Muslims have never been the sole 'others' of the West."

129. Uitermark, Mepschen, and Duyvendak, "Populism, Sexual Politics, and the Exclusion of Muslims," 235–36.

130. Uitermark, Mepschen, and Duyvendak, "Populism, Sexual Politics, and the Exclusion of Muslims," 242. Some Muslims also perceive an opposition between Islam and modernity. According to a 2006 survey, 28 percent of Muslims in France, 36 percent of Muslims in Germany, and 47 percent of Muslims in Britain agreed with the statement that there is a "natural conflict between being a devout Muslim and living in a modern society." Jikeli, *European Muslim Antisemitism*, 23.

131. Cesari, *Why the West Fears Islam*, 11–12. See also Joppke and Torpey, *Legal Integration of Islam*, 121–24.

132. Alternative discourses exist in Europe and the United States, but they have not gained widespread support. One alternative can be found among far-left radicals who consider Islamist elements within the Muslim population to be at the forefront of an emancipatory struggle against Western imperialism. On the radical left and Islamism, see Küntzel, *Jihad and Jew-Hatred*, 141–50; Laqueur, *Changing Face of Antisemitism*, 185–86; Judaken, "So What's New," 544–48; Shepherd, *State beyond the Pale*, 218–25; Wistrich, *Lethal Obsession*, 399–434; Shindler, *Israel and the European Left*, 272–76; and Walzer, "Islamism and the Left." The far-left radicals who see Islamists as allies in a shared struggle against Western imperialism retain the binary structure of Orientalist thinking while reversing the value signs; they think they are taking the Muslim side in a struggle against Western imperialism, but in fact they are taking sides in a struggle among Muslims over the meaning of Islam. Some academics have sought to challenge the binary opposition between Islam and the West by emphasizing the diversity of Europe's Muslim population, its mutability, or the transnational or hybrid character of Muslim identities. Appeals to a shared Abrahamic religious tradition or to multiculturalism also seek to challenge this opposition.

133. Most contemporary scholarship comes to similar conclusions about the Western association of Muslims with premodernity. Buijs and Rath note in "Muslims in Europe" that "Muslim[s] are often associated with pre-modern attitudes and practices. . . . A lot of attention is dedicated to . . . the compatibility of Islam and modernity" (28). A study of antisemitism in

contemporary Spain confirms this finding while also underscoring how representations of Jews and Muslims differ: it found that Muslims were perceived as religious, backward, sexist, and medieval, while Jews were perceived as intelligent, rational, business-oriented, and ultramodern. Baer and López, "Blind Spots of Secularization."

134. These figures come from the *Jewish Daily Forward*, "Who Speaks for the Jews," which adds: "The only population that comes close [to Israel's Jewish population] is the 5.3 million [Jews] here in the United States according to the Pew Research Center's 2013 survey, and the numbers are not increasing anywhere near the level of growth in Israel, which has the highest birth rate in the developed world." The concentration of most of the world's Jews in Israel and America in the twenty-first century is surely relevant to the linkage of antisemitism (or anti-Zionism) and anti-Americanism.

135. Weintraub, "Some Thoughts on Anti-Zionism & Anti-Semitism."

136. Cohen, "Auto-Emancipation and Antisemitism," 74. Just as one can distinguish criticism of the United States from anti-Americanism (Buruma and Margalit, *Occidentalism*, 8–11; Markovits, *Uncouth Nation*, 1–4), so it is important to distinguish criticism of Israel from anti-Zionism as an ideological formation. Anti-Zionism functions as an interpretive frame. Thus, while it may be a response to Israel's policies, it is a symbolically mediated and not a direct response. Furthermore, while there are good reasons to be critical of Israeli policies, what Israel's government does or does not do is often beside the point because anti-Zionism rejects not only Israeli policies but the idea of the Jewish state itself. As Jeff Weintraub has noted in a private communication: "Someone is 'against Israel's existence,' more or less strongly, if they hold one or more of the following cluster of beliefs (which many people do actually believe): that the creation of Israel was mistaken and/or unjust and shouldn't have happened; that Israel's existence (not its policies or its occupation of territories captured in 1967, but its existence) continues to be unjust and illegitimate and pernicious; that it is therefore proper and necessary to promote or support actions and policies leading to the elimination of Israel, through means ranging from 'armed struggle' against what used to be routinely called 'the Zionist entity' or the 'Zionist regime' to the absorption of Israel into an Arab-majority country via some version of a 'one-state' agenda; etc. Efforts to isolate, undermine, stigmatize, and demonize Israel are often practical expressions of such beliefs and desires." As a corollary of such demonization, Israel tends to occupy a subject position in this ideology that goes far beyond its actual empirical role (Buruma and Margalit, *Occidentalism*, 138–39; Postone, "History and Helplessness"). Weintraub, "Some Thoughts on Anti-Zionism & Anti-Semitism"; Hirsh, "Anti-Zionism and Antisemitism"; Hirsh, "Hostility to Israel and Antisemitism"; Judaken, "So What's New"; Shepherd, *State beyond the Pale*; and Shindler, *Israel and the European Left* provide helpful analyses of anti-Zionism and its relation to antisemitism, though I do not necessarily agree with them in all details.

137. According to Judt, "Israel: The Alternative," Israel "imported a characteristically late-nineteenth-century separatist project into a world that has moved on, a world of individual rights, open frontiers, and international law." Israel thus became an "anachronism" in a world of "pluralist states which have long since become multiethnic and multicultural." Sociologist Göran Therborn expressed a similar view in "Three Epochs of European Anti-Semitism," where he suggested that "the state of Israel runs on European time," which is to say, the time of ethnic nationalism and imperialism, but "world time was moving away from the European calendar, into de-colonization, universal rights, and the assertion and recognition of indigenous peoples and of non-European religions and cultures" (163). Traverso provides another variation on the theme of Jewish backwardness in *La fin de la modernité juive*. From 1750 to 1950, he argues, Jews exhibited a predominantly progressive, critical, nonconformist, and cosmopolitan outlook

rooted in their experience of dispersion and exclusion. But since the mid-twentieth century, he contends, they have taken a conservative turn: "The Jews have abandoned their old condition of pariahs. . . . The old trouble-makers and disturbers of order have become its pillars" (76–77). He traces this supposed reversal to two events: the Shoah, the consecration and memory of which has allegedly eliminated antisemitism as a serious problem, and the establishment of Israel on a purported foundation of ethnoreligious nationalism "when, in the Old World, national sovereignties were coming into crisis," Germany was freeing itself from its "chauvinist past," and the construction of "European unity" had begun (24). All translations from Traverso are my own. Shepherd's gloss on this perspective makes explicit its connection to old motifs: "Embodied in the State of Israel, the Jews had, to use the lexicon of Engels, become a 'reactionary people'" (Shepherd, *State beyond the Pale*, 221).

138. Badiou, "Uses of the Word 'Jew,'" 234.

139. Badiou, "Uses of the Word 'Jew,'" 165, 184–85. To be sure, Badiou does not conceive Pauline universalism as entailing the obliteration of difference or the exclusion of the particular (165, 188–94). As he points out, Paul fully intended to include Jews in the "universality of the Announcement." In his view, Paul merely sought to displace the "privileging" of Jewish particularity and to "remind us that it is absurd to believe oneself a proprietor of God" (193–94). Badiou adds that Paul was wary of making "universalist militantism" the "bearer of differences and particularities in turn" (190). Regrettably, however, this is precisely what Badiou does: he makes the Jews (and the Jewish state) the other of the universal. In calling for the displacement of Israel and Jewish communitarianism by a "new Palestine" and a "new Jew" (202–7), Badiou recapitulates the logic of Jewish emancipation, which made inclusion conditional upon moral *régénération*. Badiou, too, wishes to encompass the Jews in his universalism—not real or everyday Jews as they actually exist, but rather the Jews as he thinks they ought to be. Baptism (now figurative) is once again the price of admission to European culture; the Church of Saint Badiou is open only to the converted.

140. Badiou, "Uses of the Word 'Jew,'" 158, 160, 193, 217–29.

141. Badiou, "Uses of the Word 'Jew,'" 218–19.

142. Badiou, "Uses of the Word 'Jew,'" 223.

143. Badiou, "Uses of the Word 'Jew,'" 209, 229.

144. Badiou, "Uses of the Word 'Jew,'" 162, 214.

145. Badiou, "Uses of the Word 'Jew,'" 163.

146. Badiou, "Uses of the Word 'Jew,'" 214.

147. Badiou, "Uses of the Word 'Jew,'" 212. The formation of the European Union did not, of course, fuse France and Germany into a single state. No matter for Badiou, whose answer to this objection is that Israel must be held to a higher standard: "The Zionist state must . . . become the least racial, the least religious and the least nationalist of all states. It must become the most universal of all" (209). Elsewhere Badiou appears to back away from a conceptual opposition between Europe and Israel. In one instance, he concedes that Europe, too, has "'national' states (Croat, Serb, Slovene, etc.) that are totally archaic," but only because it "accepted" the breakup of Yugoslavia (214). In regard to his native France, Badiou bizarrely insists that "it was only in the sorry period of the Nazi occupation, with the Pétain government, that France was defined as the 'French state'" (214). But elsewhere he says: "I have always been especially severe on all the inegalitarian characteristics that mark the uses of the signifier 'French' in contemporary polemics, especially when it comes to the so-called 'republican' camp. For one must start putting one's own house in order" (243). Badiou also concedes in at least one instance that Israeli policies are "neither more nor less cynical and particularist than those of any other States" (242). However,

even if Israel's alleged wickedness is not exceptional, it remains exceptional in his view by virtue of the talismanic power of its Jewish name, shared by no other state, which supposedly shields it from criticism, his own notwithstanding.

148. Badiou, "Uses of the Word 'Jew,'" 163–64.

149. Quotation from Said, *Orientalism*, 287. Mearsheimer and Walt, *Israel Lobby and U.S. Foreign Policy*. *Times of Israel*, "Ex-UK FM: 'Unlimited' Jewish Funds Control US Policy."

150. Quotation from Said, *Orientalism*, 107.

151. Said, *Orientalism*, 309.

152. Buruma and Margalit, *Occidentalism*, 138–39. Shepherd, *State beyond the Pale*, 218–25.

153. It is incorrect to say that Jews are viewed in Western Europe as "the veritable embodiment of the postnational order" (Bunzl, "Between Anti-Semitism and Islamophobia," 502) and misleading to assert that Jews, "after having historically embodied a figure of otherness internal to the Western world," now symbolize the Western world (Traverso, *La fin de la modernité juive*, 116, my translation). The implication of such claims is that Jews have become privileged insiders of a dominant Judeo-Christian, European, or Western order at the expense of new outgroups, particularly Muslims. These claims fail to recognize how the positive image of a modern, postnational Europe is constructed in opposition not only to the Muslim other but also to the Jewish state. Bunzl overstates European support for Zionism in "Between Anti-Semitism and Islamophobia" because he fails to distinguish, as Shepherd does in *State beyond the Pale*, intergovernmental relations between Europe and Israel from the discourse of Europe's opinion-forming classes.

154. Shepherd, *State beyond the Pale*, 55–60.

155. With the end of the Cold War, "intellectuals and publics" began to identify nationalism with "the negative antimonies of civil society," while counterposing it to a "newly universalized discourse of the good" that gave "new legitimacy" to the United Nations and the European Community. Alexander, "Modern, Anti, Post and Neo," 93. This is especially true of Jewish nationalism. Undoubtedly, like all nationalisms, Jewish nationalism can and does take anticivil forms. What I question is the assumption that it can take no other form. Others have made arguments similar to my own about Israel and European postnationalism, to which I am indebted, though I do not necessarily agree with them in all details. Strauss, "Antiglobalism's Jewish Problem," 65. Ottolenghi, "Europe's 'Good' Jews." Fine, "Fighting with Phantoms," 475–76. Shepherd, *State beyond the Pale*, 144–66. Fine, "On Doing the Sociology of Antisemitism." Hirsh, "Hostility to Israel and Antisemitism," 1418. Friedman, "An Insider's Guide." For a different view, see J. J. Goldberg, "Israeli Right's 'Post-Nationalism' Excuse." Goldberg criticizes what he calls the "nationalism-vs.-post-nationalism argument" on two grounds: first, that American and Israeli rightists use it to dismiss criticism of the Israeli occupation of the West Bank—as examples he points to Hazony, "Israel through European Eyes," and Will, "Netanyahu, the Anti-Obama"—and second, that it overstates the extent to which Europeans have abandoned or transcended the old nation-state paradigm. Goldberg is right on both points. However, the use of the argument to defend right-wing policies does not make it inherently right-wing, as Goldberg himself acknowledges when he attributes a left-wing version to Judt, "Israel: The Alternative." As with any binary opposition, the value signs of the two terms (*nationalism* and *postnationalism*) can be reversed to legitimize antithetical political stances. Moreover, the postnational paradigm may attract support as a normative ideal, aspiration, and political project among elites in what Shepherd calls Europe's opinion-making classes even though it elicits less enthusiasm among European voters and mass publics, and actual European realities fall short of it. To the extent that Israel serves as Europe's other, European anti-Zionism functions similarly

to anti-Americanism. Alexander, "'Globalization' as Collective Representation," 87–88. Heins, "Orientalising America?" Markovits, *Uncouth Nation.*

156. Jeffay, "Chinese Discover Jews and Israel." See also Sebag-Montefiore, "Chinese Believe That the Jews Control America"; Ross and Song, *Image of Jews in Contemporary China.*

157. On Jews as social winners, see Muller, *Capitalism and the Jews,* 72–132. Chua and Rubenfeld, *Triple Package.*

158. Küntzel, *Jihad and Jew-Hatred,* 32–34, 84, 94–95, 99–100, 131–32, 146. Postone, "History and Helplessness."

159. Küntzel, *Jihad and Jew-Hatred,* 141–50. Strauss, "Antiglobalism's Jewish Problem." Laqueur, *Changing Face of Antisemitism,* 186–89. Weitzman, *Magical Logic, Globalization, Conspiracy Theory.* Wistrich, *Lethal Obsession,* 600–608. The antiglobalization movement is best understood as a protective countermovement that seeks to check, control, or modify the harmful and destructive consequences of unrestrained market forces. As Polanyi noted in *Great Transformation,* such countermovements can take right-wing as well as left-wing forms.

160. Bové quoted in Strauss, "Antiglobalism's Jewish Problem," 65. Mahler quoted in Weitzman, *Magical Logic, Globalization, Conspiracy Theory,* 6. Hale quoted in Strauss, "Antiglobalism's Jewish Problem," 63.

161. Strauss, "Antiglobalism's Jewish Problem," 65. Judaken, "So What's New," 545. Quotation from Wistrich, *Lethal Obsession,* 606.

162. French diplomat Daniel Bernard reportedly said in 2001 that "the current troubles in the world were all because of 'that shitty little country Israel.'" "Why," he reportedly added, "should the world be in danger of World War Three because of those people?" Amiel, "Islamists Overplay Their Hand." BBC News, "'Anti-Semitic' French Envoy under Fire." In a poll of seventy-five hundred Europeans conducted by the European Commission in October 2003, respondents identified Israel as the biggest threat to world peace. Fuller, "European Poll Calls Israel a Big Threat to World Peace." In 2015, Irish statesman Dermot Ahern reportedly referred to "the destabilising of the entire region, because of the Israeli-Palestinian issue, and that has been the source of all the problems in that part of the world." Ó Raghallaigh, "Israel-Palestine Conflict Is Not the Source."

163. Hirsh, "Corbyn Left." Maltz Bovy, "Comparing Syrian and Jewish Refugees."

Bibliography

Abbott, Andrew. *Department & Discipline: Chicago Sociology at One Hundred.* Chicago: University of Chicago Press, 1999.

Abbott, Andrew, and Rainer Egloff. "The Polish Peasant in Oberlin and Chicago: The Intellectual Trajectory of W. I. Thomas." *American Sociologist* 39, no. 4 (December 2008): 217–58.

Abraham, Gary A. *Max Weber and the Jewish Question.* Urbana: University of Illinois Press, 1992.

———. "Max Weber on 'Jewish Rationalism' and the Jewish Question." *International Journal of Politics, Culture and Society* 1, no. 3 (Spring 1988): 358–91.

Achinger, Christine. "Threats to Modernity, Threats of Modernity: Racism and Antisemitism through the Lens of Literature." *European Societies* 14, no. 2 (2012): 240–58.

Adams, Julia, Elisabeth S. Clemens, and Ann Shola Orloff. "Social Theory, Modernity, and the Three Waves of Historical Sociology." In *Remaking Modernity: Politics, History, and Sociology*, edited by Julia Adams, Elisabeth S. Clemens, and Ann Shola Orloff, 1–72. Durham, NC: Duke University Press, 2005.

Aho, James Alfred. *German Realpolitik and American Sociology: An Inquiry into the Sources and Political Significance of the Sociology of Conflict.* Lewisburg, PA: Bucknell University Press, 1975.

Al-Azmeh, Aziz. "Afterword." In *Islam in Europe: Diversity, Identity and Influence*, edited by Aziz Al-Azmeh and Effie Fokas, 208–15. New York: Cambridge University Press, 2007.

Alatas, Syed Farid, and Vineeta Sinha. "Teaching Classical Sociological Theory in Singapore: The Context of Eurocentrism." *Teaching Sociology* 29, no. 3 (July 2001): 316–31.

Alba, Richard, and Victor Nee. *Remaking the American Mainstream: Assimilation and Contemporary Immigration.* Cambridge, MA: Harvard University Press, 2003.

———. "Rethinking Assimilation Theory for a New Era of Immigration." *International Migration Review* 31, no. 4 (1997): 826–74.

Alexander, Jeffrey C. *The Civil Sphere.* New York: Oxford University Press, 2006.

———. *The Dark Side of Modernity.* Malden, MA: Polity, 2013.

———. "Durkheimian Sociology and Cultural Studies Today." In *Durkheimian Sociology: Cultural Studies*, edited by Jeffrey C. Alexander, 1–21. New York: Cambridge University Press, 1988.

———. "'Globalization' as Collective Representation: The New Dream of a Cosmopolitan Civil

Sphere." *International Journal of Politics, Culture, and Society* 19, no. 1–2 (December 2005): 81–90.

———. "Modern, Anti, Post and Neo." *New Left Review* 210 (March 1995): 63–101.

———. "On the Centrality of the Classics." In *Structure and Meaning: Relinking Classical Sociology*, 8–67. New York: Columbia University Press, 1989.

———. *Remembering the Holocaust: A Debate.* New York: Oxford University Press, 2009.

———. "Rethinking Strangeness: From Structures in Space to Discourses in Civil Society." *Thesis Eleven* 79 (November 2004): 87–104.

———. "Struggling Over the Mode of Incorporation: Backlash against Multiculturalism in Europe." *Ethnic and Racial Studies* 36, no. 4 (2013): 531–56.

Almog, Shmuel. "What's in a Hyphen?" *SICSA Report: Newsletter of the Vidal Sassoon International Center for the Study of Antisemitism* (Summer 1989): 1–2. http://sicsa.huji.ac.il/hyphen.htm

Altgeld, Wolfgang. "German Catholics." In *The Emancipation of Catholics, Jews and Protestants*, edited by Rainer Liedtke and Stephan Wendehorst, 100–21. New York: Manchester University Press, 1999.

Amiel, Barbara. "Islamists Overplay Their Hand but London Salons Don't See It." *Daily Telegraph*, December 17, 2001. http://www.telegraph.co.uk/comment/personal-view/3570981/Islamists-overplay-their-hand-but-London-salons-dont-see-it.html

Anderson, Benedict. *Imagined Communities: Reflections on the Origin and Spread of Nationalism.* Revised ed. New York: Verso, 1991.

Arendt, Hannah. *The Origins of Totalitarianism.* New York: World Publishing, [1951] 1958.

Arkush, Allan. "Judaism as Egoism: From Spinoza to Feuerbach to Marx." *Modern Judaism* 11, no. 2 (May 1991): 211–23.

Atkin, Maurice, Lloyd P. Gartner, Arden J. Geldman, Isaiah Kenen, Jacob Rader Marcus, and Sefton D. Temkin. "United States of America." *Encyclopaedia Judaica.* Edited by Michael Berenbaum and Fred Skolnik. 2nd ed. Vol. 20. Detroit, MI: Macmillan, 2007.

Avineri, Shlomo. "Marx and Jewish Emancipation." *Journal of the History of Ideas* 25, no. 3 (July–September 1964): 445–50.

Backhaus, Jürgen. "Sombart's Modern Capitalism." *Kyklos* 42, no. 4 (November 1989): 599–611.

———, ed. *Werner Sombart (1863–1941): Social Scientist.* 3 vols. Marburg, Germany: Metropolis, 1996.

Badiou, Alain. "Uses of the Word 'Jew.'" In *Polemics*, 155–254. Translated by Steve Corcoran. New York: Verso, 2006.

Baer, Alejandro, and Paula López. "The Blind Spots of Secularization: A Qualitative Approach to the Study of Antisemitism in Spain." *European Societies* 14, no. 2 (2012): 203–21.

Barbalet, Jack. *Weber, Passion and Profits: 'The Protestant Ethic and the Spirit of Capitalism' in Context.* New York: Cambridge University Press, 2008.

Baron, Salo W., Arcadius Kahan, and Nachum Gross. *Economic History of the Jews.* New York: Schocken, 1975.

Bauer, Bruno. *The Jewish Problem.* Translated by Helen Lederer. Cincinnati, OH: Hebrew Union College-Jewish Institute of Religion, [1843] 1958.

Bauer, Yehuda. "In Search of a Definition of Antisemitism." In *Approaches to Antisemitism: Context and Curriculum*, edited by Michael Brown, 10–23. New York: American Jewish Committee, 1994.

Bauman, Zygmunt. "'Antisemitism' Reassessed." In *Life in Fragments: Essays in Postmodern Morality*, 206–22. Cambridge, UK: Blackwell, 1995.

———. "Exit Visas and Entry Tickets: Paradoxes of Jewish Assimilation." *Telos* 77 (Fall 1988): 45–77.

———. *Modernity and Ambivalence.* Ithaca, NY: Cornell University Press, 1991.

BBC News. "'Anti-Semitic' French Envoy under Fire." December 20, 2001. http://news.bbc.co.uk/2/hi/europe/1721172.stm

Ben-Sasson, Haim Hillel, Samuel Miklos Stern, Robert Weltsch, Michael Berenbaum, Jacob S. Levinger, and Chaim Yahil. "Germany." *Encyclopaedia Judaica.* Edited by Michael Berenbaum and Fred Skolnik. 2nd ed. Vol. 7. Detroit, MI: Macmillan, 2007.

Benbassa, Esther. *The Jews of France: A History from Antiquity to the Present.* Translated by M. B. DeBevoise. Princeton, NJ: Princeton University Press, 1999.

Berman, Lila Corwin. *Speaking of Jews: Rabbis, Intellectuals, and the Creation of an American Public Identity.* Berkeley: University of California Press, 2009.

Bhabha, Homi K. *The Location of Culture.* London: Routledge, 1994.

Bhambra, Gurminder K. "Sociology and Postcolonialism: Another 'Missing' Revolution?" *Sociology* 41, no. 5 (October 2007): 871–84.

Bingham, Theodore A. "Foreign Criminals in New York." *North American Review* 188, no. 634 (September 1908): 383–94.

Birnbaum, Pierre. "French Jewish Sociologists between Reason and Faith: The Impact of the Dreyfus Affair." *Jewish Social Studies* 2, no. 1 (Fall 1995): 1–35.

———. *Geography of Hope: Exile, the Enlightenment, Disassimilation.* Translated by Charlotte Mandell. Stanford, CA: Stanford University Press, [2004] 2008.

———. *Jewish Destinies: Citizenship, State, and Community in Modern France.* Translated by Arthur Goldhammer. New York: Hill & Wang, [1995] 2000.

———. *The Jews of the Republic: A Political History of State Jews in France from Gambetta to Vichy.* Translated by Jane Marie Todd. Stanford, CA: Stanford University Press, [1992] 1996.

Blackbourn, David. "The Discrete Charm of the Bourgeoisie: Reappraising German History in the Nineteenth Century." In *The Peculiarities of German History: Bourgeois Society and Politics in Nineteenth-Century Germany*, edited by David Blackbourn and Geoff Eley, 159–292. New York: Oxford University Press, 1984.

Blackbourn, David, and Geoff Eley. *The Peculiarities of German History: Bourgeois Society and Politics in Nineteenth-Century Germany.* New York: Oxford University Press, 1984.

Blanchard, William H. "Karl Marx and the Jewish Question." *Political Psychology* 5, no. 3 (September 1984): 365–74.

Bloemraad, Irene, Anna Korteweg, and Gökçe Yurdakul. "Citizenship and Immigration: Multiculturalism, Assimilation, and Challenges to the Nation-State." *Annual Review of Sociology* 34 (2008): 153–79.

Bloom, Solomon F. "Karl Marx and the Jews." *Jewish Social Studies* 4, no. 1 (January 1942): 3–16.

Bodemann, Y. Michal. "Coldly Admiring the Jews: Werner Sombart and Classical German Sociology on Nationalism and Race." In *Antisemitism and the Constitution of Sociology*, edited by Marcel Stoetzler, 110–34. Lincoln: University of Nebraska Press, 2014.

———. "Ethnos, Race and Nation: Werner Sombart, the Jews and Classical German Sociology." *Patterns of Prejudice* 44, no. 2 (2010): 117–36.

Boer, Roland. *Criticism of Earth: On Marx, Engels and Theology.* Boston: Brill, 2012.

Bouglé, Célestin. "Philosophie de l'antisémitisme (l'idée de race)." *La Grande Revue* 9 (January 1, 1899): 143–58.

Bourdieu, Pierre. "Les conditions sociales de la production sociologique: Sociologie coloniale et décolonisation de la sociologie." In *Le Mal de voir*, 416–27. Paris: Union générale d'éditions, 1976.

———. "Intellectual Field and Creative Project." *Social Science Information* 8, no. 2 (1969): 89–120.

———. *Language and Symbolic Power*. Edited by John B. Thompson. Translated by Gino Raymond and Matthew Adamson. Cambridge, MA: Harvard University Press, 1991.

———. *The Logic of Practice*. Stanford, CA: Stanford University Press, [1980] 1990.

———. *Pascalian Meditations*. Translated by Richard Nice. Stanford, CA: Stanford University Press, [1997] 2000.

———. *Political Interventions: Social Science and Political Action*. Translated by David Fernbach. New York: Verso, [2002] 2008.

Bourne, Randolph S. "The Jew and Trans-National America." In *War and the Intellectuals*, edited by Carl Resek, 124–33. New York: Harper & Row, [1916] 1964.

Bowen, John R. *Why the French Don't Like Headscarves: Islam, the State, and Public Space*. Princeton, NJ: Princeton University Press, 2007.

Brenner, Michael. "Between Revolution and Legal Equality." In *German-Jewish History in Modern Times*, vol. 2. Edited by Michael A. Meyer, 279–318. New York: Columbia University Press, 1997.

Bressler, Marvin. "Jewish Behavior Patterns as Exemplified in W. I. Thomas' Unfinished Study of the *Bintl Brief*." PhD diss., University of Pennsylvania, 1952.

———. "Selected Family Patterns in W. I. Thomas' Unfinished Study of the *Bintl Brief*." *American Sociological Review* 17, no. 5 (October 1952): 563–71.

Brocke, Bernhard vom. "Werner Sombart, 1863–1941. Capitalism—Socialism. His Life, Works and Influence." In *Werner Sombart (1863–1941): Social Scientist*, vol. 1, edited by Jürgen Backhaus, 19–102. Marburg, Germany: Metropolis, 1996.

Brubaker, Rogers. *Citizenship and Nationhood in France and Germany*. Cambridge, MA: Harvard University Press, 1992.

———. "The Return of Assimilation? Changing Perspectives on Immigration and Its Sequels in France, Germany, and the United States." *Ethnic and Racial Studies* 24, no. 4 (July 2001): 531–48.

Brubaker, Rogers, Mara Loveman, and Peter Stamatov. "Ethnicity as Cognition." *Theory and Society* 33, no. 1 (February 2004): 31–64.

Brunetière, F. "Revue Littéraire, *La France juive*." *Revue des deux mondes* 75 (June 1, 1886): 693–704.

Brustein, William I. *Roots of Hate: Anti-Semitism in Europe before the Holocaust*. New York: Cambridge University Press, 2003.

Brustein, William I., and Louisa Roberts. *The Socialism of Fools? Leftist Origins of Modern Anti-Semitism*. New York: Cambridge University Press, 2015.

Buijs, Frank J., and Jan Rath. "Muslims in Europe: The State of Research." IMISCOE Working Paper, 2006. http://www.imiscoe.org/workingpapers/documents/muslims_in_europe

Bunzl, Matti. "Between Anti-Semitism and Islamophobia: Some Thoughts on the New Europe." *American Ethnologist* 32, no. 4 (November 2005): 499–508.

Burner, David. *The Politics of Provincialism: The Democratic Party in Transition, 1918–1932*. New York: Knopf, 1967.

Burns, Michael. *Dreyfus: A Family Affair, 1789–1945*. New York: Harper Collins, 1991.

Burr, Clinton Stoddard. *America's Race Heritage*. New York: National Historical Society, 1922.

Buruma, Ian, and Avishai Margalit. *Occidentalism: The West in the Eyes of Its Enemies.* New York: Penguin, 2004.

Cahnman, Werner J. *Jews & Gentiles: A Historical Sociology of Their Relations.* Edited by Judith T. Marcus and Zoltan Tarr. New Brunswick, NJ: Transaction, 2004.

Calhoun, Craig. "Nationalism, Political Community and the Representation of Society: Or, Why Feeling at Home Is Not a Substitute for Public Space." *European Journal of Social Theory* 2, no. 2 (1999): 217–31.

Camic, Charles. "Classical Sociological Theory as a Field of Research." In *Reclaiming the Sociological Classics,* edited by Charles Camic, 1–10. Malden, MA: Blackwell, 1997.

———. "Weber and the Judaic Economic Ethic: A Comment on Fahey." *American Journal of Sociology* 89, no. 6 (May 1984): 1410–16.

Camic, Charles, and Neil Gross. "The New Sociology of Ideas." In *The Blackwell Companion to Sociology,* edited by Judith R. Blau, 236–49. Malden, MA: Blackwell, 2001.

Carey, James T. *Sociology and Public Affairs: The Chicago School.* London: Sage, 1975.

Carlebach, Julius. *Karl Marx and the Radical Critique of Judaism.* Boston: Routledge, 1978.

Cesarani, David. "Why Muslims Are Not the New Jews." *Jewish Chronicle,* October 22, 2009. http://www.thejc.com/comment/comment/21173/why-muslims-are-not-new-jews

Cesari, Jocelyne. "Muslim Identities in Europe: The Snare of Exceptionalism." In *Islam in Europe: Diversity, Identity and Influence,* edited by Aziz Al-Azmeh and Effie Fokas, 49–67. New York: Cambridge University Press, 2007.

———. *When Islam and Democracy Meet: Muslims in Europe and in the United States.* New York: Palgrave Macmillan, 2013.

———. *Why the West Fears Islam: An Exploration of Muslims in Liberal Democracies.* New York: Palgrave Macmillan, 2013.

Chabauty, E. A. *Les juifs, nos maîtres! Documents et dévelopments nouveaux sur la question juive.* Paris: Victor Palmé, 1882.

Chirac, Auguste. *Les rois de la république: Histoire des juiveries.* 2 vols. Paris: Éditions du Trident, [1883–1886] 1987.

Choate, Mark I. *Emigrant Nation: The Making of Italy Abroad.* Cambridge, MA: Harvard University Press, 2008.

Chua, Amy, and Jed Rubenfeld. *The Triple Package: How Three Unlikely Traits Explain the Rise and Fall of Cultural Groups in America.* New York: Penguin, 2014.

Chua, Peter. "Orientalism as Cultural Practices and the Production of Sociological Knowledge." *Sociology Compass* 2, no. 4 (2008): 1179–91.

Clapham, J. H. "Review of *Die Zukunft der Juden* by Werner Sombart." *The Economic Journal* 22, no. 86 (June 1912): 294–96.

Clark, Terry Nichols. "Émile Durkheim and the Institutionalization of Sociology in the French University System." *European Journal of Sociology* 9 (1968): 37–71.

———. *Prophets and Patrons: The French University and the Emergence of the Social Sciences.* Cambridge, MA: Harvard University Press, 1973.

Cohen, Mitchell. "Auto-Emancipation and Antisemitism (Homage to Bernard-Lazare)." *Jewish Social Studies* 10, no. 1 (Autumn 2003): 69–77.

Collins, Randall. "The Durkheimian Movement in France and in World Sociology." In *The Cambridge Companion to Durkheim,* edited by Jeffrey C. Alexander and Philip Smith, 101–35. New York: Cambridge University Press, 2005.

———. *Max Weber.* Newbury Park, CA: Sage, 1986.

———. "Weber's Last Theory of Capitalism: A Systematization." *American Sociological Review* 45, no. 6 (December 1980): 925–42.

Commons, John R. *Races and Immigrants in America.* New York: Augustus M. Kelley Publishers, [1907] 1967. First edition originally published by Macmillan in 1907. Second edition published in 1920.

Conn, Peter. *The Divided Mind: Ideology and Imagination in America, 1898–1917.* New York: Cambridge University Press, 1983.

Connell, R. W. "Why Is Classical Theory Classical?" *American Journal of Sociology* 102, no. 6 (May 1997): 1511–57.

Cooley, Charles H. *Social Organization: A Study of the Larger Mind.* New York: Scribner, [1909] 1925.

Coser, Lewis A. "Georg Simmel's Style of Work: A Contribution to the Sociology of the Sociologist." *American Journal of Sociology* 63, no. 6 (May 1958): 635–41.

———. "Introduction." In *Georg Simmel*, edited by Lewis A. Coser, 1–26. Englewood Cliffs, NJ: Prentice-Hall, 1965.

———. *Masters of Sociological Thought.* 2nd ed. San Diego, CA: Harcourt Brace Jovanovich, 1971.

Cuddihy, John Murray. *The Ordeal of Civility: Freud, Marx, Lévi-Strauss, and the Jewish Struggle with Modernity.* Boston: Beacon, 1974.

Davenport, Charles Benedict. *Heredity in Relation to Eugenics.* New York: Henry Holt, 1911.

Davies, Peter. *The Extreme Right in France, 1789 to the Present.* New York: Routledge, 2002.

Davis, Natalie Zemon. "Religion and Capitalism Once Again? Jewish Merchant Culture in the Seventeenth Century." *Representations* 59 (Summer 1997): 56–84.

Deegan, Mary Jo. *Jane Addams and the Men of the Chicago School, 1892–1918.* New Brunswick, NJ: Transaction, 1988.

———. *Race, Hull-House, and the University of Chicago.* Westport, CT: Praeger, 2002.

Derks, Hans. "Nomads, Jews, and Pariahs: Max Weber and Anti-Judaism." *European Legacy* 4, no. 4 (1999): 24–48.

Dewey, John. "Nationalizing Education." In *The Middle Works, 1899–1924*, vol. 10, edited by Jo Ann Boydston, 202–10. Carbondale: Southern Illinois University Press, [1916] 1980.

———. *The Public and Its Problems.* New York: Henry Holt, 1927.

DiMaggio, Paul. "Culture and Cognition." *Annual Review of Sociology* 23 (1997): 263–87.

DiMaggio, Paul J., and Walter W. Powell. "The Iron Cage Revisited: Institutional Isomorphism and Collective Rationality in Organizational Fields." *American Sociological Review* 48, no. 2 (April 1983): 147–60.

Diner, Hasia R. "Introduction: Louis Wirth and the Making of *The Ghetto.*" In *The Ghetto*, ix–lxiii. New Brunswick, NJ: Transaction, 1998.

Douglas, Mary. *Purity and Danger: An Analysis of the Concepts of Pollution and Taboo.* New York: Routledge, 1966.

Draper, Hal. "Marx and the Economic-Jew Stereotype." In *Karl Marx's Theory of Revolution*, vol. 1, 591–608. New York: Monthly Review Press, 1977.

Drumont, Édouard. *La fin d'un monde.* Paris: Albert Savine, 1889.

———. *La France juive.* 2 vols. Paris: Éditions du Trident, [1886] 1986.

Du Bois, W. E. Burghardt. *The Souls of Black Folk: Essays and Sketches.* 3rd ed. Chicago: A. C. McClurg & Co, 1903.

Durkheim, Émile. *L'Allemagne au-dessus de tout: La mentalité allemande et la guerre.* Paris: Librairie Armand Colin, 1915.

———. "The Determination of the Moral Fact." In *Sociology and Philosophy*. Translated by D. F. Pocock. New York: Free Press, [1906] 1974.

———. *The Division of Labor in Society*. Translated by W. D. Halls. New York: Free Press, [1893] 1984.

———. *The Elementary Forms of Religious Life*. Translated by Karen E. Fields. New York: Free Press, [1912] 1995.

———. *Emile Durkheim: Contributions to* L'Année Sociologique. Edited by Yash Nandan. Translated by John French, Andrew P. Lyons, Yash Nandan, John Sweeney, and Kennerly Woody. New York: Free Press, 1980.

———. "Individualism and the Intellectuals." In *Émile Durkheim: On Morality and Society*, edited by Robert N. Bellah. Chicago: University of Chicago Press, [1898] 1973.

———. "The Intellectual Elite and Democracy." In *Émile Durkheim: On Morality and Society*, edited by Robert N. Bellah, 58–60. Chicago: University of Chicago Press, [1904] 1973.

———. *Lettres à Marcel Mauss*. Edited by Philippe Besnard and Marcel Fournier. Paris: Presses Universitaires de France, 1998.

———. "Lettres de Durkheim." *Revue française de sociologie* 20, no. 1 (January–March 1979): 113–21.

———. *Moral Education*. Translated by Everett K. Wilson and Herman Schnurer. Edited by Everett K. Wilson. New York: Free Press, 1961.

———. "The Principles of 1789 and Sociology." In *Émile Durkheim: On Morality and Society*, edited by Robert N. Bellah. Chicago: University of Chicago Press, [1890] 1973.

———. *Professional Ethics and Civic Morals*. Translated by Cornelia Brookfield. New York: Routledge, 1957.

———. *The Rules of Sociological Method*. Edited by Steven Lukes. Translated by W. D. Halls. New York: Free Press, [1895] 1982.

———. *Socialism and Saint-Simon*. Edited by Alvin W. Gouldner. Translated by Charlotte Sattler. Yellow Springs, OH: Antioch Press, 1958.

———. *Suicide*. Translated by John A. Spaulding and George Simpson. Edited by George Simpson. New York: Free Press, [1897] 1951.

———. *Textes*. 3 vols. Paris: Editions de Minuit, 1975.

Durkheim, Émile, and Ernest Denis. *Qui a voulu la guerre? Les origines de la guerre d'après les documents diplomatiques*. Paris: Librairie Armand Colin, 1915.

Eagles, Charles W. *Democracy Delayed: Congressional Reapportionment and Urban-Rural Conflict in the 1920s*. Athens: University of Georgia Press, 1990.

Edgeworth, F. Y. "Economists on War." *The Economic Journal* 25, no. 100 (December 1915): 604–10.

Eisenstadt, S. N. "The Format of Jewish History. Some Reflections on Weber's *Ancient Judaism*." *Modern Judaism* 1, no. 1 (May 1981): 54–73.

———. "The Format of Jewish History. Some Reflections on Weber's *Ancient Judaism*: Transformations in the Second Temple Era and the Subsequent Course of Jewish History. Part II." *Modern Judaism* 1, no. 2 (September 1981): 217–34.

———. *Jewish Civilization: The Jewish Historical Experience in a Comparative Perspective*. Albany: State University of New York Press, 1992.

———. "Multiple Modernities." *Daedalus* 129, no. 1 (Winter 2000): 1–29.

———. "Multiple Modernities in an Age of Globalization." *Canadian Journal of Sociology/Cahiers canadiens de sociologie* 24, no. 2 (Spring 1999): 283–95.

———. "Pluralism and the Multiple Forms of Modernity." *European Journal of Social Theory* 7, no. 3 (August 2004): 391–404.

Elias, Norbert. *The Civilizing Process: The Development of Manners.* Translated by Edmund Jephcott. New York: Urizen Books, [1939] 1978.

Emirbayer, Mustafa. "Manifesto for a Relational Sociology." *American Journal of Sociology* 103, no. 2 (September 1997): 281–317.

———. "Useful Durkheim." *Sociological Theory* 14, no. 2 (July 1996): 109–30.

Epstein, M. "The Teaching of Economics in Germany after the War." *The Economic Journal* 27, no. 107 (September 1917): 432–35.

Etzioni, Amitai. "The Ghetto: A Re-Evaluation." *Social Forces* 37, no. 3 (March 1959): 255–62.

Fahey, Tony. "Max Weber's *Ancient Judaism.*" *American Journal of Sociology* 88, no. 1 (July 1982): 62–87.

Fairchild, Henry Pratt. *The Melting Pot Mistake.* Boston: Little, Brown, 1926.

Faris, Robert E. L. *Chicago Sociology, 1920–1932.* Chicago: University of Chicago Press, 1967.

Feuerbach, Ludwig. *The Essence of Christianity.* Translated by George Eliot. New York: Harper & Row, [1841] 1957.

Fine, Robert. "Fighting with Phantoms: A Contribution to the Debate on Antisemitism in Europe." *Patterns of Prejudice* 43, no. 5 (2009): 459–79.

———. "On Doing the Sociology of Antisemitism." December 21, 2012. https://engageonline.wordpress.com/2012/12/21/robert-fine-on-doing-the-sociology-of-antisemitism/

———. "Rereading Marx on the 'Jewish Question': Marx as a Critic of Antisemitism?" In *Antisemitism and the Constitution of Sociology,* edited by Marcel Stoetzler, 137–59. Lincoln: University of Nebraska Press, 2014.

Fink, Leon. "Progressive Reformers, Social Scientists, and the Search for a Democratic Public." In *Progressive Intellectuals and the Dilemmas of Democratic Commitment,* 13–51. Cambridge, MA: Harvard University Press, 1997.

Fischer, Lars. *The Socialist Response to Antisemitism in Imperial Germany.* New York: Cambridge University Press, 2007.

Fish, Isaac Stone. "Is China Still a 'Developing' Country?" *Foreign Policy,* September 25, 2014. http://foreignpolicy.com/2014/09/25/is-china-still-a-developing-country/

Fitzgerald, David. *A Nation of Emigrants: How Mexico Manages Its Migration.* Berkeley: University of California Press, 2009.

Foner, Nancy, and Richard Alba. "Immigrant Religion in the U.S. and Western Europe: Bridge or Barrier to Inclusion?" *International Migration Review* 42, no. 2 (Summer 2008): 360–92.

Fournier, Marcel. "Durkheim's Life and Context: Something New about Durkheim?" In *The Cambridge Companion to Durkheim,* edited by Jeffrey C. Alexander and Philip Smith, 41–69. New York: Cambridge University Press, 2005.

———. *Émile Durkheim.* Paris: Fayard, 2007.

———. *Émile Durkheim: A Biography.* Translated by David Macey. Malden, MA: Polity, [2007] 2013.

———. *Marcel Mauss: A Biography.* Princeton, NJ: Princeton University Press, [1994] 2006.

Frazier, E. Franklin. "Theoretical Structure of Sociology and Sociological Research." *British Journal of Sociology* 4, no. 4 (December 1953): 293–311.

Freud, Sigmund. *Three Essays on the Theory of Sexuality.* Translated and edited by James Strachey. New York: Basic Books, [1905] 1962.

Friedman, Matti. "An Insider's Guide to the Most Important Story on Earth." *Tablet Maga-*

zine, August 26, 2014. http://tabletmag.com/jewish-news-and-politics/183033/israel-insider-guide

Frisby, David. *Georg Simmel.* London: Tavistock, 1984.

Fukuyama, Francis. "The End of History?" *National Interest* 16 (Summer 1989): 3–18.

———. *The End of History and the Last Man.* New York: Free Press, 1992.

Fuller, Thomas. "European Poll Calls Israel a Big Threat to World Peace." *New York Times*, October 31, 2003. http://www.nytimes.com/2003/10/31/news/31iht-poll_ed3_.html

Gartner, Lloyd P. *History of the Jews in Modern Times.* New York: Oxford University Press, 2001.

Geller, Jay. *The Other Jewish Question: Identifying the Jew and Making Sense of Modernity.* New York: Fordham University Press, 2011.

Gerstle, Gary. *American Crucible: Race and Nation in the Twentieth Century.* Princeton, NJ: Princeton University Press, 2001.

Giddens, Anthony. *Capitalism and Modern Social Theory: An Analysis of the Writings of Marx, Durkheim and Max Weber.* New York: Cambridge University Press, 1971.

———. "Durkheim's Political Sociology." *Sociological Review* 19, no. 4 (November 1971): 477–519.

Gillespie, Michael Allen. *The Theological Origins of Modernity.* Chicago: University of Chicago Press, 2008.

Gilman, Sander L. "Karl Marx and the Secret Language of Jews." *Modern Judaism* 4, no. 3 (October 1984): 275–94.

Gilroy, Paul. *The Black Atlantic: Modernity and Double Consciousness.* Cambridge, MA: Harvard University Press, 1993.

Go, Julian. "For a Postcolonial Sociology." *Theory and Society* 42, no. 1 (January 2013): 25–55.

———, ed. *Postcolonial Sociology.* Bingley, UK: Emerald, 2013.

Goldberg, Chad Alan. "Introduction to Émile Durkheim's 'Antisemitism and Social Crisis.'" *Sociological Theory* 26, no. 4 (December 2008): 299–323.

———. "The Two Marxes: From Jewish Domination to Supersession of the Jews." *Journal of Classical Sociology* 15, no. 4 (November 2015): 415–34.

Goldberg, David Theo. "Racial Europeanization." *Ethnic and Racial Studies* 29, no. 2 (2006): 331–64.

Goldberg, Harvey. "Jean Jaurès and the Jewish Question: The Evolution of a Position." *Jewish Social Studies* 20, no. 2 (April 1958): 67–94.

Goldberg, J. J. "The Israeli Right's 'Post-Nationalism' Excuse." *Jewish Daily Forward*, August 25, 2010. http://forward.com/articles/130674/the-israeli-right-s-post-nationalism-excus

Goldberg, Milton M. "A Qualification of the Marginal Man Theory." *American Sociological Review* 6, no. 1 (February 1941): 52–58.

Goldenweiser, E. A. "Review of *Die Zukunft der Juden* by Werner Sombart." *American Economic Review* 2, no. 3 (September 1912): 678–79.

Goldstein, Eric L. *The Price of Whiteness: Jews, Race, and American Identity.* Princeton, NJ: Princeton University Press, 2006.

Golovensky, David I. "The Marginal Man Concept: An Analysis and Critique." *Social Forces* 30, no. 3 (March 1952): 333–39.

Goren, Arthur A. *New York Jews and the Quest for Community: The Kehillah Experiment, 1908–1922.* New York: Columbia University Press, 1970.

Gould, Charles W. *America: A Family Matter.* New York: Scribner, 1922.

Grant, Madison. *The Conquest of a Continent; or, The Expansion of Races in America.* New York: Scribner, 1933.

———. *The Passing of the Great Race.* New York: Scribner, 1916.

Green, Arnold W. "A Re-Examination of the Marginal Man Concept." *Social Forces* 26, no. 2 (December 1947): 167–71.

———. "Why Americans Feel Insecure: The Sense of Alienation Is Not Exclusively Jewish." *Commentary* 6 (1948): 18–28.

Greifer, Julian L. "Attitudes to the Stranger: A Study of the Attitudes of Primitive Society and Early Hebrew Culture." *American Sociological Review* 10, no. 6 (December 1945): 739–45.

Grundmann, Reiner, and Nico Stehr. "Why Is Werner Sombart Not Part of the Core of Classical Sociology?" *Journal of Classical Sociology* 1, no. 2 (2001): 257–87.

Gusfield, Joseph R. *Symbolic Crusade: Status Politics and the American Temperance Movement.* Urbana: University of Illinois Press, 1963.

Habermas, Jürgen, and Jacques Derrida. "February 15, or What Binds Europeans Together: A Plea for a Common Foreign Policy, Beginning in the Core of Europe." *Constellations* 10, no. 3 (September 2003): 291–97.

Halbwachs, M. "Review of *Die Juden und das Wirtschaftsleben* by Werner Sombart." *L'Année sociologique* 12 (1909–1912): 623–28.

Hall, Stuart. "Cultural Identity and Diaspora." In *Colonial Discourse and Post-Colonial Theory: A Reader*, 392–401, edited by Patrick Williams and Laura Chrisman. London: Harvester Wheatsheaf, 1993.

———. "When Was 'the Post-Colonial'? Thinking at the Limit." In *The Post-Colonial Question*, 242–60. Edited by Iain Chambers and Lidia Curti. New York: Routledge, 1996.

Harris, Abram L. "Sombart and German (National) Socialism." *Journal of Political Economy* 50, no. 6 (December 1942): 805–35.

Hart, Mitchell B. "Jews, Race, and Capitalism in the German-Jewish Context." *Jewish History* 19, no. 1 (2005): 49–63.

———. *Social Science and the Politics of Modern Jewish Identity.* Stanford, CA: Stanford University Press, 2000.

Haynes, Stephen R. *Reluctant Witnesses: Jews and the Christian Imagination.* Louisville, KY: Westminster John Knox Press, 1995.

Hazony, Yoram. "Israel through European Eyes." *Jerusalem Letters*, July 14, 2010. http://jerusalemletters.com/israel-through-european-eyes/

Hegel, G. W. F. *Introduction to the Philosophy of History.* Translated by Leo Rauch. Indianapolis, IN: Hackett, [1840] 1988.

Heilbron, Johan. *French Sociology.* Ithaca, NY: Cornell University Press, 2015.

Heins, Volker. "Orientalising America? Continental Intellectuals and the Search for Europe's Identity." *Millennium: Journal of International Studies* 34, no. 2 (February 2006): 433–48.

Heinze, Andrew R. *Jews and the American Soul: Human Nature in the Twentieth Century.* Princeton, NJ: Princeton University Press, 2004.

Herberg, Will. "The Christian Mythology of Socialism." *Antioch Review* 3, no. 1 (Spring 1943): 125–32.

Herf, Jeffrey. *Reactionary Modernism: Technology, Culture, and Politics in Weimar and the Third Reich.* New York: Cambridge University Press, 1984.

Hertz, Robert. "The Pre-Eminence of the Right Hand: A Study in Religious Polarity." In *Death and the Right Hand.* Translated by Rodney Needham and Claudia Needham, 89–113. Glencoe, IL: Free Press, [1909] 1960.

Hertzberg, Arthur. *The French Enlightenment and the Jews.* New York: Columbia University Press, 1968.

Herzl, Theodor. *Old-New Land.* 2nd ed. Translated by Lotta Levensohn. New York: Bloch, [1902] 1960.

Heschel, Susanah. *Abraham Geiger and the Jewish Jesus.* Chicago: University of Chicago Press, 1998.

———. "Revolt of the Colonized: Abraham Geiger's *Wissenschaft des Judentums* as a Challenge to Christian Hegemony in the Academy." *New German Critique* 77 (Spring–Summer 1999): 61–85.

Hess, Jonathan M. *Germans, Jews and the Claims of Modernity.* New Haven, CT: Yale University Press, 2002.

Higham, John. *Strangers in the Land: Patterns of American Nativism, 1860–1925.* 2nd ed. New Brunswick, NJ: Rutgers University Press, [1955] 1992.

Hilferding, Rudolf. *Finance Capital: A Study of the Latest Phase of Capitalist Development.* Edited by Tom Bottomore, Morris Watnick, and Sam Gordon. Boston: Routledge & Kegan Paul, [1910] 1981.

Hirsh, David. "Anti-Zionism and Antisemitism: Cosmopolitan Reflections." Yale Initiative for the Interdisciplinary Study of Antisemitism Working Paper Series, 2007. http://isgap.org/wp-content/uploads/2013/08/ISGAP-Working-Papers-David-Hirsh.pdf

———. "The Corbyn Left: The Politics of Position and the Politics of Reason." *Fathom* (Autumn 2015). http://fathomjournal.org/the-corbyn-left-the-politics-of-position-and-the-politics-of-reason/

———. "Hostility to Israel and Antisemitism: Toward a Sociological Approach." *Journal for the Study of Antisemitism* 5 (2013): 1401–22. http://research.gold.ac.uk/8734/

Hobsbawm, Eric J. *The Age of Capital, 1848–1875.* New York: Scribner, 1975.

———. *The Age of Empire, 1875–1914.* New York: Vintage, 1987.

———. *The Age of Extremes: The Short Twentieth Century, 1914–1991.* New York: Viking Penguin, 1994.

———. *The Age of Revolution, 1789–1848.* Cleveland, OH: World Publishing, 1962.

Hofstadter, Richard. "The Pseudo-Conservative Revolt." In *The Paranoid Style in American Politics and Other Essays*, 41–65. New York: Knopf, [1954] 1966.

Hughes, Everett C. "Dilemmas and Contradictions of Status." *American Journal of Sociology* 50, no. 5 (March 1945): 353–59.

———. "Social Change and Status Protest: An Essay on the Marginal Man." *Phylon* 10, no. 1 (1949): 58–65.

Huntington, Samuel P. "The Clash of Civilizations?" *Foreign Affairs* 72, no. 3 (Summer 1993): 22–49.

———. *The Clash of Civilizations and the Remaking of World Order.* New York: Simon & Schuster, 1996.

Hutton, Patrick H. *The Cult of the Revolutionary Tradition: The Blanquists in French Politics, 1864–1893.* Berkeley: University of California Press, 1981.

Hyman, Paula E. *From Dreyfus to Vichy: The Remaking of French Jewry, 1906–1939.* New York: Columbia University Press, 1979.

———. *The Jews of Modern France.* Berkeley: University of California Press, 1998.

Jacobs, Joseph. "Statistics." *The Jewish Encyclopedia.* Edited by Isidore Singer. Vol. 11. New York: Funk & Wagnalls, 1905.

Janowitz, Morris. "Introduction." In *On Social Organization and Social Personality*, edited by Morris Janowitz, vii–lviii. Chicago: University of Chicago Press, 1966.

———. "Sociological Theory and Social Control." *American Journal of Sociology* 81, no. 1 (July 1975): 82–108.

Jeffay, Nathan. "The Chinese Discover Jews and Israel and Can't Seem to Get Enough." *Jewish Daily Forward*, January 26, 2011. http://forward.com/articles/134962/the-chinese-discover-jews-and-israel-and-can-t-s/

Jennings, Jeremy. "Anti-Semitic Discourse in Dreyfus-Affair France." In *The Development of the Radical Right in France*, translated and edited by Edward J. Arnold, 16–32. New York: St. Martin's, 2000.

Jersch-Wenzel, Stefi. "Population Shifts and Occupational Structure." In *German-Jewish History in Modern Times*, vol. 2., edited by Michael A. Meyer, 50–89. New York: Columbia University Press, 1997.

Jewish Daily Forward. "Who Speaks for the Jews?" February 11, 2015. http://forward.com/opinion/editorial/214527/who-speaks-for-the-jews/

Jikeli, Günther. *European Muslim Antisemitism: Why Young Urban Males Say They Don't Like Jews*. Bloomington: Indiana University Press, 2015.

Joas, Hans. *Pragmatism and Social Theory*. Chicago: University of Chicago Press, 1993.

Jones, Robert Alun. "Ambivalent Cartesians: Durkheim, Montesquieu, and Method." *American Journal of Sociology* 100 (July 1994): 1–39.

———. *The Development of Durkheim's Social Realism*. New York: Cambridge University Press, 1999.

———. "Durkheim, Frazer, and Smith: The Role of Analogies and Exemplars in the Development of Durkheim's Sociology of Religion." *American Journal of Sociology* 92 (November 1986): 596–627.

———. "On Understanding a Sociological Classic." *American Journal of Sociology* 83 (September 1977): 279–319.

———. "The Other Durkheim: History and Theory in the Treatment of Classical Sociological Thought." In *Reclaiming the Sociological Classics*, edited by Charles Camic, 142–72. Malden, MA: Blackwell, 1997.

———. "The Positive Science of Ethics in France: German Influences on 'De la division du travail social.'" *Sociological Forum* 9 (March 1994): 37–57.

Jones, Robert Alun, and Douglas A. Kibbee. "Durkheim, Language, and History: A Pragmatist Perspective." *Sociological Theory* 11 (July 1993): 152–70.

Joppke, Christian, and John Torpey. *Legal Integration of Islam: A Transatlantic Comparison*. Cambridge, MA: Harvard University Press, 2013.

Judaken, Jonathan. "So What's New? Rethinking the 'New Antisemitism' in a Global Age." *Patterns of Prejudice* 42, nos. 4–5 (2008): 531–60.

Judt, Tony. "Israel: The Alternative." *New York Review of Books*, October 23, 2003. http://www.nybooks.com/articles/archives/2003/oct/23/israel-the-alternative/

———. *Marxism and the French Left*. Oxford: Clarendon Press, 1986.

Kagan, Robert. *Of Paradise and Power: America and Europe in the New World Order*. New York: Knopf, 2003.

———. "Power and Weakness." *Policy Review* 113 (June and July 2002): 3–28.

Kallen, Horace M. "Democracy versus the Melting-Pot." In *Culture and Democracy in the United States*, 67–125. New York: Boni & Liveright, [1915] 1924.

———. "Review of *A New Social Philosophy* by Werner Sombart." *Annals of the American Academy of Political and Social Science* 194 (November 1937): 223–24.

Kant, Immanuel. *Anthropology from a Pragmatic Point of View*. Translated and edited by Robert B. Louden. New York: Cambridge University Press, [1798] 2006.

Karady, Victor. "The Prehistory of Present-Day French Sociology (1917–1957)." In *French Sociology: Rupture and Renewal since 1968*, edited by Charles C. Lemert, 33–47. New York: Columbia University Press, 1981.

Kaufmann, Eric P. *The Rise and Fall of Anglo-America*. Cambridge, MA: Harvard University Press, 2004.

Kemple, Thomas M., and Renisa Mawani. "The Sociological Imagination and Its Imperial Shadows." *Theory, Culture & Society* 26, nos. 7–8 (2009): 228–49.

Khazzoom, Aziza. "The Great Chain of Orientalism: Jewish Identity, Stigma Management, and Ethnic Exclusion in Israel." *American Sociological Review* 68, no. 4 (August 2003): 481–510.

King, Richard H. "The Rise of Sociology, Antisemitism, and the Jewish Question: The American Case." In *Antisemitism and the Constitution of Sociology*, edited by Marcel Stoetzler, 183–205. Lincoln: University of Nebraska Press, 2014.

Kivisto, Peter. "What Is the Canonical Theory of Assimilation?" *Journal of the History of the Behavioral Sciences* 40, no. 2 (2004): 149–63.

Klausen, Jytte. *The Islamic Challenge: Politics and Religion in Western Europe*. New York: Oxford University Press, 2005.

Kohler, Max J. "Review of *Die Juden und das Wirtschaftsleben* by Werner Sombart." *American Economic Review* 2, no. 1 (March 1912): 81–84.

Kumar, Krishan. "The Nation-State, the European Union, and Transnational Identities." In *Muslim Europe or Euro-Islam: Politics, Culture, and Citizenship in the Age of Globalization*, edited by Nezar AlSayyad and Manuel Castells, 53–68. Lanham, MD: Rowman & Littlefield, 2002.

Küntzel, Matthias. *Jihad and Jew-Hatred: Islamism, Nazism and the Roots of 9/11*. New York: Telos Press, [2002] 2007.

Kurasawa, Fuyuki. "The Durkheimian School and Colonialism." In *Sociology and Empire: The Imperial Entanglements of a Discipline*, edited by George Steinmetz, 188–209. Durham, NC: Duke University Press, 2013.

Lal, Barbara. *The Romance of Culture in an Urban Civilisation: Robert E. Park on Race and Ethnic Relations in Cities*. New York: Routledge, 1990.

Landes, David S. "The Jewish Merchant: Typology and Stereotypology in Germany." *Leo Baeck Yearbook* 14 (1974): 11–23.

———. *The Unbound Prometheus: Technological Change and Industrial Development in Western Europe from 1750 to the Present*. New York: Cambridge University Press, 1969.

Lange, Matthew. *Antisemitic Elements in the Critique of Capitalism in German Culture, 1850–1933*. Oxford: Peter Lang, 2007.

Laqueur, Walter. *The Changing Face of Antisemitism*. New York: Oxford University Press, 2006.

Lasch, Christopher. *The New Radicalism in America, 1889–1963: The Intellectual as a Social Type*. New York: Knopf, 1965.

Laurence, Jonathan. *The Emancipation of Europe's Muslims: The State's Role in Minority Integration*. Princeton, NJ: Princeton University Press, 2012.

Lazare, Bernard. *Antisemitism: Its History and Causes*. London: Britons Publishing, [1894] 1967.

Lears, T. J. Jackson. *No Place of Grace: Antimodernism and the Transformation of American Culture, 1880–1920*. Chicago: University of Chicago Press, [1981] 1994.

Lebovics, Herman. *Social Conservatism and the Middle Classes in Germany, 1914–1933*. Princeton, NJ: Princeton University Press, 1969.

Leff, Lisa Moses. *Sacred Bonds of Solidarity: The Rise of Jewish Internationalism in Nineteenth-Century France.* Stanford, CA: Stanford University Press, 2006.

Lehmann, Jennifer M. *Durkheim and Women.* Lincoln: University of Nebraska Press, 1994.

Lémann, Joseph. *La prépondérance juive, première partie, ses origines (1789–1791).* Paris: Victor Lecoffre, 1889.

Leuchtenburg, William E. *The Perils of Prosperity, 1914–32.* Chicago: University of Chicago Press, 1958.

Lévi-Strauss, Claude. *Totemism.* Translated by Rodney Needham. Boston: Beacon, [1962] 1963.

Levine, Donald N. "Simmel at a Distance: On the History and Systematics of the Sociology of the Stranger." *Sociological Focus* 10, no. 1 (January 1977): 15–29.

———. "Some Key Problems in Simmel's Work." In *Georg Simmel*, edited by Lewis A. Coser, 97–115. Englewood Cliffs, NJ: Prentice-Hall, 1965.

———. *Visions of the Sociological Tradition.* Chicago: University of Chicago Press, 1995.

Levine, Donald N., Ellwood B. Carter, and Eleanor Miller Gorman. "Simmel's Influence on American Sociology. I." *American Journal of Sociology* 81, no. 4 (January 1976): 813–45.

Levy, Richard S. "Forget Webster." *German Studies Review* 29, no. 1 (February 2006): 145–146.

Lewis, J. David, and Richard L. Smith. *American Sociology and Pragmatism: Mead, Chicago Sociology, and Symbolic Interaction.* Chicago: University of Chicago Press, 1980.

Liebersohn, Harry. *Fate and Utopia in German Sociology, 1870–1923.* Cambridge, MA: MIT Press, 1988.

Lindner, Rolf. *The Reportage of Urban Culture: Robert Park and the Chicago School.* Translated by Adrian Morris, Jeremy Gaines, and Martin Chalmers. New York: Cambridge University Press, [1990] 1996.

Lippmann, Walter. "The Causes of Political Indifference Today." In *Men of Destiny*, 18–34. New York: Macmillan, 1927.

Loader, Colin. "Werner Sombart's *The Jews and Modern Capitalism.*" *Society* 39, no. 1 (November/December 2001): 71–77.

Löwy, Michael. *Georg Lukács: From Romanticism to Bolshevism.* Translated by Patrick Camiller. London: NLB, 1979.

Ludwig, Heinz. "Sombart and the Jews." In *Werner Sombart (1863–1941): Social Scientist*, vol. 1, edited by Jürgen Backhaus, 205–10. Marburg, Germany: Metropolis, 1996.

Lukes, Steven. *Émile Durkheim: His Life and Work.* New York: Harper & Row, 1973.

Mack, Michael. *German Idealism and the Jew: The Inner Anti-Semitism of Philosophy and German Jewish Responses.* Chicago: University of Chicago Press, 2003.

Magubane, Zine. "Overlapping Territories and Intertwined Histories: Historical Sociology's Global Imagination." In *Remaking Modernity: Politics, History, and Sociology*, edited by Julia Adams, Elisabeth S. Clemens, and Ann Shola Orloff, 92–108. Durham, NC: Duke University Press, 2005.

Maltz Bovy, Phoebe. "'Embrasser les Juifs': Jews and Intermarriage in Nineteenth-Century France (1792–1906)." PhD diss., New York University, 2013.

———. "The Problem with Comparing Syrian and Jewish Refugees." *New Republic*, November 20, 2015. https://newrepublic.com/article/124298/problem-comparing-syrian-jewish-refugees

Markovits, Andrei S. *Uncouth Nation: Why Europe Dislikes America.* Princeton, NJ: Princeton University Press, 2007.

Marshall, Bruce D. "Christ and the Cultures: The Jewish People and Christian Theology." In *The*

Cambridge Companion to Christian Doctrine, edited by Colin E. Gunton, 81–118. New York: Cambridge University Press, 1997.

Marx, Karl. *Grundrisse: Foundations of the Critique of Political Economy*. Translated by Martin Nicolaus. New York: Vintage Books, 1973.

Marx, Karl, and Frederick Engels. *Collected Works*. 50 vols. New York: International Publishers, 1975–2004.

Matthews, Fred H. *Quest for an American Sociology: Robert E. Park and the Chicago School*. Montreal: McGill-Queen's University Press, 1977.

Maurras, Charles. *Quand les Français ne s'aimaient pas: Chronique d'une renaissance, 1895–1905*. 2nd ed. Paris: Nouvelle Librairie Nationale, 1916.

———. *Les vergers sur la mer: Attique, Italie et Provence*. Paris: E. Flammarion, 1937.

Mayer, Arno J. *The Persistence of the Old Regime*. New York: Pantheon Books, 1981.

Mearsheimer, John J., and Stephen M. Walt. *The Israel Lobby and U.S. Foreign Policy*. New York: Farrar, Straus and Giroux, 2007.

Mendelsohn, Ezra. *The Jews of East Central Europe between the World Wars*. Bloomington: Indiana University Press, 1983.

Mendes-Flohr, Paul. *Divided Passions: Jewish Intellectuals and the Experience of Modernity*. Detroit, MI: Wayne State University Press, 1991.

———. "Werner Sombart's 'The Jews and Modern Capitalism': An Analysis of Its Ideological Premises." *Leo Baeck Yearbook* 21 (1976): 97–107.

Meyer, John W., and Brian Rowan. "Institutionalized Organizations: Formal Structure as Myth and Ceremony." *American Journal of Sociology* 83, no. 2 (September 1977): 340–63.

Miller, Herbert A. "A Social Contribution: *The Marginal Man* by Everett V. Stonequist." *Journal of Higher Education* 9, no. 6 (June 1938): 349–50.

Mitzman, Arthur. *The Iron Cage: An Historical Interpretation of Max Weber*. New York: Knopf, 1969.

———. *Sociology and Estrangement: Three Sociologists of Imperial Germany*. New York: Knopf, 1973.

Momigliano, Arnaldo. "A Note on Max Weber's Definition of Judaism as a Pariah-Religion." *History and Theory* 19, no. 3 (October 1980): 313–18.

Mommsen, Wolfgang. *Max Weber and German Politics, 1890–1920*. Translated by Michael S. Steinberg. Chicago: University of Chicago Press, 1984.

Moore, Deborah Dash. "David Émile Durkheim and the Jewish Response to Modernity." *Modern Judaism* 6, no. 3 (October 1986): 287–300.

Morris, Aldon D. *The Scholar Denied: W. E. B. Du Bois and the Birth of Modern Sociology*. Oakland: University of California Press, 2015.

Morris-Reich, Amos. "From Assimilationist Antiracism to Zionist Anti-Antisemitism: Georg Simmel, Franz Boas, and Arthur Ruppin." In *Antisemitism and the Constitution of Sociology*, edited by Marcel Stoetzler, 160–82. Lincoln: University of Nebraska Press, 2014.

———. "Three Paradigms of 'The Negative Jew': Identity from Simmel to Žižek." *Jewish Social Studies* 10, no. 2 (Winter 2004): 179–214.

Mosbah-Natanson, Sébastien. "Facing Antisemitism Politically and Scientifically: Durkheimian Sociology around 1900." Paper presented at the International Conference on Antisemitism and the Emergence of Sociological Theory, Manchester, UK, November 2–3, 2008.

———. "La sociologie comme 'mode'? Usages éditoriaux du label 'sociologie' en France à la fin du XIXe siècle." *Revue française de sociologie* 52, no. 1 (January–March 2011): 103–32.

Mosse, George L. *The Crisis of German Ideology: Intellectual Origins of the Third Reich.* New York: Grosset & Dunlap, 1964.

Mosse, Werner Eugen. *Jews in the German Economy: The German-Jewish Economic Elite, 1820–1935.* New York: Oxford University Press, 1987.

———. "Judaism, Jews and Capitalism: Weber, Sombart and Beyond." *Leo Baeck Yearbook* 24 (1979): 3–15.

Muller, Jerry Z. *Capitalism and the Jews.* Princeton, NJ: Princeton University Press, 2010.

———. *The Mind and the Market: Capitalism in Western Thought.* New York: Random House, 2002.

Myrdal, Gunnar. *An American Dilemma: The Negro Problem and Modern Democracy.* New York: Harper, 1944.

Nachmani, Amikam. *Europe and Its Muslim Minorities: Aspects of Conflict, Attempts at Accord.* Brighton, UK: Sussex Academic Press, 2009.

Nandan, Yash. "Editor's Introduction." In *Emile Durkheim: Contributions to* L'Année Sociologique, edited by Yash Nandan, 1–44. New York: Free Press, 1980.

Nelson, Benjamin. *The Idea of Usury, from Tribal Brotherhood to Universal Otherhood.* 2nd ed. Chicago: University of Chicago Press, [1949] 1969.

New York Times. "Wrong about Jews, Bingham Admits." September 17, 1908.

Niebuhr, Gustav. "All Need Toleration: Some Observations about Recent Differences in the Experiences of Religious Minorities in the United States and Western Europe." *Annals of the American Academy of Political and Social Science* 612 (July 2007): 172–86.

Nirenberg, David. *Anti-Judaism: The Western Tradition.* New York: Norton, 2013.

———. "The Birth of the Pariah: Jews, Christian Dualism, and Social Science." *Social Research* 70, no. 1 (Spring 2003): 201–36.

Nisbet, Robert A. *Émile Durkheim.* Englewood Cliffs, NJ: Prentice-Hall, 1965.

———. "The French Revolution and the Rise of Sociology in France." *American Journal of Sociology* 49, no. 2 (September 1943): 156–64.

———. *The Sociological Tradition.* New York: Basic Books, 1966.

Noland, Aaron. *The Founding of the French Socialist Party (1893–1905).* Cambridge, MA: Harvard University Press, 1956.

Nussbaum, Frederick L. *A History of the Economic Institutions of Modern Europe: An Introduction to* Der moderne Kapitalismus *of Werner Sombart.* New York: Crofts, 1933.

Oelsner, Toni. "The Place of the Jews in Economic History as Viewed by German Scholars." *Leo Baeck Yearbook* 7 (1962): 183–212.

Offe, Claus. *Reflections on America: Tocqueville, Weber and Adorno in the United States.* Translated by Patrick Camiller. Malden, MA: Polity, [2004] 2005.

Ó Raghallaigh, Ciarán. "Israel-Palestine Conflict Is Not the Source of All Troubles in Mideast." *Irish Examiner,* November 19, 2015. http://www.irishexaminer.com/viewpoints/yourview/israel-palestine-conflict-is-not-the-source-of-all-troubles-in-mideast-365740.html

Ottolenghi, Emanuele. "Europe's 'Good' Jews." *Commentary* 120, no. 5 (December 2005): 42–46.

Park, Robert Ezra. "Assimilation, Social." *Encyclopaedia of the Social Sciences,* vol. 1. Edited by Edwin R. A. Seligman, 281–83. New York: Macmillan, [1930] 1937.

———. "The Bases of Race Prejudice." In *Race and Culture,* edited by E. C. Hughes, C. S. Johnson, J. Masuoka, R. Redfield, and L. Wirth, 230–43. Glencoe, IL: Free Press, [1928] 1950.

———. "Behind Our Masks." In *Race and Culture,* edited by E. C. Hughes, C. S. Johnson, J. Masuoka, R. Redfield, and L. Wirth, 244–55. Glencoe, IL: Free Press, [1926] 1950.

———. "The Career of the Africans in Brazil." In *Race and Culture*, edited by E. C. Hughes, C. S. Johnson, J. Masuoka, R. Redfield, and L. Wirth, 196–203. Glencoe, IL: Free Press, [1942] 1950.

———. "The City: Suggestions for the Investigation of Human Behavior in the City Environment." *American Journal of Sociology* 20, no. 5 (March 1915): 577–612.

———. "The City: Suggestions for the Investigation of Human Behavior in the Urban Environment." In *The City*, by Robert E. Park, Ernest W. Burgess, and Roderick D. McKenzie, 1–46. Chicago: University of Chicago Press, [1925] 1967.

———. Collection. Special Collections Research Center, University of Chicago Library.

———. "Community Organization and the Romantic Temper." *Journal of Social Forces* 3, no. 4 (May 1925): 673–77.

———. "The Crowd and the Public." In *The Crowd and the Public and Other Essays*, edited by Henry Elsner Jr. Translated by Charlotte Elsner, 1–81. Chicago: University of Chicago Press, [1904] 1972.

———. "Culture and Civilization." In *Race and Culture*, edited by E. C. Hughes, C. S. Johnson, J. Masuoka, R. Redfield, and L. Wirth, 15–23. Glencoe, IL: Free Press, 1950.

———. "Culture and Cultural Trends." In *Race and Culture*, edited by E. C. Hughes, C. S. Johnson, J. Masuoka, R. Redfield, and L. Wirth, 24–35. Glencoe, IL: Free Press, [1925] 1950.

———. "Education in Its Relation to the Conflict and Fusion of Cultures." In *Race and Culture*, edited by E. C. Hughes, C. S. Johnson, J. Masuoka, R. Redfield, and L. Wirth, 261–83. Glencoe, IL: Free Press, [1918] 1950.

———. "The Etiquette of Race Relations in the South." In *Race and Culture*, edited by E. C. Hughes, C. S. Johnson, J. Masuoka, R. Redfield, and L. Wirth, 177–88. Glencoe, IL: Free Press, [1937] 1950.

———. "Human Migration and the Marginal Man." *American Journal of Sociology* 33, no. 6 (May 1928): 881–93.

———. "Immigrant Community and Immigrant Press." In *Society, Collective Behavior, News and Opinion, Sociology and Modern Society*, vol. 3 of *The Collected Papers of Robert Ezra Park*, edited by E. C. Hughes, C. S. Johnson, J. Masuoka, R. Redfield, and L. Wirth, 152–164. Glencoe, IL: Free Press, [1925] 1955.

———. *The Immigrant Press and Its Control.* New York: Harper, 1922.

———. "Mentality of Racial Hybrids." In *Race and Culture*, edited by E. C. Hughes, C. S. Johnson, J. Masuoka, R. Redfield, and L. Wirth, 377–92. Glencoe, IL: Free Press, [1931] 1950.

———. "Missions and the Modern World." In *Race and Culture*, edited by E. C. Hughes, C. S. Johnson, J. Masuoka, R. Redfield, and L. Wirth, 331–41. Glencoe, IL: Free Press, [1944] 1950.

———. "The Negro and His Plantation Heritage." In *Race and Culture*, edited by E. C. Hughes, C. S. Johnson, J. Masuoka, R. Redfield, and L. Wirth, 66–78. Glencoe, IL: Free Press, [1934] 1950.

———. "Negro Race Consciousness as Reflected in Race Literature." In *Race and Culture*, edited by E. C. Hughes, C. S. Johnson, J. Masuoka, R. Redfield, and L. Wirth, 284–300. Glencoe, IL: Free Press, [1923] 1950.

———. "Our Racial Frontier on the Pacific." In *Race and Culture*, edited by E. C. Hughes, C. S. Johnson, J. Masuoka, R. Redfield, and L. Wirth, 138–51. Glencoe, IL: Free Press, [1926] 1950.

———. "Personality and Cultural Conflict." In *Race and Culture*, edited by E. C. Hughes, C. S. Johnson, J. Masuoka, R. Redfield, and L. Wirth, 357–71. Glencoe, IL: Free Press, [1931] 1950.

———. "Politics and 'The Man Farthest Down.'" In *Race and Culture*, edited by E. C. Hughes, C. S. Johnson, J. Masuoka, R. Redfield, and L. Wirth, 166–76. Glencoe, IL: Free Press, [1935] 1950.

———. "The Problem of Cultural Differences." In *Race and Culture*, edited by E. C. Hughes, C. S. Johnson, J. Masuoka, R. Redfield, and L. Wirth, 3–14. Glencoe, IL: Free Press, [1931] 1950.

———. "Race Ideologies." In *Race and Culture*, edited by E. C. Hughes, C. S. Johnson, J. Masuoka, R. Redfield, and L. Wirth, 301–15. Glencoe, IL: Free Press, [1943] 1950.

———. "Race Relations and Certain Frontiers." In *Race and Culture*, edited by E. C. Hughes, C. S. Johnson, J. Masuoka, R. Redfield, and L. Wirth, 117–37. Glencoe, IL: Free Press, [1934] 1950.

———. "The Race Relations Cycle in Hawaii." In *Race and Culture*, edited by E. C. Hughes, C. S. Johnson, J. Masuoka, R. Redfield, and L. Wirth, 189–95. Glencoe, IL: Free Press, [1937] 1950.

———. "A Race Relations Survey." In *Race and Culture*, edited by E. C. Hughes, C. S. Johnson, J. Masuoka, R. Redfield, and L. Wirth, 158–65. Glencoe, IL: Free Press, [1923] 1950.

———. "Racial Assimilation in Secondary Groups." In *Race and Culture: Essays in the Sociology of Contemporary Man*, edited by E. C. Hughes, C. S. Johnson, J. Masuoka, R. Redfield, and L. Wirth, 204–20. Glencoe, IL: Free Press, [1913] 1950.

———. "Review of *Jews in a Gentile World* by Isacque Graeber and Steuart Henderson Britt." *American Sociological Review* 9, no. 6 (December 1944): 710–11.

Park, Robert Ezra, and Ernest W. Burgess. *Introduction to the Science of Sociology*. 3rd ed. revised. Chicago: University of Chicago Press, [1921] 1924.

Park, Robert Ezra, and Herbert A. Miller. *Old World Traits Transplanted*. New York: Harper, 1921.

Parsons, Talcott. "'Capitalism' in Recent German Literature: Sombart and Weber." *Journal of Political Economy* 36, no. 6 (December 1928): 641–61.

———. "The Role of Theory in Social Research." *American Sociological Review* 3, no. 1 (February 1938): 13–20.

———. *The Structure of Social Action*. 2 vols. New York: Free Press, [1937] 1968.

Pasto, James. "Islam's 'Strange Secret Sharer': Orientalism, Judaism, and the Jewish Question." *Comparative Studies in Society and History* 40, no. 3 (July 1998): 437–74.

Peach, Ceri, and Günther Glebe. "Muslim Minorities in Western Europe." *Ethnic and Racial Studies* 18, no. 1 (1995): 26–45.

Peled, Yoav. "From Theology to Sociology: Bruno Bauer and Karl Marx on the Question of Jewish Emancipation." *History of Political Thought* 13, no. 3 (Autumn 1992): 463–85.

Penslar, Derek J. *Shylock's Children: Economics and Jewish Identity in Modern Europe*. Berkeley: University of California Press, 2001.

Persons, Stow. *Ethnic Studies at Chicago, 1905–45*. Urbana: University of Illinois Press, 1987.

Pew Research Center. *The Future of the Global Muslim Population: Projections for 2010–2030*. Washington, DC: Pew Research Center, 2011.

———. *Muslim Americans: Middle Class and Mostly Mainstream*. Washington, DC: Pew Research Center, 2007.

Picard, Edmond. *Synthèse de l'antisémitisme*. Paris: Albert Savine, 1892.

Pickering, W. S. F. "The Enigma of Durkheim's Jewishness." In *Debating Durkheim*, edited by W. S. F. Pickering and H. Martins, 10–39. New York: Routledge, 1994.

Pickering, W. S. F., and H. Martins, eds. *Debating Durkheim*. New York: Routledge, 1994.

Plummer, Ken, ed. *The Chicago School: Critical Assessments*. 4 vols. New York: Routledge, 1997.

Pocock, J. G. A. "Modernity and Anti-Modernity in the Anglophone Political Tradition." In *Patterns of Modernity, Vol. 1. The West*, edited by S. N. Eisenstadt, 44–59. New York: New York University Press, 1987.

Poggi, Gianfranco. *Money and the Modern Mind: Georg Simmel's* Philosophy of Money. Berkeley: University of California Press, 1993.

Polanyi, Karl. *The Great Transformation*. Boston: Beacon, [1944] 1957.

Porter, Jack Nusan. "The Jewish Presence in Sociology." In *The Jew as Outsider: Historical and Contemporary Perspectives*, 65–107. Washington, DC: University Press of America, 1981.

Portes, Alejandro, and Min Zhou. "The New Second Generation: Segmented Assimilation and Its Variants." *Annals of the American Academy of Political and Social Science* 530 (November 1993): 74–96.

Postone, Moishe. "History and Helplessness: Mass Mobilization and Contemporary Forms of Anticapitalism." *Public Culture* 18, no. 1 (2006): 93–110.

Proudhon, P.-J. *Carnets*. 4 vols. Paris: Marcel Rivière, [1809–1865] 1961.

———. *Césarisme et christianisme*. 2nd ed. 2 vols. Paris: C. Marpon and E. Flammarion, 1883.

———. *De la justice dans la révolution et dans l'église*. 6 vols. Brussels: A. LaCroix, Verboeckhoven, [1858] 1868–1870.

———. *Résumé de la question sociale; banque d'échange*. Paris: Garnier Frères, 1849.

———. "Si les traités de 1815 ont cessé d'exister?" In *Oeuvres complètes*, new ed., 327–428. Paris: Marcel Rivière, [1863] 1952.

Pulzer, Peter. "Legal Equality and Public Life." In *German-Jewish History in Modern Times*, vol. 3, edited by Michael A. Meyer, 153–195. New York: Columbia University Press, 1997.

———. *The Rise of Political Anti-Semitism in Germany and Austria*. New York: Wiley, 1964.

Radkau, Joachim. *Max Weber: A Biography*. Translated by Patrick Camiller. Malden, MA: Polity, [2005] 2009.

Raphaël, Freddy. "L'Étranger et le paria dans l'œuvre de Max Weber et de Georg Simmel." *Archives de sciences sociales des religions* 61, no. 1 (January–March 1986): 63–81.

———. *Judaïsme et capitalisme: Essai sur la controverse entre Max Weber et Werner Sombart*. Paris: Presses Universitaires de France, 1982.

———. "Les Juifs en tant que peuple paria dans l'œuvre de Max Weber." *Social Compass* 23, no. 4 (December 1976): 397–426.

Raushenbush, Winifred. *Robert E. Park: Biography of a Sociologist*. Durham, NC: Duke University Press, 1979.

Reed, Adolph L. Jr. *W. E. B. Du Bois and American Political Thought*. New York: Oxford University Press, 1997.

Rémond, René. *The Right Wing in France: From 1815 to de Gaulle*. 2nd American ed. Translated by James M. Laux. Philadelphia: University of Pennsylvania Press, 1969.

Repp, Kevin. *Reformers, Critics, and the Paths of German Modernity: Anti-Politics and the Search for Alternatives, 1890–1914*. Cambridge, MA: Harvard University Press, 2000.

Richarz, Monika. "Demographic Developments." In *German-Jewish History in Modern Times*, vol. 3, edited by Michael A. Meyer, 7–34. New York: Columbia University Press, 1997.

———. "Occupational Distribution and Social Structure." In *German-Jewish History in Modern Times*, vol. 3, edited by Michael A. Meyer, 35–67. New York: Columbia University Press, 1997.

Riesman, David. "Marginality, Conformity, and Insight." In *Individualism Reconsidered and Other Essays*, 166–78. Glencoe, IL: Free Press, 1954.

———. "Some Observations Concerning Marginality." *Phylon* 12, no. 2 (1951): 113–27.

Rieß, Rolf. "Werner Sombart under National Socialism: A First Approximation." In *Werner Sombart (1863–1941): Social Scientist*, vol. 1, edited by Jürgen Backhaus, 193–204. Marburg, Germany: Metropolis, 1996.

Ringer, Fritz K. *The Decline of the German Mandarins: The German Academic Community, 1890–1933*. Cambridge, MA: Harvard University Press, 1969.

———. *Fields of Knowledge: French Academic Culture in Comparative Perspective, 1890–1920*. New York: Cambridge University Press, 1992.

———. "The Intellectual Field, Intellectual History, and the Sociology of Knowledge." *Theory and Society* 19, no. 3 (1990): 269–94.

———. *Max Weber: An Intellectual Biography*. Chicago: University of Chicago Press, 2004.

Rock, Paul. *The Making of Symbolic Interactionism*. Totowa, NJ: Rowman & Littlefield, 1979.

Rodgers, Daniel T. *Atlantic Crossings: Social Politics in a Progressive Age*. Cambridge, MA: Harvard University Press, 1998.

Ross, Edward Alsworth. *The Old World in the New*. New York: Century, 1914.

Ross, James, and Song Lihong, eds. *The Image of Jews in Contemporary China*. Boston: Academic Studies Press, 2016.

Rotenstreich, Nathan. *Jews and German Philosophy: The Polemics of Emancipation*. New York: Schocken Books, 1984.

———. *The Recurring Pattern: Studies in Anti-Judaism in Modern Thought*. New York: Horizon Press, 1963.

Roth, Guenther. "Max Weber's Views on Jewish Integration and Zionism: Some American, English and German Contexts." *Max Weber Studies* 3, no. 1 (2002): 56–73.

———. "Weber the Would-Be Englishman: Anglophilia and Family History." In *Weber's Protestant Ethic: Origins, Evidence, Context*, edited by Hartmut Lehmann and Guenther Roth, 3–121. New York: Cambridge University Press, 1993.

Roudiez, Léon. *Maurras jusqu'à l'Action Française*. Paris: Éditions André Bonne, 1957.

Rourke, Francis E. "Urbanism and American Democracy." *Ethics* 74, no. 4 (July 1964): 255–68.

Rucker, Darnell. *The Chicago Pragmatists*. Minneapolis: University of Minnesota Press, 1969.

Said, Edward W. *Orientalism*. New York: Pantheon, 1978.

Saint-Simon, Henri Comte de. *Selected Writings*. Edited and translated by F. M. H. Markham. New York: Macmillan, 1952.

Salerno, Roger A. *Louis Wirth: A Bio-Bibliography*. New York: Greenwood, 1987.

Salomon, Albert. "Georg Simmel Reconsidered." *International Journal of Politics, Culture, and Society* 8, no. 3 (Spring 1995): 361–78.

Sarna, Jonathan D. "The Cult of Synthesis in American Jewish Culture." *Jewish Social Studies* 5, no. 1/2 (Autumn–Winter 1998–1999): 52–79.

Schechter, Ronald. *Obstinate Hebrews: Representations of Jews in France, 1715–1815*. Berkeley: University of California Press, 2003.

Schluchter, Wolfgang. "The Approach of Max Weber's Sociology of Religion as Exemplified in His Study of Ancient Judaism." *Archives de sciences sociales des religions* 49, no. 127 (July–September 2004): 33–56.

Sebag-Montefiore, Clarissa. "The Chinese Believe That the Jews Control America: Is That a Good Thing?" *Tablet Magazine*, March 27, 2014. http://www.tabletmag.com/jewish-arts-and-culture/books/167289/nanjing-jewish-studies

Seidman, Steven. "The Colonial Unconscious of Classical Sociology." In *Postcolonial Sociology*, edited by Julian Go, 35–54. Bingley, UK: Emerald, 2013.

Sewell, William H. Jr. "A Theory of Structure: Duality, Agency, and Transformation." *American Journal of Sociology* 98, no. 1 (July 1992): 1–29.

Sharlin, Allan N. "Werner Sombart: A Study in the Relationship between Social Science and Politics." MA thesis, University of Wisconsin, 1972.

Shepherd, Robin. *A State beyond the Pale: Europe's Problem with Israel.* London: Weidenfeld & Nicolson, 2009.

Shils, Edward A. "Center and Periphery." In *The Constitution of Society*, 93–109. Chicago: University of Chicago Press, 1982.

Shindler, Colin. *Israel and the European Left: Between Solidarity and Delegitimization.* New York: Continuum, 2012.

Shmueli, Efraim. "The 'Pariah-People' and Its 'Charismatic Leadership': A Revaluation of Max Weber's 'Ancient Judaism.'" *Proceedings of the American Academy for Jewish Research* 36 (1968): 167–247.

Silberner, Edmund. "Charles Fourier on the Jewish Question." *Jewish Social Studies* 8 (1946): 245–66.

———. "French Socialism and the Jewish Question, 1865–1914." *Historia Judaica* 16, pt. 1 (April 1954): 3–38.

———. "Proudhon's Judeophobia." *Historia Judaica* 10, no. 1 (April 1948): 61–80.

———. "Was Marx an Anti-Semite?" *Historia Judaica* 11, no. 1 (April 1949): 3–52.

Simmel, Georg. "The Adventure." In *Simmel on Culture: Selected Writings*, edited by David Frisby and Mike Featherstone, 221–32. London: Sage, [1911] 1997.

———. "The Concept and Tragedy of Culture." In *Simmel on Culture: Selected Writings*, edited by David Frisby and Mike Featherstone, 55–75. London: Sage, [1911] 1997.

———. "Money in Modern Culture." In *Simmel on Culture: Selected Writings*, edited by David Frisby and Mike Featherstone, 243–55. London: Sage, [1896] 1997.

———. "On the Psychology of Money." In *Simmel on Culture: Selected Writings*, edited by David Frisby and Mike Featherstone, 233–43. London: Sage, [1889] 1997.

———. *The Philosophy of Money.* Translated by Tom Bottomore, David Frisby, and Kaethe Mengelberg. New York: Routledge, [1900] 2004. English translation based on the second German edition of 1907.

———. "The Stranger." In *On Individuality and Social Forms*, edited by Donald N. Levine, 143–49. Chicago: University of Chicago Press, [1908] 1971.

———. "The Web of Group-Affiliations." In *Conflict and the Web of Group-Affiliations*, 125–95. Translated by Kurt H. Wolff and Reinhard Bendix. New York: Free Press, [1922] 1955.

Sklare, Marshall. "The Sociology of Contemporary Jewish Studies." In *The Jew in American Society*, edited by Marshall Sklare, 1–27. New York: Behrman House, 1974.

Slezkine, Yuri. *The Jewish Century.* Princeton, NJ: Princeton University Press, 2004.

Smith, Dennis. *The Chicago School: A Liberal Critique of Capitalism.* London: Macmillan, 1988.

Smith, Rogers M. *Civic Ideals: Conflicting Visions of Citizenship in U.S. History.* New Haven, CT: Yale University Press, 1997.

Sombart, Werner. *Der Bourgeois: Zur Geistesgeschichte des modernen Wirtschaftsmenschen.* Munich and Leipzig: Duncker & Humblot, 1913.

———. *Economic Life in the Modern Age.* Edited by Nico Stehr and Reiner Grundmann. New Brunswick, NJ: Transaction, 2001.

———. *The Jews and Modern Capitalism.* Translated by M. Epstein. New Brunswick, NJ: Transaction, [1911] 1951.

———. *Die Juden und das Wirtschaftsleben.* Munich and Leipzig: Duncker & Humblot, 1911.

———. *A New Social Philosophy.* Translated and edited by Karl F. Geiser. Princeton, NJ: Princeton University Press, [1934] 1937.

———. *The Quintessence of Capitalism: A Study of the History of the Modern Business Man.* Translated and edited by M. Epstein. New York: E. P. Dutton, [1913] 1915.

———. *Why Is There No Socialism in the United States?* Edited by C. T. Husbands. White Plains, NY: M. E. Sharpe, [1906] 1976.

Sorlin, Pierre. *"La Croix" et les Juifs (1880–1899): Contribution à l'histoire de l'antisémitisme contemporain.* Paris: Éditions Bernard Grasset, 1967.

Sperber, Jonathan. *Karl Marx: A Nineteenth-Century Life.* New York: Norton, 2013.

Spykman, Nicholas J. *The Social Theory of Georg Simmel.* New York: Russell & Russell, [1925] 1964.

Stehr, Nico, and Reiner Grundmann. "Introduction." In *Economic Life in the Modern Age*, by Werner Sombart. Edited by Nico Stehr and Reiner Grundmann, ix–lxii. New Brunswick, NJ: Transaction, 2001.

Steinmetz, George. "Decolonizing German Theory: An Introduction." *Postcolonial Studies* 9, no. 1 (2006): 3–13.

———. *The Devil's Handwriting: Precoloniality and the German Colonial State in Qingdao, Samoa, and Southwest Africa.* Chicago: University of Chicago Press, 2007.

———. "The Sociology of Empires, Colonies, and Postcolonialism." *Annual Review of Sociology* 40 (2014): 77–103.

Stern, Fritz. *The Politics of Cultural Despair: A Study in the Rise of the Germanic Ideology.* Berkeley: University of California Press, 1961.

Stoddard, Lothrop. *The Rising Tide of Color against White World-Supremacy.* New York: Scribner, 1920.

Stoetzler, Marcel, ed. *Antisemitism and the Constitution of Sociology.* Lincoln: University of Nebraska Press, 2014.

Stonequist, Everett Verner. "The Marginal Character of the Jews." In *Jews in a Gentile World: The Problem of Anti-Semitism*, 296–310. Westport, CT: Greenwood Press, [1942] 1979.

———. *The Marginal Man: A Study in Personality and Culture Conflict.* New York: Russell & Russell, [1937] 1965.

———. "The Marginal Man: A Study in Personality and Culture Conflict." In *Contributions to Urban Sociology*, edited by Ernest W. Burgess and Donald J. Bogue, 327–45. Chicago: University of Chicago Press, 1964.

———. "The Marginal Man: A Study in the Subjective Aspects of Cultural Conflict." PhD diss., University of Chicago, 1930.

———. "The Problem of the Marginal Man." *American Journal of Sociology* 41, no. 1 (July 1935): 1–12.

Strauss, Mark "Antiglobalism's Jewish Problem." *Foreign Policy* 139 (November–December 2003): 58–67.

Strenski, Ivan. *Durkheim and the Jews of France.* Chicago: University of Chicago Press, 1997.

Swatos, William H. Jr., and Peter Kivisto. "Max Weber as 'Christian Sociologist.'" *Journal for the Scientific Study of Religion* 30, no. 4 (December 1991): 347–62.

Swedberg, Richard. *Max Weber and the Idea of Economic Sociology.* Princeton, NJ: Princeton University Press, 1998.

Szajkowski, Zosa. "The Jewish Saint-Simonians and Socialist Antisemites in France." *Jewish Social Studies* 9, no. 1 (January 1947): 33–60.

Therborn, Göran. "Three Epochs of European Anti-Semitism." *European Societies* 14, no. 2 (2012): 161–65.

Thomas, William I. "Analytical Types: Philistine, Bohemian, and Creative Man." Originally published as "The Persistence of Primary Group Norms in Present Day Society." Reprinted in *On Social Organization and Social Personality*, edited by Morris Janowitz, 168–81. Chicago: University of Chicago Press, [1917] 1966.

———. Papers. Special Collections Research Center, University of Chicago Library.

Thomas, William I., and Florian Znaniecki. *The Polish Peasant in Europe and America.* 2 vols. New York: Farrar, Straus and Giroux, [1918–1921] 1974. Reprint of 2nd ed. published in 1927 by Knopf.

Tilly, Charles. *Big Structures, Large Processes, Huge Comparisons.* New York: Russell Sage, 1984.

Times of Israel. "Ex-UK FM: 'Unlimited' Jewish Funds Control US Policy, Block Mideast Peace." October 27, 2013. http://www.timesofisrael.com/ex-uk-fm-unlimited-jewish-funds-control-us-policy-block-mideast-peace/

Tocqueville, Alexis de. *The Old Regime and the French Revolution.* Translated by Stuart Gilbert. New York: Doubleday, [1856] 1955.

Tönnies, Ferdinand. *Fundamental Concepts of Sociology (Gemeinschaft und Gesellschaft).* Translated by Charles P. Loomis. New York: American Book, [1887] 1940.

———. "The Individual and the World in the Modern Age." In *On Sociology: Pure, Applied, and Empirical*, edited by Werner J. Cahnman and Rudolf Heberle, 288–317. Chicago: University of Chicago Press, [1913] 1971.

Torpey, John. "A (Post-) Secular Age? Religion and the Two Exceptionalisms." *Social Research* 77, no. 1 (Spring 2010): 269–96.

Toussenel, Alphonse. *Les Juifs, rois de l'époque: Histoire de la féodalité financière.* 2 vols. Paris: Gabriel de Gonet, 1847.

Traverso, Enzo. *La fin de la modernité juive: Histoire d'un tournant conservateur.* Paris: La Découverte, 2013.

———. *The Marxists and the Jewish Question: The History of a Debate, 1843–1943.* Translated by Bernard Gibbons. Amherst, MA: Humanities Press, [1990] 1994.

Tridon, Gustave. *Du molochisme juif: Études critiques et philosophiques.* Brussels: E. Maheu, 1884.

Tucker, Robert C., ed. *The Marx-Engels Reader.* 2nd ed. New York: Norton, 1978.

Uitermark, Justus, Paul Mepschen, and Jan Willem Duyvendak. "Populism, Sexual Politics, and the Exclusion of Muslims in the Netherlands." In *European States and Their Muslim Citizens: The Impact of Institutions on Perceptions and Boundaries*, edited by John R. Bowen, Christophe Bertossi, Jan Willem Duyvendak, and Mona Lena Krook, 235–55. New York: Cambridge University Press, 2014.

US Bureau of the Census. *Historical Statistics of the United States, Colonial Times to 1970.* Bicentennial ed., pt. 1. Washington, DC: US Government Printing Office, 1975.

Veblen, Thorstein. "The Intellectual Pre-Eminence of Jews in Modern Europe." *Political Science Quarterly* 34, no. 1 (March 1919): 33–42.

Vital, David. *A People Apart: The Jews in Europe, 1789–1939.* New York: Oxford University Press, 1999.

Vlach, Michael J. *The Church as a Replacement of Israel: An Analysis of Supersessionism.* Frankfurt: Peter Lang, 2009.

Vogt, W. Paul. "Political Connections, Professional Advancement, and Moral Education in Durkheimian Sociology." *Journal of the History of the Behavioral Sciences* 27 (January 1991): 56–75.

Wacker, R. Fred. *Ethnicity, Pluralism, and Race: Race Relations Theory in America Before Myrdal.* Westport, CT: Greenwood, 1983.

Walzer, Michael. "Islamism and the Left," *Dissent Magazine* (Winter 2015). http://www.dissentmagazine.org/article/islamism-and-the-left

Wander, Paul. "Review of *Die Juden und das Wirtschaftsleben* by Werner Sombart." *American Journal of Sociology* 17, no. 6 (May 1912): 838–41.

Wasserman, Henry. "Prussia." *Encyclopaedia Judaica.* Edited by Michael Berenbaum and Fred Skolnik. 2nd ed. Vol. 16. Detroit, MI: Macmillan, 2007.

Wasserstein, Bernard. *On the Eve: The Jews of Europe before the Second World War.* New York: Simon & Schuster, 2012.

Wax, Murray. "Ancient Judaism and the Protestant Ethic." *American Journal of Sociology* 65, no. 5 (March 1960): 449–55.

Weber, Marianne. *Max Weber: A Biography.* Translated and edited by Harry Zohn. New York: Wiley, 1975.

Weber, Max. *Ancient Judaism.* Translated and edited by Hans H. Gerth and Don Martindale. New York: Free Press, [1917] 1952.

———. *Economy and Society.* 2 vols. Edited by Guenther Roth and Claus Wittich. Berkeley: University of California Press, [1922] 1978.

———. *General Economic History.* Translated by Frank H. Knight. Mineola, NY: Dover, 1927.

———. *The Protestant Ethic and the Spirit of Capitalism.* Translated by Talcott Parsons. New York: Scribner, [1920] 1958.

———. *The Protestant Ethic and the Spirit of Capitalism with Other Writings on the Rise of the West.* 4th ed. Translated by Stephen Kalberg. New York: Oxford University Press, 2009.

———. "The Protestant Sects and the Spirit of Capitalism." In *From Max Weber: Essays in Sociology,* translated and edited by H. H. Gerth and C. Wright Mills, 302–22. New York: Oxford University Press, [1906] 1946.

———. *The Religion of China: Confucianism and Taoism.* Translated and edited by H. H. Gerth. New York: Macmillan, [1915] 1964.

———. "Religious Rejections of the World and Their Directions." In *From Max Weber: Essays in Sociology,* translated and edited by H. H. Gerth and C. Wright Mills, 323–59. New York: Oxford University Press, [1915] 1946.

———. "Science as a Vocation." In *From Max Weber: Essays in Sociology,* translated and edited by H. H. Gerth and C. Wright Mills, 129–156. New York: Oxford University Press, [1919] 1946.

Weingartner, Rudolph H. "Theory and Tragedy of Culture." In *Georg Simmel,* edited by Lewis A. Coser, 122–34. Englewood Cliffs, NJ: Prentice-Hall, 1965.

Weintraub, Jeff. "Some Thoughts on Anti-Zionism & Anti-Semitism," *Commentaries and Controversies,* April 25, 2006. http://jeffweintraub.blogspot.com/2006/04/some-thoughts-on-anti-zionism-anti.html

Weitzman, Mark. *Magical Logic, Globalization, Conspiracy Theory, and the Shoah.* Jerusalem: Vidal Sassoon International Center for the Study of Antisemitism, 2008.

Westbrook, Robert B. *John Dewey and American Democracy.* Ithaca, NY: Cornell University Press, 1991.

Wilcken, Patrick. *Claude Lévi-Strauss: The Poet in the Laboratory*. New York: Penguin, 2010.

Will, George F. "Netanyahu, the Anti-Obama," *Washington Post*, August 12, 2010. http://www.washingtonpost.com/wp-dyn/content/article/2010/08/11/AR2010081104747.html

Wilson, Stephen. *Ideology and Experience: Antisemitism in France at the Time of the Dreyfus Affair*. London: Associated University Presses, 1982.

Wirth, Louis. "Consensus and Mass Communication." In *On Cities and Social Life*, edited by Albert J. Reiss Jr., 18–43. Chicago: University of Chicago Press, [1948] 1964.

———. "Culture Conflict and Misconduct." In *On Cities and Social Life*, edited by Albert J. Reiss Jr., 229–43. Chicago: University of Chicago Press, [1931] 1964.

———. "Culture Conflicts in the Immigrant Family." MA thesis, University of Chicago, 1925.

———. "Education for Survival: The Jews." *American Journal of Sociology* 48, no. 6 (May 1943): 682–691.

———. *The Ghetto*. Chicago: University of Chicago Press, [1928] 1956.

———. "The Ghetto: A Study in Isolation." PhD diss., University of Chicago, 1926.

———. Papers. Special Collections Research Center, University of Chicago Library.

———. "The Problem of Minority Groups." In *On Cities and Social Life*, edited by Albert J. Reiss Jr., 244–69. Chicago: University of Chicago Press, [1945] 1964.

———. "Types of Nationalism." In *On Cities and Social Life*, edited by Albert J. Reiss Jr., 106–21. Chicago: University of Chicago Press, [1936] 1964.

———. "Urbanism as a Way of Life." *American Journal of Sociology* 44, no. 1 (July 1938): 1–24.

Wirth, Louis, and Herbert Goldhamer. "The Hybrid and the Problem of Miscegenation." In *Characteristics of the American Negro*, edited by Otto Klineberg, 249–369. New York: Harper, 1944.

Wirth Marvick, Elizabeth. "Louis Wirth: A Biographical Memorandum." In *On Cities and Social Life*, edited by Albert J. Reiss Jr., 333–40. Chicago: University of Chicago Press, 1964.

Wistrich, Robert S. *A Lethal Obsession: Anti-Semitism from Antiquity to the Global Jihad*. New York: Random House, 2010.

Wyndham, H. A. "Review of *The Marginal Man* by Everett C. Stonequist." *International Affairs* 17, no. 6 (November–December 1938): 831.

Yovel, Yirmiyahu. *Dark Riddle: Hegel, Nietzsche, and the Jews*. University Park: Pennsylvania State University Press, 1998.

———. *The Other Within: The Marranos. Split Identity and Emerging Modernity*. Princeton, NJ: Princeton University Press, 2009.

Zangwill, Israel. *The Melting-Pot: Drama in Four Acts*. New York: Macmillan, [1908] 1923.

Zelizer, Viviana A. *The Social Meaning of Money*. New York: Basic Books, 1994.

Zimmerman, Andrew. "Decolonizing Weber." *Postcolonial Studies* 9, no. 1 (2006): 53–79.

Index